"Although there are many good books that introduce us to the Four Gospels, they rarely focus on the spirituality of the Gospels; that is, what the Gospels mean for our lives in Christ. Father Peter Feldmeier has admirably filled that need by providing us with a reliable reading of the Four Gospels that shows how they call us to live our lives in, with, and for Christ. This book will be of immense value to all who want a better understanding of how the story of each Gospel calls them to Christian holiness."

—Frank J. Matera, Professor Emeritus, The Catholic University of America

"Through a masterful weaving of scholarship, theological insight, and spiritual wisdom, Peter Feldmeier leads us on a new type of adventure through the Gospels. He walks us through each of the four Gospels, providing opportunities to learn anew not only the power of engaging the living Word of God, but perhaps more valuably, the power of a vocation to 'live Christ.'"

—Virginia Herbers, author of *Gifts from Friends We've Yet to Meet*

"Pope Francis has frequently reminded Christians that we need to renew our approaches to Scripture and to be challenged by the radicality of Jesus's preaching in the Gospels. Too often Christians have become complacent with tired interpretations and preconceptions about the Gospels. In this book, Peter Feldmeier offers readers a way to engage with the Gospels in a deep, theologically rich, and pragmatic way that answers Pope Francis's call to spiritual renewal. No matter how well you think you know the Gospels, Feldmeier invites us to rethink our assumptions in order to enter into the Word of God with new eyes and an open heart. I highly recommend this book, not only for Christians looking for a great scriptural resource but also for preachers seeking new inspiration."

—Daniel P. Horan, OFM, Professor of Philosophy, Religious Studies, and Theology at Saint Mary's College, Notre Dame, Indiana

Living Christ

A Spiritual Reading of the Gospels

Peter Feldmeier

LITURGICAL PRESS
Collegeville, Minnesota

www.litpress.org

Cover design by Monica Bokinskie. *Jesus Christ Pantocrator*, detail of the Deësis Mosaic, Hagia Sophia, Istanbul. Image courtesy of Wikimedia Commons (CC BY-SA 2.0).

Scripture quotations are from New Revised Standard Version Bible: Catholic Edition © 1989, 1993 National Council of the Churches of Christ in the United States of America. Used by permission. All rights reserved worldwide.

Excerpt from the English translation of *The Roman Missal* © 2010, International Commission on English in the Liturgy Corporation. All rights reserved.

1	2	3	4	5	6	7	8	9

Library of Congress Cataloging-in-Publication Data

Names: Feldmeier, Peter, author.
Title: Living Christ : a spiritual reading of the gospels / Peter Feldmeier.
Description: Collegeville, Minnesota : Liturgical Press, [2023] | Includes
   bibliographical references. | Summary: "Living Christ unites up-
   to-date biblical scholarship to a deep spiritual engagement with the
   Gospels"— Provided by publisher.
Identifiers: LCCN 2022038313 (print) | LCCN 2022038314 (ebook)
   | ISBN 9780814668214 (trade paperback) | ISBN 9780814668221
   (epub) | ISBN 9780814668221 (pdf) | ISBN 9780814669198 (pdf)
Subjects: LCSH: Jesus Christ—Example. | Bible—Use. | Spiritual life.
Classification: LCC BT304.2 .F453 2023 (print) | LCC BT304.2
   (ebook) | DDC 232—dc23/eng/20221207
LC record available at https://lccn.loc.gov/2022038313
LC ebook record available at https://lccn.loc.gov/2022038314

Contents

into this truth, the best we can get from the Bible is knowledge of important first-century Christian documents. But if our focus of the text is to know Christ, then the Bible becomes a vehicle to understand and know the Word himself. This is how the fathers of Vatican II frame it:

> It pleased God, in his goodness and wisdom, to reveal himself and to make known the mystery of his will . . . , which was that people can draw near to the Father, through Christ, the Word made flesh, in the holy Spirit, and thus become sharers in the divine nature. . . . The most intimate truth thus revealed about God and human salvation shines forth for us in Christ, who is himself both the mediator and the sum total of revelation. . . . Hence, Jesus Christ . . . "speaks the words of God," . . . and accomplishes the saving work which the Father gave him to do. . . . As a result, he himself—to see whom is to see the Father . . . —completed and perfected revelation and confirmed it with divine guarantees.[2]

The Bible is foundational and indispensable for Christianity and for our own souls. But it is a complicated book, or, literally, set of books. In it we find different theologies and different visions of faithfulness. These do not always cohere neatly to each other. Some even seem to exist in a creative tension with each other. This fact, however, ought not to frustrate us or undermine the Bible's authority. Ultimately, God transcends words and concepts, and we should not mistake the finger pointing to the moon to be the moon itself. Ultimately too, the kingdom of God that Jesus preached will not be reduced to a formula. God will not be housetrained. Further, there are various ways to consider faithfulness, and the Bible witnesses to these in different ways.

This book is not a work of original biblical scholarship, but it relies on scholars who have investigated the historical, religious, and cultural situation from which the texts emerged, and it draws on insights that come from these studies. Scholars use an array of tools to understand the intent of the author and even how texts themselves work, both in the ancient world as well as ours. Biblical scholars pay attention to literary genres (*form criticism*) such as myth, poetry, historical narrative, exhortation, and so on. They also incorporate historical analysis to their interpretation (*historical-critical method*), where they identify cultural assumptions of the day and how these affect the text and help us to understand it better. They also address whether and how the text was edited (*redaction criticism*). For example, Mark was a central source for Matthew and Luke, and sometimes they cite Mark verbatim. But other times, they clearly change Mark to meet their own literary or theological interests. There is also *source criticism*, which looks at where the text or tradition came from; *narrative criticism*, which investigates how the text is structured and what themes are emphasized; *ideological criticism*, which addresses how the text imagines power relations; and the list could continue. Among biblical scholars there is often quite a consensus when addressing these various issues.

Many lay Christians resist biblical scholarship, and this is for several reasons. One reason is that the various tools mentioned above tend to make for a very dry reading of the text. One of my students once remarked, "This kind of study just takes the romance right out of the Bible." It certainly can do that. Others have responded with a wariness that they might "lose their faith"; that is, the Bible gets reduced to critical analysis that seems to gut its revelatory quality altogether. They also seem to fear learning, for example, that some of the narrative may not have happened as written. For them, it undermines the Bible of its assurance of truth. "Can I now even trust the Bible?" they seem to be asking.

One way of dealing with these concerns is to recognize that what we understand as *historical accuracy* is a modern idea. As I have noted in another publication, "When the Bible describes historical figures or events, these descriptions are laden with history, theology, themes of national identity, intercultural conflicts, and so on."[3] The evangelists believed they were writing a true account of the life and ministry of Jesus. They also believed, like everyone else in their day, that they had narrative license in describing the true Jesus. Further, they wrote in the context of their own Christian communities in the late first century. The concerns, piety, conflicts, and religious experiences that these communities had often get set into the narrative itself. This is not a foul, but an opportunity to see how Jesus's ministry can be even more relevant to them and, by extension, to us.

Even if these worries can be allayed, biblical scholarship can take us only so far. What does the biblical word mean for us? How can the Gospels be revelatory in my life? These questions cannot be fully answered by biblical scholarship alone. One of the leading thinkers of interpretation theory (hermeneutics), Paul Ricoeur, argues that texts such as the Bible have a *surplus of meaning*.[4] Ricoeur means by this that once the text has been removed from its author and initial audience, it allows new audiences access to its truths that go beyond its original context. Here, interpretation involves entering into a proposed world unfolded by the text. To interpret is to try to understand the type of being-in-the-world provided by the text. What must be interpreted is the proposed world, which one could inhabit and wherein one could project one's own possibilities. So the text becomes a medium through which we understand ourselves anew. Real appropriation of the text's truths is found in wrestling with this proposed world in one's own life. For Ricoeur, this is how religious texts become revelatory: they occasion an event of encounter with God in the world the text brings us.

The great challenge for an authentic Christian use of the Bible is to honor and respect the original intent of the author and its original circumstance—this is the primary role of scholarship—and how the text can speak to us now, many cultures different and centuries away from that original circumstance. This is where biblical spirituality comes to the fore. This book is a creative expression of biblical spirituality; it is a spiritual reading. As such, I will endeavor always to be an honest broker regarding biblical scholarship, and indeed I am relying on that scholarship to guide me. That will be our foundation. But I also intend this book to express a living text, a living revelation; one that facilitates an encounter with the living Word through the word. *This is what I strongly recommend to the reader: First, read a particular Gospel as a complete story. Then, read my commentary for that particular Gospel. Do this for each of the four Gospels.* In this way, you will first encounter the word of God as it is and as a complete rendering. Then allow my own reading to help you walk through it a second time.

What Is Biblical Spirituality?

The term *spirituality* is used ubiquitously in our culture. Any major bookstore will have a large number of books devoted to the subject, ranging from the New Age movement to mysticism to self-help books. Some seem exotic, others esoteric, and many have little to do with the spiritual life and more to do with skillful activity, from learning how to play golf to gaining business strategies. In my book *Christian Spirituality*, I suggest that even scholars in the field struggle to agree with what it is. I note, "The famous Anglican theologian John Macquarrie considers that spiritualty 'has to do with becoming a person in the fullest sense.' Leading Protestant spirituality scholar Gordon Wakefield says that it 'describes those attitudes, beliefs, and practices which animate people's lives and help them reach out towards super-sensible realities.' And finally, the former Archbishop of Canterbury Rowan Williams speaks of 'each believer making his or her own that engagement with the questioning at the heart of faith.'"[5] Ewert Cousins, the general editor of the World Spirituality series, concludes that spirituality is "that inner dimension of the person called by certain traditions 'the spirit.' This spiritual core is the deepest center of the person. It is here that the person is open to the transcendent dimension; it is here that the person experiences ultimate reality."[6] This last definition seems the most useful. Augmenting Cousins's definition, I would add that spirituality is about religious experience, religious commitments, and interior transformation. Authentic spirituality is also deeply invested in everything that gives meaning to human growth and flourishing. Given this broader set of considerations, spirituality ought to be understood as something holistic that encompasses the environment, justice, prayer, community, and even global relations. It ought not to be purely individualistic.

The English word "spirituality" derives from the Latin *spiritualitas*. This Latin term translates the biblical Greek noun *pneuma* (spirit). We find in the New Testament that *Pneuma Hagion* (Holy Spirit) dwells in us, transforming us to be spiritual (*pneumatikos*) persons (Rom 8:9-11). In John's Gospel, believers are promised a rebirth in the Spirit and in truth (John 3:2-8; 4:23). The Spirit even establishes the Christian community (Acts 2:32-33). St. Paul understands the very nature of a Christian as being "one spirit" with Christ (1 Cor 6:17), and the indwelling presence of God makes one a "spiritual person" (1 Cor 2:14-15).

Every Christian's spirituality is necessarily going to be particular, as everyone is unique with different personality qualities, experiences, and lifestyles. I think we can also say, however, that a Christian spirituality has universal and biblically grounded elements. Here are some of the most central. A Christian spirituality is:

1. A life of grace and faith: God's gift of himself and the whole entrusting of oneself to God;

2. A life in the Spirit: living in and through the Holy Spirit and knowing what Paul calls the fruit of the Spirit (love, joy, peace, patience, kindness, generosity, faithfulness, gentleness, and self-control—Gal 5:22-23);

3. Christocentric: real intimacy with Christ and conforming ourselves to Christ in both cross and resurrection;

4. Trinitarian: living through the divine interchange of love;

5. Communal: we know and serve God as a body of Christ;

6. Just: one that advocates actively for those marginalized and seeks the common good;

7. Prayerful: seeking intimacy with God who indwells; and

8. Divinized: ultimately seeking full union with God where one lives in and through the divine.[7]

The Bible is decisive and foundational for a Christian spirituality because it offers core religious framings or patterns of thought that structure Christian identity. Themes in the Old and New Testaments create ways of looking at our lives, our relationships with each other, and, most important, our relationship with God. These patterns are woven throughout the biblical text, and they imply and draw on each other. Taking on these patterns involves making them part of our own spiritual horizon. Consider that the Bible is telling us: "Imagine God *this* way," "Consider your soul like *this*," "Engage each other through *these* values." These themes ground the Christian character and thus Christian spirituality. As I note in *Christian Spirituality*, these themes include the following:

Creation: God made the world out of love, God deemed it "good," and God created humanity in God's very image and likeness.

Covenant: In God's providence, he chose a people for himself with binding faithfulness and with both expectations and promises.

Sin and Redemption: From the start, humanity sought a kind of independence from God that has deeply wounded our souls and our relationship with him and each other, though God also always sought to heal those wounds and right our relationship with him.

Monarchy: God ceded Israel's wish to form a kingdom, and through David God has promised an eternal reign, which Jesus will fulfill.

Temple and Priesthood: God formed a priesthood and supported a temple for worship where he would be particularly present to his people.

Sacrifice: God ordered sacrifices that atoned for sin, provided divine communion, and sealed covenants.

Prophecy: God has chosen holy men and women to speak God's will and demand covenant fidelity.

Wisdom: The universe was created with an order imbued with purpose and life, and God's Torah or law represents divine wisdom at its height.

Law and Grace: God's favor and blessings can be found in his Torah, and Christ will ultimately complete the Torah.

Kingdom of God: Ultimately, God is king, and God desires a kingdom of justice, flourishing, devotion, and peace.

Prayer: Israel prays to God, praises God, and finds intimacy with God through prayer, with the Psalms being foremost.[8]

A Brief Introduction to the Gospels[9]

The Gospel of Matthew

Scholars generally place the origins of the Gospel of Matthew around 85–90 CE, written in Palestine or Syria for a community of believers that was primarily Jewish. It is overwhelmingly interested in showing how Jesus fulfills Old Testament prophecies and expectations, and it assumes its audience knows and follows Jewish Torah or law. In fact, it is here more than any other Gospel where Jesus shows himself the authentic interpreter of Torah in contrast to the Pharisees and scribes of Jesus's day (and rabbis in Matthew's day). As already noted, one of Matthew's key sources is Mark, whom he freely uses and yet whose text he also edits for his own purpose. We also see an additional source that Luke uses as well. Scholars refer to this as "Q," a shorthand for the German word *quelle*, which simply means "source." Many of Jesus's sayings were orally transmitted and almost certainly written down by the Christian community. Matthew also has his own independent sources that are unique to his Gospel. Matthew is not Matthew the tax collector, whom we meet in 9:9 and who then becomes an apostle in 10:3. Nowhere does the author suggest having been an eyewitness to Jesus's ministry, and the ascription of Matthew was appended to the manuscript only in the second century. But he is certainly Jewish, as is most of his believing community. Actually, none of the Gospels originally had the authors' names assigned to them. None were eyewitnesses, and the ascriptions Matthew, Mark, Luke, and John all came only in the second century.

Matthew begins his Gospel with Jesus as *Immanuel*, God is with us (1:23), and ends it with "And remember, I am with you always, to the end of the age" (28:20). The ongoing presence of God through Jesus is a dominant theme. The presence of Christ with them allows Matthew's readers to embody Christ in who they are and in what they do. His is a Gospel of *doing*. God demands that our lives show concrete fruits of discipleship, evidenced in acts of compassion, love, forgiveness, and attention to those in need. But it is also a Gospel of *being*. One's inner disposition overwhelmingly matters. Anyone with a modicum of self-discipline can act in certain ways. Jesus demands interior transformation that reveals the deepest message of the kingdom. Jesus calls his listeners to become pure of heart, to live out the fullness of the Torah that he provides, and to live a life whereby "I was hungry and you gave me food, I was thirsty and you gave me something to drink, I was a stranger and you welcomed me, I was naked and you gave me clothing, I was sick and you took care of me, I was in prison and you visited me. . . . Truly I tell you, just as you did it to the least of these . . . you did it to me" (25:35-40).

The Gospel of Mark

Most scholars place Mark's Gospel as originating in Rome around the time shortly after Caesar Nero's persecution of Christians. This persecution happened during the mid-to-late 60s. Given Mark's references to the temple's destruction and the apocalyptic language and urgency throughout the Gospel, it is usually placed around 70. The world for Christians seemed to be falling apart. Unlike the Jewish audience of Matthew, Mark seems to be primarily addressing a Gentile group of believers, as he has to explain Aramaic terms (5:41; 7:34) and Jewish customs as he understands them (7:3-4).

Jesus tells few parables in Mark's Gospel, but Jesus himself is something of a parable. He is the truth, but an expression of the truth that seems strange to them. Those who follow him, including the twelve apostles, find him an enigma. He knows he is the Son of God: "You are my Son, the Beloved; with you I am well pleased" (1:11). And demons know this: "What have you to do with us, Jesus of Nazareth? Have you come to destroy us? I know who you are, the Holy One of God" (1:24). But the people never really get it, and even the disciples grow in only some understanding. After Jesus calms the sea Mark notes, "And they were utterly astounded . . . but their hearts were hardened" (6:51-52).

Mark's Gospel is meant to *grab* the reader. There is a "you were there" quality to his account. He gives specific names to secondary characters and provides more dialogue for them. Mark also presents those closest to Jesus in very human and flawed ways. His disciples often confound Jesus: "Why are you afraid? Have you still no faith?" (4:40), and his family even tried to restrain him (3:21). Mark also provides expressions of Jesus's emotional life, such as compassion, surprise, indignation, and love (1:41; 6:6; 10:14; 10:21).

In Mark there are two great themes: first, Jesus is a Messiah who will die as a ransom for humanity (10:45); second, disciples must take on this very way of the cross as well. Mark is a meditation on suffering as the way to glory. Discipleship is learning this. Mark refers to Jesus's disciples as *mathātās*, learners, and what they must learn is the way of the cross. The context of these two themes is apocalypticism. Jesus is opposed by all who resist the kingdom. His first miracle is an exorcism of a demon, and yet soon enough, "The Pharisees went out and immediately conspired with the Herodians against him, how to destroy him" (3:6). Jesus seems to frame it all in apocalyptic terms, anticipating that "the sun will be darkened, and the moon will not give its light, and the stars will be falling from heaven, and the powers in the heavens will be shaken" (13:24-25). Earlier he proclaimed, "Truly I tell you, there are some standing here who will not taste death until they see that the kingdom of God has come with power" (9:1). I once noted, "To understand Mark's spirituality is to understand Jesus as mightier than any of these powers even as one might fall victim to them. Christ has ultimately conquered them. In Mark's Gospel, faith is perseverance especially in times of trial, and confidence that even in one's suffering the victorious Christ walks with the faithful."[10]

The Gospel of Luke

Like Matthew's Gospel, the Gospel of Luke is generally believed to have been written late in the first century (85–90), though in his case he primarily addresses a Gentile audience. Like Matthew, Luke draws on Mark and Q along with other sources. In contrast to Mark, he downplays the apocalypticism and sees the Greco-Roman world as ripe for evangelization. Luke, who also wrote Acts, quotes the risen Jesus as promising, "You will receive power when the Holy Spirit has come upon you; and you will be my witnesses in Jerusalem, in all Judea and Samaria, and to the ends of the earth" (Acts 1:8).

The presence of the Holy Spirit dominates both Luke and Acts. John the Baptist promises that "One who is more powerful than I is coming. . . . He will baptize you with the Holy Spirit and fire" (3:16). Upon Jesus's baptism, he was "full of the Holy Spirit" (4:1), and "filled with the power of the Spirit," he began his ministry quoting Isaiah, "The Spirit of the Lord is upon me, because he has anointed me to bring good news to the poor. He has sent me to proclaim release to the captives and recovery of sight to the blind, to let the oppressed go free, to proclaim the year of the Lord's favor. . . . Today this scripture has been fulfilled in your hearing" (4:14, 18-21).

The kingdom of God Jesus proclaims is one of reversal of fortunes. Here the poor and the marginalized will be raised. These are the ones who can depend only on God. In contrast, those wealthy and those in power often resist the kingdom of God, as they seem content relying on their wealth and status. Mary's Magnificat sets the tone for the whole Gospel:

> My soul magnifies the Lord, and my spirit rejoices in God my Savior; for he has looked with favor on the lowliness of his servant. . . . His mercy is for those who fear him from generation to generation. He has shown strength with his arm; he has scattered

the proud in the thoughts of their hearts. He has brought down the powerful from their thrones, and lifted up the lowly; he has filled the hungry with good things, and sent the rich away empty. He has helped his servant Israel, in remembrance of his mercy, according to the promise he made to our ancestors, to Abraham and to his descendants forever. (1:46-55)

God is faithful to his covenantal promises, and Jesus has come to fulfill them, bringing salvation to his people. This salvation is marked as feeding the hungry and lifting up the poor. Here in Luke we see God's preferential option for the poor played out particularly in his parables. While Jesus certainly calls for repentance from all, it is notable that in many parables, the poor are asked only to believe in the greatness of God's mercy and love for them. The rich, on the other hand, are challenged to see their fate connected to how they have aligned themselves and their goods in service to those in need. Jesus has come "to seek out and save the lost" (19:10). Christians are servants, just as Jesus is a servant: "The kings of the Gentiles lord it over them; and those in authority over them are called benefactors. But not so with you; rather the greatest among you must become like the youngest, and the leader like one who serves. . . . I am among you as one who serves" (22:25-27).

In the Gospel of Luke, God's universal love is expressed best by care for the masses, almost all of whom were poor peasants. Luke's spiritual message is one that requires deep examination of one's values and priorities. Jesus demands repentance and faith, and that faith is borne out by taking the side of the poor and marginalized and by identifying with their plight.

The Gospel of John

The Gospel of John is very different from Matthew, Mark, and Luke. These are known as the *Synoptic* (literally "same eye") Gospels, as they present the teaching and ministry of Jesus similarly. John is different. There are few miracles in John, no parables, and Jesus's teaching style is very different. It is widely believed to have been written around the year 100 and reflects a situation where "Judaism, early Christianity, the complex religions of the Hellenistic and Greek world, and incipient Gnosticism rubbed shoulders—often painfully."[11] Many Jews who believed in Jesus were, by the late first

The Gospel
of Matthew

Living the Torah of Jesus

Jesus in Infancy (1:1–2:23)

Throughout Matthew's Gospel we find Jesus variously identified. Jesus is the "Son of David" (21:9) and more. Jesus is the Messiah and Son of God (16:16) and perhaps even more. Jesus is the "Son of Man" (19:28), an apocalyptic figure who will establish God's everlasting kingdom, and more. As we shall see, Jesus is also a *type* of Moses and even Israel, and even Israel's Torah (teaching and law), symbolically embodying them and expressing their fulfillment. Matthew's first title for Jesus is "Emmanuel, which means 'God is with us'" (1:23). Matthew begins his Gospel with a genealogy of Jesus. Jesus was born at the right place at the right time: "So all the generations from Abraham to David are fourteen generations; and from David to the deportation to Babylon, fourteen generations; and from the deportation to Babylon to the Messiah, fourteen generations" (1:17). This was all part of God's providence, a providence that includes Perez's mother Tamar disguising herself as a prostitute to entice Judah (her father-in-law!) to impregnate her; Boaz, whose mother was Rahab, a non-Jew and actual prostitute; the Moabite woman Ruth, the great-grandmother of King David; and Bathsheba, the wife of Uriah whom David had killed to conceal his adultery. God draws straight with crooked lines, and nothing need be outside God's providence. This is not to say that God wills chaos or sin to bring order or good but rather that God's providential grace works in human history with all its brokenness and frailties. Again and again, Matthew will tell us that Jesus and his ministry fulfilled prophecies and sayings from the Hebrew Bible.[1] Prophecy can mean something predicted that will come to pass. Matthew typically sees it differently. For Matthew, *fulfilled* usually means *filled full of meaning*, here uniting images and truths of the past with the truths of the present.

Matthew tells us that the Holy Family dwells in a house in Bethlehem when the three wise men from the east journey to venerate the newly born "king of the Jews." They come following a star,[2] as this is a cosmic event, with gifts of gold, frankincense, and myrrh, gifts fit for a king, for a priest, and perhaps an anticipation of his death. "When King Herod heard this, he was frightened, and all Jerusalem with him" (2:3). Herod was infamous for striking down any possible claimant to his throne, including some of his own children. A joke attributed to his contemporary was, "Better to be Herod's pig than his son."[3] And so Joseph took the mother and child and fled to Egypt to await the time of a safe return; and Jesus is now a type of Israel. Matthew quotes the prophet Hosea, "Out of Egypt I called my son" (Hos 11:1). Jesus is also a type of Moses. Consider their parallels: Both lived under a despot (Pharaoh and Herod) who killed children they feared (Hebrews and the infants of Bethlehem). Both fled to another country to escape the tyrant, and both returned when he died. Just to be on the safe side, the Holy Family moved far north to avoid Herod's eldest son, the tyrant Archelaus, who took the throne of Judea (2:22-23).

I have often marveled at despots who would do anything to retain their power. What is it worth? What is it for? The real tyrant is the intoxication that power brings and the fear of being exposed as nothing more or less than a human being, come up from dust and to dust return. It is a life of nothing less than enslavement. And yet, so many want to be enslaved by it. We might also consider our own spheres of influence or power. Do we carry them lightly and humbly and as an expression of service? Or do we love to cling to and to inflate our own egos? Much later Jesus tells his disciples, "You know that the rulers of the Gentiles lord it over them, and their great ones are tyrants over them. It will not be so among you; but whoever wishes to be great among you must be your servant, and whoever wishes to be first among you must be your slave; just as the Son of Man came not to be served but to serve, and to give his life a ransom for many" (20:25-28).

Baptism and Testing (3:1–4:11)

The great prophet Elijah challenged King Ahab and Queen Jezebel to cease worshiping the god Baal and commit to the living God. His prophetic ministry was harrowing, though he survived the threats against his life. According to the Bible, he never died but was swept up to heaven. He was with his disciple Elisha: "As they continued walking and talking, a chariot of fire and horses of fire separated the two of them, and Elijah ascended in a whirlwind into heaven" (2 Kgs 2:11). Three centuries later (sixth century BCE), the prophet Malachi foresaw a judgment day of the Lord: "See, the day is coming, burning like an oven, when all the arrogant and all evildoers will be stubble; the day that comes shall burn them up, says the LORD of hosts. . . . Lo, I will send you the prophet Elijah before the great and terrible day of the LORD comes" (Mal 4:1-5). The day of the Lord that Malachi saw was healing and joy for the righteous but terror for those who would not repent.

John the Baptist is a type of Elijah who demanded repentance before that great and terrible day. Jesus anticipates his own ministry by participating in John's. Like a perfected Israel, he entered the waters of John's baptism, and all present heard the voice from heaven, "This is my Son, the Beloved, with whom I am well pleased" (3:17). Often Christians wonder why Jesus would need to be baptized, since he was without sin. Pope Francis remarks that Jesus intended to show "solidarity with the repentant people. . . . Jesus receives approval from the heavenly Father, who sent him precisely that he might share our condition, our poverty."[4]

Jesus is preparing for his ministry. It begins with John and then takes him to the desert. As Israel passed forty years in the desert of testing and purification, so now God's Son enters.[5] The tempter appeals to his divine Sonship: prove it, he says. "If you are the Son of God, command these stones to become loaves of bread" (4:3). Prove it, he says. "If you are the Son of God, throw yourself down [from the pinnacle of the temple]" (4:5-6). Won't God hold you up? Become a world king, he says; just do me homage and I will make it happen (4:9). Jesus's responses all cite Deuteronomy (8:3; 6:16; 6:13), referring to Israel's time in the desert. Where Israel faltered, Jesus does not. Jesus becomes Israel now perfected.

The Sermon on the Mount (5:1–7:29)

The Sermon on the Mount is the first of Jesus's teaching discourses. Matthew provides us with five total, which some scholars consider an echo of the five books of Moses, the Pentateuch.[6] Just as Moses received the Torah (law) of God on Mount Sinai, Jesus delivers a sermon on a mountain regarding true Torah piety. "The crowds were astounded at his teaching, for he taught them as one having authority, and not as their scribes" (7:28-29). Jesus spoke with *exousia*, with divine power and authority. The first part of Jesus's sermon is what is famously known as the *Beatitudes* (derived from the Latin *beatus*: blessed or fortunate). Matthew's Greek is *makarios*, blessed or happy.

> Blessed are the poor in spirit, for theirs is the kingdom of heaven. Blessed are those who mourn, for they will be comforted. Blessed are the meek, for they will inherit the earth. Blessed are those who hunger and thirst for righteousness, for they will be filled. Blessed are the merciful, for they will receive mercy. Blessed are the pure in heart, for they will see God. Blessed are the peacemakers, for they will be called children of God. Blessed are those who are persecuted for righteousness' sake, for theirs is the kingdom of heaven. Blessed are you when people revile you and persecute you and utter all kinds of evil against you falsely on my account. Rejoice and be glad, for your reward is great in heaven, for in the same way they persecuted the prophets who were before you. (5:3-12)

The poor in spirit, the mourners, the meek—all three reference those who are humble and gentle. It is these whose hearts are broken of pride, whose souls are softened; those not afraid of leaning in to their own suffering or that of others; those who know their nothingness in the face of God's greatness and the glory of the kingdom that they will attain. If we do not realize our own poverty, we will never experience the fullness of the undeserved grace that surpasses all and becomes our true wealth. If our hands are not open as a beggar's hands, we will not receive. In clutching and clinging to self-righteousness or control or the ego's ambitions, we walk only closefisted, receiving nothing.

To hunger and thirst for righteousness is to hunger and thirst for holiness. Jesus commands later in this sermon, "Be perfect, therefore, as your heavenly Father is perfect" (5:48). No one who strives for holiness is ever satisfied. The closer we come, the clearer it is to the soul how far we must continue to walk. St. John of the Cross describes an essential grace in this way: "God will give illumination by bestowing on the soul not only knowledge of its own misery and lowliness but also knowledge of His grandeur and majesty."[7] The humility that comes from this then becomes the foundation for loving others. It is only when our disordered loves are dissolved that we can then dwell with God in "spiritual peace and tranquility."[8]

It is a blessing to be merciful. In being so, we not only imitate God but also live God's very life of mercy. The pure of heart are promised to see God. On Sinai, Moses begs God to show him his glory. God responds, "You cannot see my face; for no one shall see me and live" (Exod 33:20). God did promise to "pass before him," but only in a cloud and only with Moses hiding in the cleft of the rock. "The LORD passed before him, and proclaimed, 'The LORD, the LORD, a God merciful and gracious'" (Exod 34:6). At the end of the day, God *as* God remains absolute mystery to us. The full vision of God is reserved for eternity, and the promise of this beatitude is ultimately a future promise. But it is also a promise bearing fruit in this life where we can, by God's grace, be sacraments of him: embodiments of his mercy, his peace. And so, blessed are the peacemakers who become now his children. Pope Francis has said: "Let us ask the Lord for the grace to be simple and humble people, the grace to be able to weep, the grace to be meek, the grace to work for justice and peace, and above all the grace to let ourselves be forgiven by God so as to become instruments of his mercy."[9]

The final two blessings are for those persecuted for being holy, for being truthful, for witnessing their faith. In Jesus's time many disciples and all the apostles suffered martyrdom. This fate is not reserved for some past, however. The twentieth century saw more martyrs for the Christian faith than the whole of the first three centuries of Christianity. Still, for many of us living in a country with religious freedom, martyrdom is not something we would fear. But persecutions are there. In our culture, if one is modestly religious, one usually has broad social support. A seriously religious person would often be considered a bit off. To seek radical holiness makes one a *fanatic*, someone privately and maybe publicly distained. *She's just taken this religion thing too far!* Truth tellers are never in the clear. To speak prophetically about today's state of affairs can garner support, but only from those who agree with one's politics or religion or morality. But to speak prophetically challenging one's own—family, community, religious tradition—is to guarantee enemies. "Let us lie in wait for the righteous man, because he is inconvenient to us and opposes our actions" (Wis 2:12). Jesus does not ask us to imagine grief as if joy or persecutions as if not harmful. But he does promise that what is suffered for God's sake will be transformed into joy in his eternal kingdom.

These are the people who are *makarios*, blessed. They are also the people who are *makarios*, happy. There is a gentle joy in living in, through, and for God. It represents living our most authentic life. Peacemakers are healers. The meek disarm and allow for reconciliation. Many years ago, when I was in the ministry and in my first assignment as a priest, I noticed at daily Mass an extremely poised elder named Mabel. I did not know anything about her, except that I was impressed with her simplicity, earnestness, and gentleness. It was only after Mabel died that I learned about her. Every morning she prayed the rosary and went to Mass. After Mass, she went to the parish school where she volunteered as the librarian. I also found out that when students were disruptive and sent out of the classroom, they more often were sent to the library rather than the principal's office. And there was Mabel. She just let them hang out. She had a calming effect, a healing effect. Often, they would tell her what was going on in their lives that caused them to act out in class. Mabel rarely had any advice; she just listened. And when they were ready to go back to class, they came back differently just for having been in Mabel's presence. Mabel was meek; she was pure of heart; she was poor in spirit. The funeral was packed: everybody loved Mabel. Mabel did nothing great in her life, and yet her life was great. She was a child of God and a sacrament of God's grace. She was a good Christian. The fathers of the Second Vatican Council assert that "the world cannot be transfigured and offered to God without the spirit of the beatitudes."[10]

Jesus continues his sermon by calling those who follow him "salt of the earth" and "light of the world." And indeed, "Let your light shine before others, so that they may see your good works and give glory to your Father in heaven" (5:16). In this brief command he says so much. The first is that what gives glory to God is our works. Matthew's Gospel is not one of "works righteousness," but Jesus demands an engaged faith that produces fruit here and now. And the second is that we must shine. It is crucial to know that our light shines from within; this is where real conversion takes place. The rest of the sermon emphasizes this interior purification that marks authentic discipleship. Jesus assures his listeners, "Do not think that I have come to abolish the law or the prophets; I have come not to abolish but to fulfill." Jesus assures them that "until heaven and earth pass away, not one letter, not one stroke of a letter, will pass from the law until all is accomplished" (5:17-18). What fulfills is the interior life. The Torah is for holiness's sake that Israel could "be holy, for I am holy" (Lev 11:45).

The prophet Jeremiah announced a new covenant would bring this about: "The days are surely coming, says the LORD, when I will make a new covenant with the house of Israel and the house of Judah. . . . I will put my law [Torah] within them, and I will write it on their hearts" (Jer 31:31-33). The Sermon on the Mount reflects this. Thus, we have the *six antitheses*: "You have heard it said . . . but I say to you . . . " Don't just avoid murder but avoid anger. Don't just avoid adultery but avoid lust. Don't follow the rules of divorce but remain faithful. Don't just avoid false oaths but speak truthfully. Don't seek redress but turn the other cheek. Don't just love the neighbor but love the enemy. All of these reflect a posture of the heart, an inner transformation that requires both God's grace and our own cultivation. Jesus then addresses the three traditional acts of piety: almsgiving, prayer, and fasting. Is it for show to others, or even show to oneself? Then it means nothing. Is it earnest and from within? Then "your Father who sees in secret will reward you" (6:18).

The Lord's Prayer

It is here where Matthew places the Lord's Prayer. We would do well to contemplate the profundity of this short prayer, particularly as it has remained central to Christian prayer since the first century.

> When you are praying, do not heap up empty phrases as the Gentiles do; for they think that they will be heard because of their many words. Do not be like them, for your Father knows what you need

And forgive our debts, as we also have forgiven our debtors. Immediately after teaching them the Lord's Prayer, Jesus says, "For if you forgive others their trespasses, your heavenly Father will also forgive you; but if you do not forgive others, neither will your Father forgive your trespasses" (6:14-15). In part, the issue here is that without forgiving others, we retain a kind of hardness of heart that does not let God's forgiving grace in. Resentments are toxic to the soul. Resentments also have a kind of narcissistic quality. They inflate the ego when we regularly mull over what so-and-so did to *ME*! But forgiveness can be complicated. How, for example, can one forgive another who refuses to acknowledge the hurt she or he has done? How can one fully forgive when one is still wounded by and suffering because of the pain another has caused? Perhaps the best way to consider sins and forgiveness is to start by realizing that I am utterly dependent on God's grace, that I too am a sinner who desperately needs God's forgiveness. This, then, does not allow me a position of power: i.e., I now deign to forgive you. Rather, it puts me in a posture of humility: i.e., I live by God's mercy and desire to be a sacrament of that same mercy in my life and with everyone, especially those who have caused me pain.

Lead us not into temptation, but deliver us from the evil one. Does God lead us into temptation? The Letter of James declares, "No one, when tempted, should say, 'I am being tempted by God'; for God cannot be tempted by evil and he himself tempts no one" (Jas 1:13). God is hardly a lure to sin. But God and life itself can *test* us, and God can even use Satan to do this. Abraham was tested by God in the offering of his son Isaac. Israel was tested in the desert for forty years to purify them. And God did not spare his Son from being tested by Satan in the desert after his baptism. The petition here clearly is about being tested beyond our capacity. Paul declares, "So if you think you are standing, watch out that you do not fall. No testing has overtaken you that is not common to everyone. God is faithful, and he will not let you be tested beyond your strength, but with the testing he will also provide the way out so that you may be able to endure it" (1 Cor 10:12-13). In Romans, Paul frames it thus: "We also boast in our sufferings, knowing that suffering produces endurance, and endurance produces character, and character produces hope, and hope does not disappoint us, because God's love has been poured into our hearts through the Holy Spirit that has been given to us" (Rom 5:3-5).

No one wants to suffer, and few look for life experiences that "test" us. But it is also true that these very experiences deepen us. It is difficult, for example, to have deep compassion for others without ourselves having suffered. This final petition of the Lord's Prayer realizes this and seeks the grace to be able to endure suffering and trials; they are not to overwhelm or crush us. The NRSV translates the final petition as being rescued from the "evil one," surely referencing Satan, but the Greek could simply be read, "deliver us from evil." We need rescue from so much, from anger, jealousy, disordered desires, and so on. Ultimately, what the Lord wants for us, and thus teaches us in the Lord's Prayer, is to live fully as children of our Father.

Other teachings in this sermon continue this theme: seek the spiritual treasure, not the temporal; be free of worry and trust in God; do not judge. The gate is narrow, and it is both demanding and freeing. We can be free from a toxic soul, but we must engage the faith robustly. In Jesus's conclusion, he demands that we bear good fruit in our lives—the tell-tale sign of authenticity—and remember, "Not everyone who says to me 'Lord, Lord,' will enter the kingdom of heaven, but only the one who does the will of my Father in heaven." For those who talk a good game and little else: "I never knew you; go away from me, you evildoers" (7:21-23).[12] Pope Francis calls these people, "Christians only in appearance . . . [who] look like Christians but . . . they are only wearing makeup."[13] The Sermon on the Mount is the most important and decisive sermon the Gospels provide. The kingdom is something of a transcendent mystery. It is something here, something to progressively realize, and something to be fulfilled in the end of time. Jesus never *exactly* tells us what he means by the kingdom. But in this sermon, we discover the kind of person we need to be to enter it.

Healing and Divine Power (8:1–9:34)

In the Sermon on the Mount, we encounter the authentic interpreter of the Torah and the kind of disciple fit for the kingdom. Here, unlike Moses, Jesus speaks with his own authority, his own *exousia*.

Now we find him a divine healer, a man with divine power. We would do best to think of these events as more than just healings or exorcisms. They point to and participate in the kingdom that is emerging by his very ministry. They are signs of the kingdom, and they help us to engage a central question: who is this man? Matthew recounts Jesus healing various persons: a leper, the centurion's servant, many who were sick or possessed while he was staying in Peter's house, two men possessed by many demons, a paralytic, a hemorrhaging woman, a girl at the point of death, two blind men, and a man who was mute and demon possessed. In addition, he stills the raging waters on the Sea of Galilee. All these can be seen as interrelated. In the world of the ancient Near East, sickness, sin, and demon attacks were not strictly distinguished; physical evil, moral evil, and supernatural evil often blended in their minds. To the paralytic man, for instance, Jesus says, "Take heart, son; your sins are forgiven." For the scribes present, this sounded like blasphemy, for who but God can forgive sins? Jesus responded to their thoughts, " 'For which is easier, to say, "Your sins are forgiven," or to say, "Stand up and walk"? But so that you may know that the Son of Man has authority on earth to forgive sins'—he then said to the paralytic—'Stand up, take your bed and go to your home.' " Matthew then tells us, "And he stood up and went to his home. When the crowds saw it, they were filled with awe, and they glorified God, who had given such authority [*exousion*] to human beings" (9:2-8).

This same power over the forces of the anti-kingdom can be seen in Jesus's stilling of the storm on the sea: "A windstorm arose on the sea, so great that the boat was being swamped by the waves; but he was asleep. And they went and woke him up, saying, 'Lord, save us! We are perishing!' And he said to them, 'Why are you afraid, you of little faith?' Then he got up and rebuked the winds and the sea; and there was a dead calm. They were amazed, saying, 'What sort of man is this, that even the winds and the sea obey him?' " (8:24-27). The sea, especially when it was stormy, often represented for the ancient Near Eastern mind a spirit of chaos and evil, certainly danger. The Psalmist proclaims, "You rule the raging of the sea; when its waves rise, you still them" (Ps 89:9).[14] Jesus has powers not only over the threatening natural world but also over the demonic and chaotic powers. The kingdom has started to arise before the disciples and it can before us as well.

The human condition is fraught. No one, for example, escapes the ravages of age and no one escapes death. But many are afraid of them. We typically hide from both, whether it is with Botox, hair coloring, plastic surgery, or just the ennui that comes from this natural aging process. And we often hide from death, ensuring that the corpses of our loved ones "look good" or "life-like." Outside of these, most people live in various levels of fear. Some have great anxiety: this could ruin me! For others it is much more subtle: what will they think of me? Perhaps the greatest fear we *ought* to have is of sin. St. Paul did not think of sin as merely a moral failing, though it is that. Rather, for him sin takes on a kind of cosmic quality. It can act as a law in the world (Rom 7:25); it can enslave us and have dominion over us (Rom 6:6, 14, 17, 20). This is where the life of faith comes in. Paul also assures us that in Christ we are free from the law of sin (Rom 8:2). "For freedom Christ has set us free," Paul assures us (Gal 5:1). We will never be free from sin or fear without experiencing the liberating love of God through Jesus Christ. This is the new life, the life of the Spirit. It is a life of communion with the living God. "God is love, and those who abide in love abide in God, and God abides in them. . . . There is no fear in love, but perfect love casts out fear" (1 John 4:16-18). Later in the Gospel, waves are threatening the boat the disciples are in. Jesus comes to them, walking on the water. They seize with fear and his gentle response is "Take heart, it is I; do not be afraid" (Matt 14:27).

Jesus Missions His Disciples (9:35–10:42)

We begin to learn about Jesus's particular disciples, the Twelve, early in Matthew. As soon as Jesus returned to Galilee from his baptism and trials in the desert, he called Simon (Peter) and his brother Andrew who were fishing. "And he said to them, 'Follow me, and I will make you fish for people.'" Then he saw James and his brother John mending their nets, "and he called them. Immediately they left the boat and their father, and followed him" (4:18-22). In chapter 9, we find him calling the tax collector Matthew: "'Follow me.' And he got up and followed him" (9:9). Chapter 10 begins by mentioning the names of the Twelve. Now we might think of them as "apostles," a term that means "being sent." In this section, Jesus sends them out.

Why twelve? Here we must go back to the early life of Israel after Moses and Joshua. For two hundred years the Israelites lived as a confederation of tribes in the Holy Land. The tribes had judges, often called by God to lead them in war or interpret God's will for the people. The transition from the time of the judges to the monarchy of Saul, then David and Solomon, was rocky. The last "national" judge was Samuel, who was aging and whose children could not be trusted. The people asked for a king, which deflated Samuel. He went to the Lord, who conceded the request reluctantly. "Samuel prayed to the Lord, and the Lord said to Samuel, 'Listen to the voice of the people in all that they say to you; for they have not rejected you, but they have rejected me from being king over them'" (1 Sam 8:7). So, God was their king, but now they wanted a human king. Jesus preaches the kingdom of God, and he chooses the Twelve. Later in Matthew, Peter asks Jesus what will come of them for having given all to follow him. "Jesus said to them, 'Truly I tell you, at the renewal of all things, when the Son of Man is seated on the throne of his glory, you who have followed me will also sit on twelve thrones, judging the twelve tribes of Israel'" (19:28). This highly symbolic group takes us to a time when God was king.

Twice Matthew tells us that Jesus went throughout the region of Galilee proclaiming the kingdom and healing those in need (4:23; 9:35). "Then he said to his disciples, 'The harvest is plentiful, but the laborers are few; therefore ask the Lord of the harvest to send out laborers into his harvest'" (9:37-38). They were to go only "to the lost sheep of the house of Israel," now empowered to, as Jesus directed, "proclaim the good news, 'The kingdom of heaven has come near.' Cure the sick, raise the dead, cleanse the lepers, cast out demons" (10:6-8). There is urgency here in Jesus's ministry. Pope Francis compares the church to a "field hospital" where "wounds need to be treated, so many wounds! So many wounds!"[15]

In his Sermon on the Mount, Jesus challenges, "Do not store up for yourselves treasures on earth . . . where your treasure is, there your heart will be also" (6:19-21). And then two would-be disciples seek to follow him. To one he replies, "Foxes have holes, and birds of the air have nests; but the Son of Man has nowhere to lay his head" (8:20), and to the one who wants to take leave first to bury his father, Jesus simply says, "Follow me, and let the dead bury their own dead" (8:22). This latter reply seems preposterous, as though one ought not to do what one must for one's father. We need not take this literally, just as we don't take literally cutting off our hands or gouging out our eyes to avoid sin (5:29-30). This is known as *literary hyperbole*. On the other hand, we need to feel the urgency Jesus himself felt regarding the kingdom. So his Twelve are given marching orders: no money, no bag for the journey, no second tunic or sandals or staff (10:9). They are to be both unreservedly free and trusting and utterly dependent on God's providence here.

Jesus also warns them about the cost of discipleship and the persecutions that come from authentic discipleship. "So have no fear of them. . . . Do not fear those who kill the body but cannot kill the soul; rather fear him who can destroy both soul and body in hell" (10:26-28). And then the paradox: "whoever does not take up the cross and follow me is not worthy of me. Those who find their life will lose it, and those who lose their life for my sake will find it" (10:38-39). If one were to take this paradox somewhat literally and tried to scheme an outcome, then it would never work. One might think, "*Because* I want to find/save my life, I will lose it; that's the only way." Then what one is doing is nothing other than trying to find/save it in the first place. Here God becomes something of a good bet, one who provides the strategy for finding/saving my own life. But then, you've never really let it go. The cross, in its many manifestations, is a real dying to one's narcissism and a real living for God and for God's sake alone. This dying to self is a lifelong project. My life ultimately has to be about God and not about me. *Only* when my life is God's and God's completely have I fully embraced the cross.

Jesus's Message Goes Unheeded (11:1–12:50)

We do not hear from Matthew how the Twelve's missionizing went, but it seems not successful enough for deep repentance and conversion, or even deep belief in the good news of the coming kingdom. "For John came neither eating nor drinking, and they say, 'He has a demon'; the Son of Man came eating and drinking, and they say, 'Look, a glutton and a drunkard, a friend of tax collectors and sinners!' Yet wisdom is vindicated by her deeds" (11:18-19).

In this section Jesus implores his listeners: "Come to me all who are weary and are carrying heavy burdens, and I will give you rest. Take my yoke upon you, and learn from me; for I am gentle and humble of heart, and you will find rest for your souls. For my yoke is easy, and my burden is light" (11:28-30). This is a central element in his good news, that is, the joy of being a disciple, of being filled with the wisdom of God. Here Jesus appeals to the Jewish Wisdom tradition where *Lady Wisdom* invites all who wish the truth to enter her banquet and be filled (Prov 9:1-6). "For wisdom will come into your heart, and knowledge will be pleasant to your soul" (Prov 2:10). The book of Wisdom describes Wisdom as "a reflection of eternal light, a spotless mirror of the working of God, and an image of his goodness" (Wis 7:26). Yet, many reject God's Wisdom and follow *Lady Folly.* "She is ignorant and knows nothing. . . . And to those without sense she says, 'Stolen water is sweet, and bread eaten in secret is pleasant.' But they do not know that the dead are there, and her guests are in the depths of Sheol" (Prov 9:13-18).

This is, then, what Jesus experienced around him. They proclaimed his mighty deeds and marveled at his authoritative teaching. But they did not really convert. "Then he began to reproach the cities in which most of his deeds of power had been done, because they did not repent. 'Woe to you, Chorazin! Woe to you, Bethsaida! . . . And you, Capernaum, will you be exalted to heaven? No, you will be brought down to Hades'" (11:20-23). Here Jesus is challenged by religious leaders about sabbath fidelity, that is to say, *their* interpretation of sabbath piety. To objections regarding plucking grain to eat, he reminds them that "the Son of Man is lord of the sabbath" (12:8). And to whether he ought to heal on the sabbath, he reminds them that doing good on the sabbath is exactly sabbath fidelity. Now the conflict has heated up: "But the Pharisees went out and conspired against him, how to destroy him" (12:14). "A corrupt person has built a self-esteem based exactly on this type of fraudulent behavior. He spends his life navigating shortcuts of opportunism at the price of his own dignity and that of others . . . and puts on a 'holier-than-thou face.' . . . He deserves a doctorate in social cosmetics. . . . This is why it is so difficult for prophecy to enter such a person's heart!"[16]

The Pharisees weirdly assert that Jesus performs exorcisms by the power of Satan himself. Absurd, Jesus responds. "If Satan casts out Satan, he is divided against himself." And then, "But if it is by the

Spirit of God that I cast out demons, then the kingdom of God has come to you" (12:26-28). Jesus then tells them that blaspheming against the Spirit is an unforgivable sin. What I think Jesus has in mind is not a specific sinful act, but rather a soul that is intent on opposing and even fighting against the very Spirit of God. This is tantamount to death to the soul.

Jesus reminds the crowd that the evidence of our souls is manifest in who we are and what we do, "for the tree is known by its fruit" (12:33). Thus, when his family seeks to see him, he reminds them (and us): "Here are my mother and brothers! For whoever does the will of my Father in heaven is my brother and sister and mother" (12:49-50).

Parables of the Kingdom (13:1-53)

Chapter 13 represents Jesus's third major discourse, and it has everything to do with his proclamation of the kingdom and its reception. We have already been told several times by Matthew that Jesus taught with *exousia*, authority and power. He is the Word of God, and he speaks the words of God. Here he tells parables of the kingdom and its reception. Jesus's first parable, that of a sower whose seeds fell variously, I will address in Mark's Gospel.

Jesus tells another agriculture parable: the kingdom is like a field with both wheat and weeds. With fear of tearing out the wheat in weeding, the master tells his servants to wait until harvest where the two will be separated, the wheat to barns and the weeds to fire (13:24-30). His final parable is like this too: a net cast where only when ashore can the fishermen toss away the bad and save the good (13:47-50). Both of these parables are important for us all to hear. All of us are only partway on our journey. We are in chapter 2 or 4 or 8 of a ten-chapter book. You don't know how it will turn out. Some *wheat* might end up looking a lot weedier in the end and some apparent weeds might end up becoming wheat. This is why we should pray daily for a "happy death," an old term for living and dying in the state of grace. And it is why we should hold back judgments. Who knows the state of another's soul or recognizes the fragility of one's own? Who knows how the future will play out for anyone?

Jesus teaches that the kingdom is like a small mustard seed that seems of little account but that grows surprisingly large. And it is like yeast, where just a little can infuse the whole loaf. A friend of mine lived most of his life with little interest in religious faith. Raised Catholic, he marginally associated with the church. When he was in high school his parish priest off-handedly but sincerely said to him, "God is mercy and God is love." He shrugged; "I guess," he replied. But he never let that go, and periodically it came back to him. When he was fifty, he was thinking about this, and he became overwhelmed with the Holy Spirit whose mercy and love he now palpably felt—more real than any reality he could perceive with his senses. Today, ten years later, he is a devout Catholic, filled with wonder and gratitude for the mercy and love that God has for him.

Jesus then tells two parables about the value of the kingdom. Someone stumbled upon a treasure in a field and paid everything he had to purchase that field. Another was a merchant who found the perfect pearl. He readily paid his life's savings for that pearl. Sell everything, pay anything for the treasure that is the kingdom. It is a gift that costs not less than everything, and it promises a richness of life that cannot be exceeded and eternal life that ultimately means everything. Both the poor man finding the treasure and the merchant in search of the finest pearl are filled with joy at their find. Gerhard Lohfink, in reflecting on this parable, writes,

> For Jesus the reign of God is tangible and visible. It does not exist only within human beings and is not hidden somewhere beyond history. It can already be seen, touched, acquired, and dealt with, and for that very reason it fascinates people and makes them willing to change their whole lives for the sake of this new thing—and all without losing their freedom. The beauty and joy of the reign of God are ultimately the force that moves Jesus' disciples and causes God's grace to prevail in the world, again and again.[17]

Peter the Rock and Jesus's First Passion Prediction (16:13-28)

Jesus asks his disciples, "Who do people say that the Son of Man is?" They reply variously: some think John the Baptist; some Elijah or other prophets returned.

> He said to them, "But who do you say that I am?" Simon Peter answered, "You are the Messiah, the Son of the living God." And

Jesus answered him, "Blessed are you, Simon son of Jonah! For flesh and blood has not revealed this to you, but my Father in heaven. And I tell you, you are Peter [rock], and upon this rock I will build my church, and the gates of Hades will not prevail against it. I will give you the keys of the kingdom of heaven, and whatever you bind on earth will be bound in heaven, and whatever you loose on earth will be loosed in heaven." (16:15-19)

This extraordinary dialogue has to be unpacked. First, we must understand that Jesus did not intend a new institution or religion. This is particularly true as seen through Matthew's eyes. *Ekklesia*, the term for "church," literally means "assembly." Jesus's assembly refers to those gathered in his name and committed to living out his kingdom. Second, one hears echoes from the Old Testament. God promised David, "I will raise up your offspring after you . . . and I will establish his kingdom. He shall build a house for my name, and I will establish the throne of his kingdom forever. I will be a father to him, and he shall be a son to me" (2 Sam 7:12-14). This originally referred to Solomon, but only in Jesus is it definitively made firm and complete. Jesus's response to Peter also draws on Old Testament history. Isaiah declares Eliakim to be the new prime minister to King Hezekiah. "I will place on his shoulder the key of the house of David; he shall open, and no one shall shut; he shall shut, and no one shall open" (Isa 22:22). Just as Eliakim controlled the entry and exit of the king's palace, so now Peter has this charge of the gates of heaven. Binding and loosing are rabbinical terms, referring to definitive decision-making. There is something apocalyptic here too. The gates of Hades hold the ungodly powers of the underworld who will threaten the church in the latter days, but the church will prevail.[18]

The authority to bind and to loose is also given to the whole of the Twelve (18:8), but to Peter alone is accorded the revelation from the Father, the role as the rock foundation of the community, and the keys to the kingdom. The future role of Peter in the Bible is complicated. In Acts, he seems to take a second seat to James at the Council at Jerusalem regarding Gentile admission into the community (Acts 15:1-21). And Paul has no qualms publicly challenging Peter in Antioch regarding the role of the Torah (Gal 2:11-14). On the other hand, consider: Peter organizes the election of a new apostle in place of Judas (Acts 1:15-22); Peter preaches the first sermon after the resurrection on the day of Pentecost (Acts 2:14-36); Peter speaks to the Sanhedrin on behalf of the whole community (Acts 4:8-12); Peter baptizes the first Gentiles into the faith (Acts 10:1-48); and it is Peter with whom Jesus privately confers after his resurrection to "Feed my lambs. . . . Tend my sheep. . . . Feed my sheep" (John 21:15-19). As is widely known, historically the bishop of Rome has been seen as holding the "chair of Peter," that is, Peter's authority. Both Eastern and Western churches understood this and regularly appealed to the bishop of Rome to settle matters. The great controversy is whether the bishop of Rome ought to have *juridical* authority over the whole of the church. This need not concern us here. What is clear enough is that Jesus saw the need for his disciples and especially Peter (and their successors) to lead the church.

We live in a world that is increasingly suspicious of authority or even rejects it as somehow an imposed limitation to one's own autonomy, even one's own dignity. Students who do not like what I am teaching sometimes tell me that it is "just your opinion," and they have a different opinion, just as valid as mine. They are both just *opinions* after all. Yes, what I say in class is what I personally believe to be the case (my opinion). But these claims are based on decades-long study and almost always represent the consensus of scholarship. An exacerbated colleague once told a student, "Look, at this stage of your education your opinions are being formed, not consulted!" Not all positions are of equal weight and certainly not of equal wisdom.

I *want* authority over me. I *want* my pastor to be my spiritual father and the leader of our community. I *want* to be guided by my church's magisterium—the teaching authority in the church. This need not be slavish, and it certainly can include respectful dialogue and even disagreements from time to time. But it is perfectly obvious to me that I've grown deeper in the faith because I've had spiritual and theological guides who led me. Sometimes this guidance came with a soft touch, a nudge, a suggestion. Other times, it felt more determined and forceful. In my youth I was taught such things as the Assumption of Mary and that the Eucharist is the transubstantiation of Jesus Christ, two claims that seemed at the time highly doubtful. But I trusted that the teaching authority was competent and needed to be respected. After years of study (and prayer), I now understand

and am grateful for the deeply important role of the Blessed Mother, who is my mother and the church's mother. I now am awed by the Eucharist and the density and mystical reality that it intrinsically has. Christ willed human leaders, always flawed, to guide his community. We should be grateful.

Jesus does not just ask the disciples, who do you think I am? He is also now asking *us*. Pope John Paul II, in a homily on this passage, says the following:

> We all know this moment in which it is no longer sufficient to speak about Jesus by repeating what others have said. You must say what you think, and not quote an opinion. You must bear witness, feel committed by the witness you have borne and carry this commitment to its extreme consequences. The best friends, followers and apostles of Christ have always been those who hear within them one day the definitive, inescapable question, before which all others become secondary and derivative: "For you, who am I?" . . . [Our life] depends on the clear, sincere and unequivocal answer, without rhetoric or subterfuge, that he gives to this question.[19]

Jesus asks: "Who am I? Who am I to you?" Besides stock answers, which themselves might be true, there is a deeper divine speaker who communicates to the depths of our existence. What does he say to us? What do we really think about him? The answers may change through life, and each change will invite (and demand) a new and deeper appropriation of our relationship with him. His question to us is really an opportunity for deeper intimacy with the Son of God.

After Jesus's exchange with Peter, he announces his first passion prediction: "Jesus began to show his disciples that he must go to Jerusalem and undergo great suffering at the hands of the elders and chief priests and scribes, and be killed, and on the third day be raised" (16:21). Peter, the rock on which Jesus will build his church, took Jesus aside and "rebuked" him. "God forbid it Lord! This must never happen to you." Jesus retorted, "Get behind me, Satan! You are a stumbling block to me; for you are setting your mind not on divine things but on human things" (16:22-23). Here, Jesus is not saying that Peter is the devil or possessed. *Satan* is a Hebrew word for "adversary" or "accuser" or "opposer." Now the rock is a stumbling stone.

The disciples, including Peter, cannot wrap their heads around the passion. It is here that Jesus, for a second time, reminds them that they too must take up the cross to follow him. "Those who want to save their life will lose it, and those who lose their life for my sake will find it" (16:25). Following Jesus is not a spectator sport but an engagement with the paschal mystery of living, dying, and resurrecting with Jesus.

The Transfiguration (17:1-13)

One of the most dramatic experiences the disciples had during Jesus's ministry was the transfiguration, though it was limited to Peter, James, and John, the very three he kept close to him in Gethsemane before his arrest (26:37). "And he was transfigured before them, and his face shone like the sun, and his clothes became dazzling white. Suddenly there appeared to them Moses and Elijah, talking with him" (17:2-3). Many commentators see Moses as representing the law and Elijah the prophetic tradition. That is, Jesus unites with representatives of the whole tradition. This alone is powerful, but there is even more depth to the episode. A mountain is a symbolic site of revelation. We have already seen this in Jesus's sermon on the mount; he becomes a *type* of Moses or lawgiver. What is particularly fascinating is that both Moses (Exod 24:9-18) and Elijah (1 Kgs 19:11-18) dramatically experienced God on Mount Sinai, and Matthew seemingly wants us to make this connection.

We saw earlier that John the Baptist is a kind of Elijah, but now we have the actual Elijah, he who did not die but was swept up in a whirlwind by a chariot of fire (2 Kgs 2:11). While Deuteronomy notes that Moses died before entering the promised land and was buried in the land of Moab (Deut 34:5-6), the rabbinic tradition imagined that he too was taken up into heaven.[20] There was also a first-century apocalyptic text called *The Assumption of Moses*, anticipating a messianic figure. In considering the transfiguration, we must join all of this in order to appreciate the depth of the vision Peter, James, and John experienced. The apostles get a glimpse of the future resurrected Lord now glorified. This is our future too, a future that has already begun in us. Paul writes, "And all of us, with unveiled faces, seeing the glory of the Lord as though reflected in a mirror, and being transformed into the same image from one degree of glory to another, for this comes from the Lord, the Spirit" (2 Cor 3:18).

God speaks to these disciples in the exact words he spoke when Jesus was baptized: "This is my Son, the Beloved; with him I am well pleased." God then adds, "Listen to him" (17:5). The disciples are trying, but they have a difficult time correlating self-offering and glory. The paschal mystery, the full ministry of Jesus, has yet to make sense to them. Peter wants this particular experience of glory to last: "Then Peter said to Jesus, 'Lord, it is good for us to be here; if you wish, I will make three dwellings here, one for you, one for Moses, and one for Elijah'" (17:4). But it does not last; spiritual highs never do. Jesus leads them back down the mountain and back to ministry.

Discipleship in the Community (18:1-35)

Chapter 18 represents Jesus's fourth teaching discourse. As I noted in the introduction, Matthew relates the story of Jesus in a way that reflects both the historical ministry of Jesus and the life of the church in the late first century. This discourse is particularly concerned with how discipleship ought to look in the believing community. It begins with the disciples asking Jesus, "Who is the greatest in the kingdom of heaven?" Jesus places a child before them and declares, "Truly I tell you, unless you change and become like children, you will never enter the kingdom of heaven" (18:1-3). We can think of children in many ways. In one sense, they are immature. Paul, for example, chastises the Corinthian community for being so spiritually immature that they are not ready for solid food (1 Cor 3:2). We might also consider that children are trusting and open in ways that adults are not. Jesus is not considering either of these. Here children represent society's nobodies, those who lack social status. In an ancient culture of pride and shame, one certainly wanted to be a "somebody," one revered, someone important. This desire remains today. "Whoever becomes humble like this child is the greatest in the kingdom of heaven" (18:4).

The early Christian community had some learned and wealthy members, but the majority of believers were of the peasant class. For Jesus and the kingdom, they had to be given particular care and concern. Indeed, any authentic discipleship involves renouncing one's pride and ego ambitions, making all disciples peers. Those with greater gifts offer them humbly for the good of the community. There is no power-playing here. Jesus insists, "If any of you put a stumbling on the Mount, Jesus had forbade divorce, "except on the ground of unchastity [adultery]" (5:32). This was Shammai's opinion. Hillel considered a much, much wider range of "something objectionable," including being a bad cook! Here the Pharisees want Jesus's opinion. Where did he stand on the debate? Jesus's answer was to return to God's original vision and intention where the two become one. "So they are no longer two, but one flesh" (19:6). With such stringency the disciples wonder out loud if it would be better not to marry at all. The apostles were married, as Paul reflects: "Do we not have the right to be accompanied by a believing wife, as do the other apostles and the brothers of the Lord and Cephas [Peter]?" (1 Cor 9:5). Jesus responds, "Not everyone can accept this teaching, but only those to whom it is given." He then describes the possibility of being "eunuchs for the sake of the kingdom of heaven" (Matt 19:11-12), that is, avowed celibates. There were, in fact, other celibates in Jesus's time, such as the ascetic community at Qumran as well as a Jewish movement known as the *Therapeutae*. Both John the Baptist and Paul (as well as Jesus himself) were unmarried. This was understood traditionally throughout Christian history as a higher, more focused religious life. Paul even reflects on this: "The unmarried man is anxious about the affairs of the Lord, how to please the Lord; but the married man is anxious about the affairs of the world, how to please his wife, and his interests are divided" (1 Cor 7:32-34).

Today, we realize that both married and celibate expressions of discipleship are honorable and mutually supportive in the church. And there is no shortage of sacrifice for the kingdom of God in marriage! It may indeed be the more challenging lifestyle in pursuing holiness and the more sacrificial one of the two. The text seems to lean toward some states of life being more heroic, as Matthew then immediately shares the story of the rich young man who approaches Jesus, "Teacher, what good deed must I do to have eternal life?" Jesus's response is "If you wish to enter into life, keep the commandments." Jesus then recounts the Ten Commandments and adds, "You shall love your neighbor as yourself." To the young man's insistence that he has followed them all, "Jesus said to him, 'If you wish to be perfect, go, sell your possessions, and give the money to the poor, and you will have treasure in heaven; then come, follow me.' When the young man heard this word, he went away grieving, for he had many possessions" (19:16-22). Here there appears to be two forms of discipleship: one of faithful obedience and one of radical renunciation. Jesus's warning to his disciples follows the short dialogue: "Truly I tell you, it will be hard for a rich person to enter the kingdom of heaven. Again I tell you, it is easier for a camel to go through the eye of a needle than for someone who is rich to enter the kingdom of God" (19:23-24).

Following Jesus in his day was a complex and multilayered affair. Jesus did not call everyone to follow him in his day-to-day ministry, and he even sent some who wanted to directly follow him back to their own town (Mark 5:19). Others retained their wealth and used some of it to support Jesus's ministry (Luke 8:1-3). Others still spoke well of him but were not direct followers, and Jesus commended them (Mark 9:38-40). Nonetheless, there does appear a kind of continuum in discipleship where "one is not perfect without sacrificing all possessions to follow Jesus."[21] Thus Peter will ask,

> "Look, we have left everything and followed you. What then will we have?" Jesus said to them, "Truly I tell you, at the renewal of all things, when the Son of Man is seated on the throne of his glory, you who have followed me will also sit on twelve thrones judging the twelve tribes of Israel. And everyone who has left houses or brothers or sisters or father or mother or children or fields, for my name's sake, will receive a hundredfold, and will inherit eternal life. But many who are first will be last, and the last will be first." (19:27-30)

The kingdom of God has a way of making everything topsy-turvy. And the assumption of who's on top and who's marginalized tends to flip. At the end of the day, what is crucial for discipleship and what makes one *perfect* is perfect obedience to whatever Jesus calls us to and perfect love in any state we are called to. Vatican II frames it thusly:

> Therefore, all in the church . . . are called to holiness. . . . This holiness of the church is shown constantly in the fruits of grace which the Spirit produces in the faithful and so it must be; it is expressed in many ways by the individuals who, each in their own state of life, tend to the perfection of charity. . . . The Lord Jesus,

divine teacher and model of all perfection, preached holiness of life, which he both initiates and brings to perfection, to each and every one of his disciples no matter what their condition of life.[22]

The Parable of the Laborers in the Vineyard

One of the most interesting parables in Matthew's Gospel is this one. Jesus begins by saying that this is what the kingdom looks like. He tells of a landowner who went to town looking for day-workers. He hired some at dawn promising the usual daily wage, then at nine, then at noon, then at three, and finally at five, promising all that he would pay "whatever is right." In the evening, he paid those last workers a full day's wage, and indeed all the workers received a full day's wage. Those who had worked the longest expected more as they worked much more, and they complained. The landowner responded, "Friend, I am doing you no wrong; did you not agree with me for the usual daily wage? Take what belongs to you and go; I choose to give this last the same as I give you. Am I not allowed to do what I choose with what belongs to me? Or are you envious because I am generous? So the last will be first and the first will be last" (20:13-16).

This parable confounds many Christians. On the surface, it simply looks unfair. Pay ought to be proportional to effort or productivity. The same pay for disproportionate work is simply no way to run a business as one would be rewarding sloth. Most imagine that this parable is about attaining heaven, where those repentant late in life will still be let in. Even here though, the Catholic belief in purgatory suggests that sins do have a cost and do require accountability and reformation before the beatific vision of heaven. So, even if the parable is about heaven, it still seems to miss the justice issue.

Maybe, however, it *is* all about justice after all. In Jesus's day, farmers owning and working their own small farms was something of a thing of the past. Because the Romans demanded such high taxes (and then there's the temple tax), the average Jewish farmer could not make the payments. The crisis in Jesus's day was that many of them had to sell their ancestral land to large landowners who could exploit cheap day labor. Those peasants then were living hand-to-mouth, and their families lived precariously. Parables about the kingdom are not necessarily or even primarily about how it works to get into heaven; the kingdom was being inaugurated before them. Parables are often about how life ought to look here and now. This does not make the parable less comprehensible, but surprisingly more so.

Amy-Jill Levine suggests the following: "To those who ask today, 'Are you saved?' Jesus might well respond, 'The better question is, do your children have enough to eat? Or do you have shelter for the night?' "[23] Consider those who are hired at five in the evening. The NRSV seems a bit misleading in its translation, which is that they were "standing idle here all day," as though loafers. The Greek is *argoi*, which literally means "those without work." This fits the context better. They want to work, and they tell the landowner their plight: "no one has hired us." One can consider how painful it would be to stand at the marketplace hoping for work, hoping to be able to feed their families, and yet not be employed for the day. The landowner, in hiring all the latter workers, promises them to pay them "what is right." The term is *dikaion*, which has the connotation of good or just. What would be good or just for these men who had to return home that evening to a concerned spouse and hungry children? Lohfink argues,

> [The parable] shows how God's new world suddenly erupts into this world of the old society. . . . In the reign of God, different rules apply. It is true that people work from morning to night here as well. God's world is not Lotusland. But here work has dignity, and no one need go home in the evening filled with worry and anxiety. No one is alone any longer. . . . It is precisely this common cause, desired by all, that creates a solidarity making it possible to share in others' suffering and rejoice in the joys of others.[24]

The Cup of Suffering (20:17-28)

Jesus's third passion prediction comes as they are on their way to Jerusalem, Jesus's fateful final week. "See, we are going up to Jerusalem, and the Son of Man will be handed over to the chief priests and scribes, and they will condemn him to death; then they will hand him over to the Gentiles to be mocked and flogged and crucified; and on the third day he will be raised" (20:17-19). Immediately, the mother of James and John seeks the favor that her sons would sit at his right and left hand in his kingdom. Jesus is noncommittal:

"But to sit at my right hand and at my left, this is not mine to grant, but it is for those for whom it have been prepared by my Father" (20:23). Jesus also chastises them by way of a question: "You do not know what you are asking. Are you able to drink the cup that I am about to drink?" He is referring to the very passion that he had just revealed. They are so sure: "We are able." In the Old Testament the term "cup" is often a metaphor for suffering, particularly God's wrath.[25] This kind of "cup" Jesus has in mind is to be drunk not at a banquet but on a cross.

In a way, James and John's mother recognized that ultimately Jesus would rule gloriously. But her request is misplaced, as was her sons' confidence. Soon, the crowds would hail Jesus as the great Messiah only to reject him days later. And instead of seeing Jesus mounted on a throne, all would see him mounted on a cross with criminals at his right and left. It is also misplaced given Jesus's passion prediction. The kingdom is about service. There is glory, but it is the glory of God they are assured to experience, not their personal glory. "But Jesus called them to him and said, 'You know that the rulers of the Gentiles lord it over them, and their great ones are tyrants over them. It will not be so among you; but whoever wishes to be great among you must be your servant, and whoever wishes to be first among you must be your slave; just as the Son of Man came not to be served but to serve, and to give his life a ransom for many'" (20:25-28).

Entering Jerusalem and Cursing a Fig Tree (21:1-22)

Jewish tradition held that the Messiah would come riding on a donkey from the Mount of Olives and reflecting Zechariah's prophecy: "Rejoice greatly, O daughter Zion! Shout aloud, O daughter Jerusalem! Lo, your king comes to you; triumphant and victorious is he, humble and riding on a donkey, on a colt, the foal of a donkey" (Zech 9:9). Jesus had been cagey about his messianic status and even ordered his disciples not to acclaim him the Messiah (Matt 16:20), but now when he is about to enter into his passion he accepts the public acclamation. The people shout "Hosanna to the Son of David! Blessed is the one who comes in the name of the Lord! Hosanna in the highest heaven!" (21:9). The next public proclamation of his messianic status will be the inscription on the cross.

Jesus enters Jerusalem not as a conquering king but as a humble one. That he is a peaceable king does not mean that he is without the prophetic bite that is also part of Jesus's ministry. Immediately upon entering Jerusalem he went to the temple and drove out those who changed money and sold doves for temple sacrifice. "My house shall be called a house of prayer; but you are making it a den of robbers" (21:13). On the surface, selling sacrificial animals and changing Roman money that carried Caesar's image for temple currency that had no idolatry would seem necessary. Further, these merchant booths would have been at the outer courts of the temple where even Gentiles could enter. Why the fuss? Why was Jesus so adamant here? I think that the very purity of the temple was at stake in Jesus's mind. Jesus's preaching often had a current of apocalypticism in it. There is the present order, and then there is the divine order. The present order is under divine judgment, and the divine order demands a complete overhaul, a total purification. In the first-century collection known as *The Psalms of Solomon* we find "And he [the Messiah] will purge Jerusalem and make it holy as it was even from the beginning."[26]

While Jesus enters Jerusalem humbly and meekly, he also comes in judgment. This is the only way to make sense of his cursing a fig tree. Matthew tells us that the next day, while Jesus was returning to Jerusalem from Bethany he was hungry and went to a fig tree by the road. "He went to it and found nothing at all on it but leaves. Then he said to it, 'May no fruit ever come from you again!' And the fig tree withered at once" (21:19). Poor fig tree! In the ancient world, figs were often a symbol of life. But in the prophetic tradition, withered fig trees represented God's judgment. Isaiah proclaims, "All the host of heaven shall rot away, and the skies roll up like a scroll. All their host shall wither like a leaf withering on a vine, or fruit withering on a fig tree" (Isa 34:4). This condemnation is not that of the whole people of Israel, but the leaders who failed to truly guide the people as we see in Jesus's conflict with the chief priests and elders (Matt 21:23-27) and the scribes and Pharisees (23:1-36). It is also a warning to us: bear fruit or whither.

This is really a glorious moment in Jesus's ministry. "When he entered Jerusalem, the whole city was in turmoil, asking, 'Who is this?' The crowds were saying, "This is the prophet Jesus from Nazareth in

messianic reign imaged as a wedding is deep in Israel's memory,[28] and the image of wearing the right garment was even used as an image in the emerging Christian community. Paul admonishes us to be "clothed in Christ" (Gal 3:27).

Consider the first half of the parable to be about those who reject Jesus and his kingdom. Like the city of Jerusalem that would soon be destroyed, those who reject his message do so at a severe cost. The second half of the parable addresses not those who have rejected Jesus but those who have accepted the invitation and entered in. In today's world, one can wear just about anything anywhere. But in the ancient world of Jesus, coming to a wedding—and a royal wedding at that—without the right attire was tantamount to a direct insult. Using this as a metaphor, Jesus warns those who merely "show up" that they will suffer the same fate as those who rejected the invitation. The new situation of the kingdom of God requires a whole new perspective, a new vision, a new relationship with God and with each other. One has to be prepared to be a full participant. We might consider the way the book of Revelation uses the same imagery: "Let us rejoice and exult and give him the glory, for the marriage of the Lamb has come, and his bride has made herself ready; to her it has been granted to be clothed with fine linen, bright and pure—for the fine linen is the righteous deeds of the saints" (Rev 19:7-8).[29]

Quarrels and the Greatest Commandment (22:15-40)

Jesus enters into challenges with religious leaders, including those trying to trip him up. Is it right to pay taxes to the emperor? And if there is a resurrection, whose wife is she if a woman marries several brothers, all of whom leave her a widow? Jesus is cagey and will not be caught in their trap. Then he is asked by a "lawyer" (scholar of Torah) as to what is the greatest of all the commandments God gave. Jesus replies, " 'You shall love your God with all your heart, and with all your soul, and with all your mind.' This is the greatest and first commandment. And the second is like it: 'You shall love your neighbor as yourself.' On these two commandments hang all the law and the prophets" (22:37-40).[30] There is much here to unpack. For the ancient Jew, one's heart referred to one's will, one's soul meant one's life, and one's mind was one's thoughts and character. So one loves God utterly. And yet, Jesus could not stop there. The "second" command in loving neighbor as oneself is inseparable from it. The two are really one commandment.

While Matthew tells us that the lawyer was trying to "test him," the question itself was not out of bounds. Other rabbis fielded this question and looked to a particular commandment that represented something of a cornerstone to all the others or a lens through which to interpret the others. Rabbi Hillel famously converted a young Gentile man by summarizing Torah as: "Do to no one what you yourself would not want to be done to you. The rest is commentary. Now go and learn it."[31] Here, he is widely interpreted as teaching that the lens to all teaching is compassion and universal empathy. Likewise, Rabbi Akiba taught that loving one's neighbor is the greatest principle of the law.

In Jesus's Jewish milieu, loving God was primarily not a feeling but a commitment to covenant fidelity. But this certainly did not exhaust the Jewish understanding of love. The psalmist writes, "Happy are those whose way is blameless, who walk in the law of the LORD. Happy are those who keep his decrees, who seek him with their whole heart" (Ps 119:1-2). What one is then seeking in following and loving God's decrees is God himself and God's love. "Let your steadfast love come to me, O LORD" (119:41). In the First Letter of John we read, "Beloved, let us love one another, because love is from God; everyone who loves is born of God and knows God . . . for God is love" (1 John 4:7-8).

Anyone with a decent degree of discipline can follow the precepts of a given religion. But to be transformed in divine love means to live love. God is love! Among all the excellences of God, such as goodness, truth, beauty, justice, compassion, and so on, the singular excellence that binds them is love. Love is God's fundamental nature. The grace of transformation into love comes from God, but the actualization in our lives comes from both God and our very souls in a synergy that involves both. James Keenan writes,

> By being in union with God, this love of God constitutes us more than even our love for ourselves. This union with God becomes the principle of our communion with others. . . . This gift is then grace itself or, as Thomas Aquinas states so clearly, no less than the divinity itself living in us. . . . Love of God supersedes

all other realities. . . . Love of God is also the foundation of our sanctification which is to love God, ourselves, and our neighbor.[32]

While loving God takes priority because God is the source and ultimate end to who we are and what we do, loving our neighbor expresses the communion we have with God and the concrete way we love God. In 1 John we read, "No one has ever seen God; if we love one another, God lives in us, and his love is perfected in us. . . . Those who say, 'I love God,' and hate their brothers or sisters, are liars; for those who do not love a brother or sister whom they have seen, cannot love God whom they have not seen. The commandment we have from him is this: those who love God must love their brothers and sisters also" (4:12, 20-21).

Jesus's command remained at the forefront of the early Christian consciousness: "Owe no one anything, except to love one another, for the one who loves another has fulfilled the law" (Rom 13:8); "For the whole law is summed up in a single commandment, 'You shall love your neighbor as yourself'" (Gal 5:14); "You do well if you really fulfill the royal law according to the scripture, 'You shall love your neighbor as yourself'" (Jas 2:8); "Whoever loves a brother or sister lives in the light" (1 John 2:10). Pope Francis observes, "The commandment to love God and neighbor is the first, not because it is at the top of the list of commandments. Jesus does not place it at the pinnacle but at the center, because it is from the heart that everything must go out and to which everything must return and refer. . . . Love is the measure of faith, and faith is the soul of love. . . . My faith is as I love. And faith is the soul of love."[33]

Truth Telling and Denunciations (23:1-39)

When I was in high school, my English teacher forbad the use of the word "nice" in any of our papers. In her words, "Nice is milquetoast." Milquetoast is a bland cracker that is rather flavorless and eaten when one has an upset stomach. It gives little nutrition but provides something to eat. Jesus was not a *nice guy*. He was compassionate. He was loving. And he healed and preached the kingdom, which should be good news to his listeners. But he was not like milquetoast; he was not "nice." In chapter 23 we see Jesus the prophet denouncing the religious authorities around him. In chapters 21 and 22 Matthew tells us that the scribes and Pharisees were hostile to him, creating disputes for the sole purpose of trying to entrap him. Earlier, he had also criticized their understanding of Torah. Now in this chapter we find the *seven woes*, much like other prophets in the Jewish tradition.[34] Here Jesus recognizes that the scribes and Pharisees have some legitimate authority; they "sit on Moses' seat" (23:2). And while he challenged some of their interpretations of Torah, his main thrust is this: "They do not practice what they teach. They tie up heavy burdens, hard to bear, and lay them on the shoulders of others; but they themselves are unwilling to lift a finger to move them. They do all their deeds to be seen by others. . . . They love to have the place of honor at banquets and the best seats in the synagogues, and to be greeted with respect in the marketplaces, and to have people call them rabbi. . . . Woe to you, scribes and Pharisees, hypocrites! . . . Woe to you, blind guides" (23:3-16). Ultimately, "Woe to you, scribes and Pharisees, hypocrites! For you are like whitewashed tombs, which on the outside look beautiful, but inside they are full of the bones of the dead and of all kinds of filth" (23:27). What we have are thirty-six verses of continual biting rebuke. And it ends with Jesus's lament over the Holy City: "Jerusalem, Jerusalem, the city that kills the prophets and stones those who were sent to it! How often I have desired to gather your children together as a hen gathers her brood under her wings, and you were not willing! See, your house is left to you, desolate" (23:37-38).

The rebuke was with little doubt a historical one of Jesus's frustration. We should be clear that many scribes and Pharisees were earnest and faithful Jews. As a movement, the Pharisee party was a popular one among the Jewish population. These are leaders who might very well have agreed with Jesus's critique about some of their own in their midst. There is an ancient Jewish saying, "Any scholar [of Torah] whose inside is not as his outside is no scholar."[35] But Jesus certainly had enemies among them who tried to undermine both him and his mission. We can also see the rebuke here to refer to the tension in the late first century between those leaders who opposed the Jesus movement and those leaders in the Matthean community. And it goes further: Jesus's rebukes act as a challenge to the leaders of Matthew's community itself. One can easily imagine the necessary self-reflection on what authentic leadership is—the Son of Man came to serve and not be served (20:28)—and conversely the all-too-human desire to be admired and wield authority as self-inflated power. Who doesn't like to be the person who has the "right" answer? Who doesn't like to be greeted with respect and honor? Who doesn't like accolades? There is an intoxicating quality to it.

But who or what gets intoxicated? We might do well to think of ourselves as having various "selves." There is a "self" of ego-attachments. This is the self of the zero-sum game. *I* am valuable insofar as I am held high and deemed better than others. This self is a bottomless pit of narcissism, always hungry, always feeding, and never satisfied. This self likes to judge others because that's one way it gets fed. This self likes honor because deep down it never really believes it is simply loved by God. It doesn't know it is loveable and is determined to prove it ought to be; this is an endless tragic game. Thomas Merton writes, "The obstacle is our 'self,' that is to say in the tenacious need to maintain our separate, external, egotistic will. It is when we refer all things to this outward and false 'self' that we alienate ourselves from reality and from God. It is then the false self that is our god, and we love everything for the sake of this self."[36]

There is another "self," one that is made in the image and likeness of God, one who knows at its depth that everything is from God and finds its completion in God. This is the self that is at rest in God and at home in the world that God made. This self, when active in the world, could be a humble laborer or a Fortune 500 CEO, a whistler or a world-class musician, a poll volunteer or a senator. It does not really matter. Living in and through and for God as the ultimate end gives this true self satisfaction and the joy that comes in using one's gifts as service and as authentic expressions of who one is in God. This is the self that might even find praise and honor challenging, because these tend to lure one back to live the life of the false self. To the extent that the true self receives such praise or honor it is solely an experience of humility—paradoxical, I know—and gratitude to Christ for the opportunity to serve him and his kingdom.

Jesus Christ challenged all to repent and believe in the good news. But he seemed to show far greater tolerance to those struggling day by day. What is apparent in all of the Gospels is that he showed no tolerance to leaders who were hypocritical, prideful, and abusers of power. The fact is that the vast majority of us have some versions of spheres of power or influence, be that in our workplace, in our homes with our children, in our group of friends, or in our church. To the degree we are, as Merton says, serving our "false self," our god, Jesus's woes fall directly on us.

The Apocalyptic Jesus (24:1-51)

In preaching about the kingdom, Jesus drew on many Jewish themes. As we saw earlier, the choice of the Twelve and the very fact that his message is the coming of the kingdom of God draws us into the time of the judges where God ruled as king and "judges" were his emissaries. The twelve apostles would then be the "judges" for the twelve tribes of Israel (19:28). He also drew on messianic expectations that God would raise up a messiah, or anointed one, to rule Israel as a descendent of David. Matthew tells us that he is of David's family line (1:6-17) and that Jesus is the fulfillment of Isaiah's prophecy (1:23). Some even rightly call him "Son of David." As one can see, these do not align. During the time of the judges there was no monarchy and God was displeased that they wanted a king (1 Sam 8:7). God relents here and concedes to a monarchy, with David being the second king after Saul. So, did Jesus have in mind something akin to before the monarchy or, in contrast, something akin to David's monarchical line? Now, Jesus prophesies something different altogether: an apocalypse!

From the second century BCE through the first century CE, Jewish writing was rife with apocalyptic literature. In such literature, the trials and persecutions of the time are seen as part of a larger war between God and supernatural evil. But the faithful Jew is promised that God will ultimately destroy evil and establish a reconstituted world of peace, justice, faithfulness, and flourishing.[37] Much of what Jesus says in this apocalyptic chapter aligns well with material found in other apocalyptic texts.[38] This is yet an additional way to approach the kingdom.

In speaking apocalyptically, Jesus cautions that there will first be "birth pangs" (24:8), including wars, famines, and earthquakes, and that many believers will fall away. "But the one who endures to the end will be saved. And this good news of the kingdom will be proclaimed throughout the world, as a testimony to all the nations; and then the end will come" (24:13-14). Further, false messiahs and false prophets will appear with impressive signs, so beware. Finally,

> The sun will be darkened, and the moon will not give its light; the stars will fall from heaven, and the powers of heaven will be shaken. Then the sign of the Son of Man will appear in heaven, and then all the tribes of the earth will mourn, and they will see "the Son of Man coming on the clouds of heaven" with power and great glory. And he will send out his angels with a loud trumpet call, and they will gather his elect from the four winds, from one end of heaven to the other. . . . But about that day and hour no one knows, neither the angels of heaven, nor the Son, but only the Father. (24:29-36)

Ultimately, Jesus warns, "Keep awake therefore, for you do not know on what day your Lord is coming" (24:42).

What are we to make of these prophecies? On one level, we might recognize that God ultimately has a future planned where God's kingdom is fully realized and sin and those who serve sin are vanquished. We can also see in the dramatic imagery that such a future will be preceded by daunting conflict and upheaval. Further, it should be obvious that trying to predict when this full conflict and subsequent divine victory will come is a fool's errand. Throughout the history of the church, claims that *this is the time of the apocalypse* were regular. This includes the first century itself. Paul even imagined that he would still be alive when the second coming would happen (1 Thess 4:17). Throughout the Roman Empire's persecution of the church, Christians regularly imagined these were the last days. When plagues came, this was the end. When the Reformation happened, this was the end. In the United States alone we've seen fever pitches about the second coming during the first great awakening (1730s–1740s) and the second great awakening in the early nineteenth century. In the mid-nineteenth century, movements that ultimately became the Seventh Day Adventist Church and the Jehovah's Witnesses preached even quite specifically when the second coming would arrive. The early twentieth-century Pentecostal movement predicted the imminent apocalypse, which went to fever pitch during the San Francisco earthquake of 1906. In the mid-to-latter twentieth century, we again saw a surge of predictions and confident anticipations of the second coming. And this continues today. So far, everyone has been dead wrong. What we can learn at least is that predicting the second coming is fruitless. If Jesus did not know, how could Christians imagine that they know?

On a deeper level, we have to understand that apocalypticism as a literary genre is not really about specific predictions in real time. Rather, it was a way of making sense of great suffering among believers, the need for them to stay strong and faithful through it all, and the assurance of God's faithful love and salvation. God gets the final word. Further, it was just one part of Jesus's preaching arsenal. As I just noted, when Jesus preached the kingdom he drew on prominent Jewish themes that do not align well. So too here. Apocalypticism is another and very different strand. This does not mean that Jesus's preaching about the kingdom was incoherent. Rather, it tells us that the kingdom is something that goes beyond all framings. Ultimately, the kingdom is a divine mystery. It is not a spiritual manual or transcendent version of the Communist Manifesto, or Mao's Little Red Book, or the US Constitution. The kingdom transcends our imagination, but we can use our imagination variously to gain a sense of it, to let it grasp us and guide us.

This is what I do personally with apocalyptic writing: I let myself get immersed in the dramatic imagery. When I am suffering, I particularly listen to its plea to stay faithful and not get drowned in despair or let my mind go toxic with acrimony. I allow it to show me that often I am not in control and do not need to be. I also see terrible suffering in the world. I see racism, sexism, systemic poverty, and violence that seems overwhelming. These apocalyptic texts remind me that God knows all of this and is present to it, and while these are human-caused evils that God hates, there is a larger spiritual battle taking place between Good and Evil. I must not give way to evil or acquiesce to it as though the battle is beyond me. I can be part of this larger spiritual battle here and now. I can *fight* these evils as a spiritual war. And finally, I have to take a sober accounting of my own life. Am I an honorable person? Am I a faithful person to what the kingdom calls me to be and do? Citing Psalm 95, the author of the Letter to the Hebrews writes, "Today, if you hear his voice, do not harden your hearts" (Heb 3:7-8), and further, "It is a fearful thing to fall into the hands of the living God" (Heb 10:31). Given God's majesty, what is my confidence in meeting my Maker today face-to-face? This is a daunting question we must regularly pose.

Four Parables about Judgment (24:45–25:46)

The Faithful and Evil Servants

Following Jesus's apocalyptic vision, he offers a parable of two servants. The faithful servant is found dutiful when the master returns. He is deemed "blessed" and thus trusted and promoted. In contrast, the evil servant abuses his power and those around him. The master comes when he is not ready, and the master demands, "Cut him in pieces and put him with the hypocrites, where there will be weeping and gnashing of teeth" (24:51). The urgency to respond that comes from apocalyptic texts is the very urgency Jesus preached to repent, believe in the good news, and transform our lives as members of the kingdom. Consider it something like this: in Greek there are two words for time, *chronos* and *kairos*. *Chronos* is time as it passes while *kairos* refers to *the* time, time in its immediate possibility. Now is the moment of decision. Everything depends on taking the challenge, the leap. Even in our day-to-day lives, we can wander through life as though sleepwalking through much of it. How is God speaking to me *now*? Am I available to the movements of the Spirit right here? You can miss the *kairos* and miss a divine opportunity.

The Wise and Foolish Bridesmaids

The parable of the ten bridesmaids has regularly challenged both preacher and parishioner. Jesus sets up a scene: Ten bridesmaids wait at the groom's gates for the groom to return, presumably with his new bride, so that the couple can be received by the bridesmaids with a brilliant illumination of torches to lead the way. But there is a delay. When it is announced that the groom is soon coming, they were all to trim their torches. But five did not bring spare oil and, with the delay, ran out. Now with the groom's imminent arrival they want the five who had wisely brought an extra supply to share theirs, but they refuse. "No! there will not be enough for you and for us; you had better go to the dealers and buy some for yourselves" (25:9).

With the maids out searching for oil, the groom finally comes, the procession begins, and all present enter the feast. When the foolish bridesmaids return, the groom does not let them in. "I do not know you," he says (25:12).

Almost everyone today would cry foul on so many levels. Shouldn't the wise maids have shared? Aren't we supposed to share? And the groom seems to act atrociously. It's his wedding night, and these are friends and relatives of the bride. And he bans them from entering? This is a parable and ought not to be taken at face value, but it does seem to correspond to ancient Jewish weddings. Consider that the dowry had already been negotiated and paid to the bride-to-be's family. But now on the wedding day, the groom and his future in-laws are haggling over the extra gifts to the bride's family. This happened regularly. So, the maids would or should have known that this could take some time and that there could very well be delays. If they wanted to be the kind of bridesmaids worthy of that honor, they would have been prepared to wet their torches regularly over a lengthy period of time. And if the "wise" bridesmaids had cut their own supply in half, there very well could be no procession. What a social humiliation for the wedding party! It could be that the wise bridesmaids saved the day by being ready for anything. It is an issue of vigilance and readiness.

One of the great metaphors for God and Israel's relationship is that of a wedding.[39] It was important enough that the church took over this metaphor, understanding Christ as the bridegroom and the church as his bride.[40] The wedding feast is the *kairos* we just saw in the previous parable. We have to be alert and ready, not just for the second coming but also for any and every time Christ our beloved appears. We cannot rely on others' readiness, something they simply cannot share with us. And we cannot say to the Lord, "Hold on, Jesus, I'll be with you in a couple of hours. I'm not available just yet." Jesus's response could only be, "I'm here, now, inviting you to my feast. Are you coming or not? Are you ready or not?"

Servants and Talents

Jesus's next parable of judgment is that of the three servants who receive talents from their master, who then leaves the country for a time. Recall that a talent is about a year's wage. The first servant is given five and in trading makes another five. The second receives two and also doubles his money. And the third is given one talent, which he buries out of fear of losing it. Upon returning, the master rejoices in his first two servants, who now are given greater charge. But the third has little to say for himself, except that he was afraid.

> "Master, I knew that you were a harsh man, reaping where you did not sow, and gathering where you did not scatter seed; so I was afraid, and I went and hid your talent in the ground. Here you have what is yours." But his master replied, "You wicked and lazy slave! . . . Then you ought to have invested my money with the bankers, and on my return I would have received what was my own with interest. So take the talent from him, and give it to the one with ten talents. For to all those who have, more will be given, and they will have an abundance; but from those who have nothing, even what they have will be taken away." (25:24-29)

The servant is then tossed into the darkness, "where there will be weeping and gnashing of teeth" (25:30).

Frequently, this parable is misrepresented as though it were about our God-given actual talents or aptitudes, where the word "talent" becomes a double entendre, at least in English. It also seems odd that the richest one gets the buried talent. Why not the second servant? And what ought we to make of "For to all those who have, more will be given, and they will have an abundance; but from those who have nothing, even what they have will be taken away"? It sounds like the rich keep getting richer and the poor poorer. Like the last parable, to our ears it sounds quite harsh and even unfair. But is it? In the first two parables, we see the imperative to be dutiful, diligent, watchful, attentive, responsible, and ready. Now we see another necessary quality for entering the kingdom; that is, it requires risk. In T. S. Eliot's poem "Little Gidding" he describes it as "A condition of complete simplicity, costing not less than everything."[41] Christianity is not for onlookers, and the kingdom of God will not flourish through cowardice.

A quick story: I was waiting around a dance studio for my stepdaughter to be done with class and started chatting with the mother of one of her friends who was in the same dance class. This very nice woman decided to let me know that she was also Catholic but did not belong to a church anymore. It happened that years ago she had a disagreement with the pastor about a school policy where this same daughter had been enrolled. Not satisfied, she pulled her daughter out the next year and never went back. But she did assure me, "We're still Catholic; we still believe. We just don't go to church anymore." Why she volunteered any of this to me I do not know. I was thinking, "You could have pulled your kid from school and still been part of the parish. Or, you could have joined another church if you couldn't stand the pastor." Instead, I said to her, "Alice, I'm not trying to lay anything on you, but Christianity isn't mainly about assenting to a set of beliefs. I think it's more of an active engagement of faith in a faith community." That was the end of the conversation. But it apparently stung her enough that she repeated the encounter with her daughter, who thought it was interesting (or shocking?) enough to tell my stepdaughter, who then told me. No onlookers in the kingdom.

Judging the Nations

In the above three parables judgment is on believers, both Jews in Jesus's day and believers in Jesus in the late first-century church, the assembly of both Jews and Gentiles that made up the early Christian community. This final judgment parable is for "all the nations" (25:32). These presumably nonbelievers will be judged as so:

> "For I was hungry and you gave me food, I was thirsty and you gave me something to drink, I was a stranger and you welcomed me, I was naked and you gave me clothing, I was sick and you took care of me, I was in prison and you visited me." Then the righteous will answer him, "Lord, when was it that we saw you hungry and gave you food, or thirsty and gave you something to drink? And when was it that we saw you a stranger and welcomed you, or naked and gave you clothing? And when was it that we saw you sick or in prison and visited you?" And the king will answer them, "Truly I tell you, just as you did it to one of the least of these who are members of my family, you did it to me." (25:35-40).

These will "inherit the kingdom prepared for you from the foundation of the world" (25:34). And those *accursed* will depart "into the eternal fire prepared for the devil and his angels" (25:41). These are

house of Judah. . . . I will put my law within them, and I will write it on their hearts" (Jer 31:31-33). Ezekiel describes it thusly: "I will make a covenant of peace with them; it shall be an everlasting covenant with them; and I will bless them and multiply them, and will set my sanctuary among them forevermore" (Ezek 37:26). For the next five hundred years, this promised covenant seemed dormant. There was, until now, no announcement, no terms, no ratification. It was almost as though it had not been not prophesied, but it had been.

"While they were eating, Jesus took a loaf of bread, and after blessing it he broke it, gave it to the disciples, and said, 'Take, eat; this is my body.' Then he took a cup, and after giving thanks he gave it to them, saying, 'Drink from it, all of you; for this is my blood of the covenant, which is poured out for many for the forgiveness of sins'" (Matt 26:26-28). We see here a double sacrifice. The first is a *communion sacrifice*, which is consumed by those involved. Here God receives the sacrifice offered, which now becomes part of the divine realm. Then those present consume the sacrifice and take on something of God's own holiness or even God's very self. The second is a *sin offering* that expiates one's own sin or even the sins of all of Israel. This was especially holy. Consider that Jesus is both offering his body and blood as a communion to his disciples, that they might share in his very holiness, and that Jesus is anticipating his crucifixion, the atonement for the sins of the world. In this holy meal, the disciples are invited and implicated in this new covenant that is both a sharing in the death of the Lord—their own dying to themselves—and a foretaste of the heavenly banquet, the full communion with the divine.

The sixth scene is the Garden of Gethsemane at the foot of the Mount of Olives. Jesus and his disciples left Jerusalem to go there. Jesus warns, "You will all become deserters because of me this night" (26:31). He even predicted to Peter that he would deny his Lord three times. "Peter said to him, 'Even though I must die with you, I will not deny you.' And so said all the disciples" (26:35). Jesus had all but Peter, James, and John stay at a distance. He then separated himself from these three: "'I am deeply grieved, even to death; remain here, and stay awake with me.' And going a little farther, he threw himself on the ground and prayed, 'My Father, if it is possible, let this cup pass from me; yet not what I want but what you want'" (26:38-39).

Jesus is not lacking nerve and not simply afraid of his imminent passion with all the physical and emotional pain that it surely will bring. I think his grief is a combination of a great deal more. He came to bring good news and to inaugurate the kingdom. He gave himself to all, often to the point of exhaustion. And what he experienced was contempt, bullying, and plots to destroy him by religious leaders. He found great acclaim, only to experience superficial conversion by the crowds.[46] Add to this the disappointments he had with his disciples who never seemed to really understand. Add to this still more that he wept over Jerusalem, which failed to recognize her divine visitation, and he foresaw its future ruin. Add that one of his own trusted Twelve sold him out for a relative pittance. Add more: his crucifixion will be a sin offering, one that takes on the sins of the world.

Matthew's seventh scene is also in Gethsemane; it is Jesus's arrest. Judas, with "a large crowd with swords and clubs" arrived. Judas leads them, approaching Jesus, " 'Greetings, Rabbi!' and kissed him. Jesus said to him, 'Friend, do what you are here to do' " (26:47-50). Jesus will soon chide them, "Have you come out with swords and clubs to arrest me as though I were a bandit? Day after day I sat in the temple teaching, and you did not arrest me. But all this has taken place, so that the scriptures of the prophets may be fulfilled" (26:55-56). This is what spiritual or moral cowardice often looks like. It works at night, in the shadows. It does not want the scrutiny of others. It is thuggish. His disciples are not cowards like this, but they were afraid indeed. And this is how Matthew ends his seventh scene: "Then all the disciples deserted him and fled" (26:56). And Jesus is truly alone.

The Spiritual Exercises of St. Ignatius is a month-long retreat that is divided into four weeks. During the first week, one meditates variously on God's purpose for creation and humanity's sinful response. Here one typically seeks the graces of "shame and confusion." It is not pleasant to stick one's face into one's own sinful condition. The second week is devoted to Christ's mission and his invitation that we join him in it. It is a hero's journey, and we seek the grace to commit unreservedly to Christ and his saving ministry. The third week involves meditations on Christ's passion and our own confrontation with the cost of discipleship. Jesus proclaims in John's Gospel, "Whoever serves me must follow me, and where I am, there will my servant be also" (John 12:26). Regarding meditating on the Gethsemane scene, Ignatius writes, "In the Passion it is proper to ask for sorrow with Christ in sorrow, anguish with Christ in anguish, tears and deep grief because of the great affliction Christ endures for me."[47]

Meditating on the Gospel is entering deeply into every moment of Jesus's ministry. And now is the time to mourn. It is truly deflating to see how shallow many who celebrated Jesus actually were. And it is aggravating to see how often he was confronted, harangued, and resisted by those leaders who should have been his greatest allies. But now we must enter a truly dark moment. Our Lord is suffering and we must suffer with him. It is also a time to do a "gut check." Are we ready to go where the master goes? "Whoever loves father or mother more than me is not worthy of me; and whoever loves son or daughter more than me is not worthy of me; and whoever does not take up the cross and follow me is not worthy of me. Those who find their life will lose it, and those who lose their life for my sake will find it" (Matt 10:37-39).

Sacrificing the Messiah, Part 2 (26:57–27:56)

The trials of Jesus were a sham. The first convenes at night in Caiaphas's house, as he was the high priest. Was it to really investigate Jesus and his ministry? Certainly not. "Now the chief priests and the whole council were looking for false testimony against Jesus so that they might put him to death, but they found none, though many false witnesses came forward" (26:59-60). Then two witnesses claimed he said that he would destroy the temple and rebuild it in three days.[48] The Gospel of John does record something like this: "Destroy this temple, and in three days I will raise it up" (John 2:19). Matthew only has Jesus imply that he is greater than the temple (12:6). Up to this point, Jesus is silent through it all, taking the form of Isaiah's *suffering servant*: "He was oppressed, and he was afflicted, yet he did not open his mouth; like a lamb that is led to the slaughter, and like a sheep that is before its shearers is silent, so he did not open his mouth" (Isa 53:7).

Finally, the chief priest loses all patience: "I put you under oath before the living God, tell us if you are the Messiah, the Son of God." Jesus finally speaks: "You have said so. But I tell you, From now on you will see the Son of Man seated at the right hand of Power and coming on the clouds of heaven" (26:63-64). Here Jesus is virtually quoting Daniel's end-of-time prophecy (Dan 7:13-14). The verdict: "He has blasphemed! . . . He deserves death" (26:65-66). "Then they spat in his face and struck him; and some slapped him, saying, 'Prophesy to us, you Messiah! Who is it that struck you?'" (26:67-68).

In the beginning of this chapter, I identified Jesus as Messiah, Son of God, and Son of Man. These realizations came out variously through the course of Jesus's ministry. Now we have them all together. Of course, the authorities either do not understand these terms as Jesus did or they simply dismissed them as false. The irony is that in sentencing him to death, they are creating the very conditions for these identifications and prophecies about him to come to full fruition. And the temple of his body, soon to be destroyed by them, will rise up on the third day gloriously. There is another irony. While Jesus is being questioned and abused, and while Jesus finally tells all, Peter in the courtyard is being questioned and harassed. And he is too afraid to admit he even knows Jesus. At first, he is vague: "I do not know what you are talking about." Finally, "Then he began to curse, and he swore an oath, 'I do not know the man!' At that moment the cock crowed" (26:69-74). Here is something for us to think about: If it were illegal to be a follower of Jesus, would the authorities have enough evidence by our lives to convict us?

Both Peter and Judas betray Jesus, though, of course, Judas's betrayal is far worse. At the time when Jesus most needed loyalty, he got none. Both regretted and were ashamed of their failure. But the difference between the two is wide. Peter will repent of his sin: "He went out and wept bitterly" (26:75). Judas will kill himself: "Throwing down the pieces of silver in the temple, he departed; and he went and hanged himself" (27:5). There is no sin that Jesus cannot forgive, but this requires facing the sin, seeking healing, addressing the harm done, and trusting in Jesus's mercy. Real repentance requires not only great faith in the mercy of God but also some courage to face who we are and what we've done. We place ourselves humbly before divine mercy. Peter humbled himself and was forgiven. Judas remained the narcissist; it was still all about him. So he took his life.

The Jewish authorities have convicted Jesus of blasphemy, but this is hardly a capital offence to the Roman Empire. For the Romans,

Jesus's life began with a cosmic sign, a star rising from the east. Now it ends with cosmic signs. The center of temple was the holy of holies. It was so sacred that only on the day of atonement would the high priest enter, and even then only when tied to a rope. God was understood as so powerfully present there that one could easily die if God's glory was directly encountered. Just in case the high priest did die, they could drag out his body without themselves entering. Now the veil that separated the holy of holies is rent. The presence of God is no longer there. If it is anywhere now particularly, it is hanging on a cross in the form of a dying just man. And accompanying this is a great earthquake. Consider what Zechariah foresaw: "On that day his [God's] feet shall stand on the Mount of Olives . . . and the Mount of Olives shall be split in two from east to west. . . . And the LORD will become king over all the earth" (Zech 14:4, 9). We have begun a new age. Even the resurrection of the saints attests to this, as many Jews expected such a resurrection event as part of the messianic age to come.[52]

Jesus is buried in the family tomb of Joseph of Arimathea, one of Jesus's disciples. "So Joseph took the body and wrapped it in a clean linen cloth and laid it in his own new tomb, which he had hewn in the rock. He then rolled a great stone to the door of the tomb and went away. Mary Magdalene and the other Mary were there, sitting opposite the tomb" (27:59-61). On behalf of the chief priests and Pharisees, Pilate ordered guards there so that the corpse would not be stolen (27:62-66). Matthew details all this in a rather dulled, unemotional manner. And why not? This is as somber as reality gets. The Messiah is dead and buried.

This raw, dark moment in salvation history is not without spiritual potency. We vigil with Jesus through his passion and next to his tomb. In the Apostles' Creed we acclaim that "he descended into hell." In 1 Peter, we find that during his transition, "he went and made a proclamation to the spirits in prison [hell], who in former times did not obey" (1 Pet 3:19-20). What this seems to mean most profoundly is that, in Jesus's sacrifice, the divine entered the arena where God is not: sin and death. St. Paul will even say that "For our sake he [God] made him [Jesus] to be sin who knew no sin, so that in him we might become the righteousness of God" (2 Cor 5:21). St. Bonaventure saw dwelling in and with the wounds of

Christ as something even mystical: "O how good it is to be with Christ crucified! I wish to make three resting places in him. One, in the feet; another, in the hands; the third perpetually in his precious side. . . . O how lovable are the wounds of our Redeemer! . . . In them too I live."[53]

The Resurrection of the Messiah (28:1-16)

Matthew tells us that the same two Marys who saw Jesus buried went to the tomb Sunday at dawn. They experience an earthquake and an angel descending from heaven who rolled back the stone. He assures them that Jesus had been raised and will meet the eleven in Galilee.

> Suddenly Jesus met them and said, "Greetings!" And they came to him, took hold of his feet, and worshiped him. . . . Now the eleven disciples went to Galilee, to the mountain to which Jesus had directed them. When they saw him, they worshiped him; but some doubted. And Jesus came and said to them, "All authority in heaven and on earth has been given to me. Go therefore and make disciples of all nations, baptizing them in the name of the Father and of the Son and of the Holy Spirit, and teaching them to obey everything that I have commanded you. And remember, I am with you always, to the end of the age." (28:9, 16-20)

Addressing chapter 26, I briefly described the Spiritual Exercises of St. Ignatius. I described the third week as confronting the cost of discipleship. There one meditates on the passion of Christ and on identifying with Jesus who suffers with and for the world's brokenness. Taking up the call of Christ, while challenging, is also exhilarating. But it is an abstract discipleship without the passion. Dietrich Bonhoeffer, the German theologian executed as a Nazi resister, coined the term *cheap grace*. "Cheap grace is the grace we bestow on ourselves. Cheap grace is the preaching of forgiveness without requiring repentance, baptism without church discipline, Communion without confession, . . . cheap grace without discipleship, grace without the cross, grace without Jesus Christ, living and incarnate."[54]

Grace without the cross is not real grace. But the story cannot end there. I once wrote, "During the fourth week, they [retreatants] meditate on his resurrected victory and share the glory of conquering evil. The retreatants experience Jesus alive, having surpassed all, and feel empowered to live in Jesus' unrestricted presence in the world. The mission and service of the Gospel must be grounded in a lived experience of his victory."[55] St. Paul reflects, "If Christ has not been raised, then our proclamation has been in vain and your faith has been in vain" (1 Cor 15:14).

The glory and power of the resurrection is ours now in part and fully ours in eternity. Paul insists, "So if anyone is in Christ, there is a new creation" (2 Cor 5:17). The Lord can mission us now because we are renewed in his resurrection by the power of the Holy Spirit. "Now the Lord is the Spirit, and where the Spirit of the Lord is, there is freedom. And all of us, with unveiled faces, seeing the glory of the Lord as though reflected in a mirror, are being transformed into the same image from one degree of glory to another; for this comes from the Lord, the Spirit" (2 Cor 3:17-18). The seal of the Spirit is God's down payment or our inheritance (Eph 1:13-14). And this is how we can be assured that we have the Spirit: "The fruit of the Spirit is love, joy, peace, patience, kindness, generosity, faithfulness, gentleness, and self-control. . . . If we live by the Spirit, let us also be guided by the Spirit" (Gal 5:22-25).

We are now empowered to be in and with the risen Christ anywhere and everywhere as his disciples, fully integrated in works and faith and the power of Christ's victory over death. The resurrected and victorious Jesus sends us forward. Alleluia!

The Gospel of Mark

Following the Suffering Messiah

Such a Beginning (1:1-13)

In Mark we have no lengthy infancy narrative. Rather, he boldly sends us into Jesus's public ministry. But he does have a short prologue, which starts, "The beginning of the good news of Jesus Christ, the Son of God" (1:1). This short sentence says much. Jesus's ministry represents "good news," *euangelion* in Greek. It was a title typically used for Greek announcements on festivals of the emperor, who was imagined to be a kind of god. Mark uses it to announce "Jesus Christ, the [actual] Son of God." And now "Christ," meaning "messiah," has become something of Jesus's surname.

Mark then introduces John the Baptist, whose mission is to "prepare the way of the Lord" (1:3). John's baptism was for repentance, an anticipation to receive the greater baptism. John's clothing, camel's hair and a belt, reminds us of Elijah, "a hairy man, with a leather belt" (2 Kgs 1:8), who was to proceed the Lord's day of visitation and judgment, as we saw in Matthew. He assured the crowd, "The one who is more powerful than I is coming after me. . . . I have baptized you with water; but he will baptize you with the Holy Spirit" (Mark 1:7-8). Jesus is *ischuroteros*—stronger and more powerful not only compared to John but, as we will see, stronger than all the powers he must confront. And this will make us stronger too, a strength Mark will progressively assure us will be necessary under persecution. "In those days Jesus came from Nazareth of Galilee and was baptized by

John in the Jordan. And just as he was coming up out of the water, he saw the heavens torn apart and the Spirit descending like a dove on him. And a voice came from heaven, 'You are my Son, the Beloved; with you I am well pleased'" (1:9-11).

In the biblical mind the "tearing open" (*schizomenous*) of the heavens allowed for God's communication or even radical presence. Ezekiel notes in his mystical experience that "the heavens were opened, and I saw visions of God" (Ezek 1:1), and Isaiah pleads, "O that you would tear open the heavens and come down" (Isa 64:1). In Jesus's baptism all this started. Note also that neither the crowd at the Jordan river nor even John experiences this. Jesus saw the heavens torn open and the Spirit descend. And the voice from the Father was heard only by Jesus: "You are my Son, the Beloved." Jesus knows who he is, and we know who he is. As we shall see, demons also know who he is. But the crowds, the leaders, his family, and even his closest disciples will find him confoundingly difficult to understand. They get it wrong almost all the time. Getting to know Jesus, as Mark shows us, is more difficult than it may seem on the surface.

Jesus's baptism is pivotal. Mark portrays this event as a "solidarity with the sinful human condition."[1] It is also an anticipation of our own faith journey. Francis Watson notes that "Jesus' baptism does not concern him alone. The new identity bestowed on him through the Spirit and the divine voice is open to participation by others . . . and Mark's Christian readers recognize in it their own experience of turning from the old life to the new."[2]

Jesus Begins His Ministry: Announcing and Calling (1:14-20)

"Now after John was arrested, Jesus came to Galilee, proclaiming the good news of God, and saying, 'The time is fulfilled, and the kingdom of God has come near; repent, and believe in the good news'" (1:14-16). Jesus begins his public ministry in his native land of Galilee. There is already a foreshadowing in John. The Greek says that John was *paradothēnai*, literally "handed over." This not only foreshadows John's death (6:14-29) but also Jesus's predictions of his own being "handing over" (9:31; 10:33), and that of his followers (13:11).

Just as Mark's first words were densely potent, so the first words of Jesus. The *time* that is fulfilled is *kairos* (exceptional moment), not *chronos* (ordinary time), and the kingdom is imminent. As we saw in the chapter on Matthew, the Jewish world of Jesus was filled with apocalyptical thinking. When the time was ripe God's kingdom would appear. This is the establishment of God's just rule over all creation.[3] As we will soon see, Jesus is not only predicting an imminent reign of God but one that he is now inaugurating by his ministry. So, what should we do? "Repent, and believe in the good news." *Metanoia*, the Greek word for repentance, is surely about repenting from our sins. But it has a richer meaning, literally "change one's mind," that is, think differently, see differently, and surely be different; this includes "believing in the good news." More Greek: *pistis*, the term for "faith" or "belief," is not simply an intellectual assent. Rather, it means entrusting oneself or committing oneself personally.

So we must ask ourselves here and now: have we fully entrusted ourselves to Christ and his kingdom, and have we really challenged ourselves to think and see differently? Most Christians think and see through the eyes of culture, a culture that includes racism, sexism, and tolerance for social injustice. Christianity can easily become just an addendum to that. In a comprehensive meta-study on religion in America, *American Grace*, authors Robert Putnam and David Campbell show that there is a correlation between religious devotedness and what they call *good neighborliness*. They found that religiously observant Americans give more, volunteer more, and are more civically active than nonreligious Americans. And the more devout, the better the citizen. This, of course, is good. The compromising fact, however, is that they are only somewhat better, not at all radically better.[4] How much actual *metanoia* have we engaged in our lives and how much *pistis* do we have? Gerhard Lohfink observes, "Jesus is not just talking *about* the reign of God. He is announcing it. He proclaims it. . . . Repentance, turning back, is a consequence of the salvation that is already present. . . . 'The time is fulfilled,' of course, appears in the garments of solemn biblical language. But it means nothing different from our expression, *the time has come*. . . . Paul means the same thing when he writes: 'See, now is the acceptable time; see, now is the day of salvation' (2 Cor 6:2)."[5]

The first thing Jesus does concretely in his ministry is to call Simon (Peter), his brother Andrew, James, and his brother John, all of whom are fishermen. Now we see something of the power of Jesus's words to Simon and Andrew: " 'Follow me and I will make you fish for people.' And immediately they left their nets and followed him" (1:17-18). The same for James and John: "Immediately he called them; and they left their father Zebedee in the boat with the hired men, and followed him" (1:20). *Immediately* he calls and *immediately* they follow. The presence of Jesus is magnetic and powerful.

Preaching and Healing (1:21-45)

Mark tells us that Jesus went to Capernaum, a fishing town on the shores of Galilee. We find him teaching in the synagogue, and "they were astounded at his teaching, for he taught them as one having authority, not like the scribes" (1:22). Immediately his power and authority are recognized by a demon who possesses a man at the synagogue. This is the first of four exorcism narratives in Mark,[6] three of which follow a pattern whereby Jesus engages the demon, the demon tries to resist his divine power, Jesus responds with the command to leave, and at the departure of the demon there is amazement. This was the world of Jesus's ministry, a struggle between God and the powers of evil. This event is really quite dramatic: "What have you to do with us, Jesus of Nazareth? Have you come to destroy us? I know who you are, the Holy One of God" (1:24). The demon literally says, "What between us and you?" This is his defense: You have your realm, and we have ours. Why are you invading ours? And that is exactly what Jesus is doing—not that he is invading alien territory but that he is taking back what was always God's. Paul Achtemeier notes, "Jesus is part of God's final, cosmic battle against the powers of evil. To miss that point is to miss the meaning of Jesus."[7]

"What between us and you?" On a much less dramatic level we see something of this in our secular culture, where religion has its place and ought to stay in its place. The separation of church and state in America was always meant to ensure religious freedom, not to force the life of faith into a private corner. "What between us and you?" The answer is, everything necessary to combat evil and allow for human flourishing, especially spiritual flourishing. This has to be our core value and perspective. "What between us and you?" Everything to live and proclaim the kingdom of God.

This part of Mark shows the beginning of the first flush of crowds that will come to Jesus for healing or spiritual freedom from evil.

Jesus entered Peter and Andrew's house, curing Peter's mother-in-law. And then, "That evening, at sunset, they brought to him all who were sick or possessed with demons. And the whole city was gathered around the door. And he cured many who were sick with various diseases, and cast out many demons; and he would not permit the demons to speak" (1:32-34). This is part of the *messianic secret* in Mark. Jesus regularly tells both demons and those he healed, and even his disciples, not to reveal him as Messiah or Son of God. He is simply not the kind of messiah (anointed king) they were looking for. We can also see here that the revelation of Jesus simply cannot be contained; it is that powerful. In curing a leper, Jesus tells him, "See that you say nothing to anyone; but go, show yourself to the priest, and offer for your cleansing what Moses commanded. . . . But he went out and began to proclaim it freely" (1:43-45). He just couldn't hold it in.

Five Controversies (2:1–3:12)

From the Greek word *skotōma* (darkening), *scotosis* refers to hardening of the heart or intellectual blindness. This section of Mark is very much about *scotosis*, that is, cultivating a way of thinking that actually blinds us from seeing what is right before us. We see *scotosis* with those scribes and Pharisees who progressively become enemies of Jesus. Mark provides us with five quick and quite different narratives of conflict. We begin with the famous story of Jesus surrounded by a crowd in his Capernaum home base. It is so packed that men who brought to Jesus a paralytic to heal cannot get access to him. So they dismantle the roof and lower him down. "Son," Jesus says to him, "your sins are forgiven" (2:5). For the scribes this is blasphemy. It technically wasn't, but it did appear to them that Jesus was assuming to himself the divine prerogative to forgive sins.[8] In this sense, they were right; Jesus was doing this. And he demonstrates his authority through healing the paralyzed man. " 'But so that you may know that the Son of Man has authority on earth to forgive sins'—he said to the paralytic—'I say to you, stand up, take your mat and go to your home' " (2:10-11). The scribes were baffled, but the people "were all amazed and glorified God" (2:12). Why wouldn't the scribes see that restoring the lame man to health is a sign of God's activity?[9]

Scotosis — a hardening of the mind against unwanted wisdom.

Following this, Jesus called the tax collector Levi and said to him, "'Follow me.' And he got up and followed him" (2:14). Levi then invites Jesus and his disciples to dine with him and his friends, who were "sinners and tax collectors." The scribes object: "Why does he eat with tax collectors and sinners?" (2:16). This is a good question looking at the tradition. Consider: "I hate the company of evildoers, and will not sit with the wicked" (Ps 26:5), and, "In company with those who work iniquity; do not let me eat of their delicacies" (Ps 141:4). Jesus's reply is "I have come to call not the righteous but sinners" (Mark 2:17). Why could they not recognize (and rejoice at!) the repentance of sinners? "This was a simple message that God loved these people and that they would be part of the kingdom being inaugurated by Jesus."[10] There is irony here, since the enemies of Jesus are exactly *not* righteous for not recognizing what is going on. And the *scotosis* deepens.

Others ask Jesus why his disciples do not fast like those of the Pharisees and John the Baptist. His answer, "As long as they have the bridegroom with them, they cannot fast" (2:19). The Hebrew Bible is filled with allusions to God calling Israel to be his faithful bride. "On that day, says the LORD, you will call me, 'My husband.' . . . I will take you for my wife in righteousness and in justice, in steadfast love, and in mercy" (Hos 2:16-20).[11] This is a new situation, a new possibility to rejoice, and one must put "new wine into fresh wineskins" (Mark 2:22). And then the Pharisees saw his disciples plucking grain and eating it on the sabbath. A violation of sabbath law, they challenge. He retorts, "The sabbath was made for human-kind, and not humankind for the sabbath; so the Son of Man is lord even of the sabbath" (2:27-28). Finally, they spied on Jesus to see "whether he would cure him on the sabbath, so that they might accuse him" (3:2). Before Jesus cures a man with a withered hand, he asks, "'Is it lawful to do good or to do harm on the sabbath, to save life or to kill?' He looked around at them with anger; he was grieved at their hardness of heart" (3:4-5). "The Pharisees went out and immediately conspired with the Herodians against him, how to destroy him" (3:6). Now the *scotosis* is complete. The controversies began with wondering whether he had blasphemed.[12] Now they begin to plot his death.

Scotosis is not merely an ancient problem, but one that threatens all of us. We can become habituated in one way of thinking that is comfortable to us. The more ingrained the habit, the less likely we are to recognize truth that comes in a package different from what we expect. "I am about to do a new thing; now it springs forth, do you not perceive it?" (Isa 43:19). We often do not see. We are more addicted to the comfort of seeing the world, our relationships, our faith, and especially God in a certain way. To any other way, we can become increasingly blind.

A New Phase of Discipleship and Parables of the Kingdom (3:13–4:34)

We've been introduced to Simon, Andrew, James, and John who were called to follow Jesus. Now Jesus ascends a mountain—a typical place for God to speak—and appoints the Twelve. "And he appointed twelve, whom he also named apostles, to be with him, and to be sent out to proclaim the message, and to have authority to cast out demons" (3:14-15). Unlike what we saw in Matthew, where the twelve were a symbolic expression of future "judges" of the twelve tribes of Israel, this Twelve is not much distinguished from other disciples in Jesus's ministry. What they do represent for us is decided disciples who learn from Jesus more than what the crowds learn. And, further, they are "apostles," that is, "those sent" to proclaim the good news. They will be given some of Jesus's authority and power that they will need to combat evil. But they will indeed have much to learn and they are only just beginning.

It is during this time that Jesus returns to his hometown of Nazareth and to immediate controversy. Crowds came as usual, but some were arguing that he "has gone out of his mind" (3:21), and his family tried to restrain him. He is also challenged that he exorcises demons through the prince of demons, Beelzebul.[13] As in Matthew, Jesus responds that Satan would not fight Satan. Here, though, we see an additional teaching: "No one can enter a strong man's house and plunder his property without first tying up the strong man; then indeed the house can be plundered" (3:27). Satan is that strong man, but Jesus is stronger, and he has tied up Satan and plundered his house. The disciples will need to receive the same strength. And so will we.

Then among the crowd is his family who call for him. " 'Who are my mother and my brothers?' And looking at those who sat around him, he said, 'Here are my mother and my brothers! Whoever does the will of God is my brother and sister and mother'" (3:33-35). This is the Jesus who demands to know on which side of the fence we stand. To do the will of God makes us part of his family. To refuse to do God's will is to not be in his family. There is a new loyalty called for here. Obviously, his was an apocalyptic framing, and this is not a manual regarding future "family values" or "family obligations." Discipleship is doing God's work, and doing God's work makes us part of Jesus's family, a place where we really belong.

Mark immediately brings us back to the shores of Galilee and the crowds there listening to Jesus preach parables of the kingdom:

> Listen! A sower went out to sow. And as he sowed, some seed fell on the path, and the birds came and ate it up. Other seed fell on rocky ground, where it did not have much soil, and it sprang up quickly, since it had no depth of soil. And when the sun rose, it was scorched; and since it had no root, it withered away. Other seed fell among thorns, and the thorns grew up and choked it, and it yielded no grain. Other seed fell into good soil and brought forth grain, growing up and increasing and yielding thirty and sixty and a hundredfold. (4:3-8)

He will soon tell his disciples what he meant. The sower is sowing the word of God. The path represents those who do not take in the word fast enough and Satan quickly snatches it. The rocky ground represents those who hear the Gospel with joy but have no staying power with the faith. The thorny ground represents those whose absorption in worldly things, particularly wealth, chokes off the Gospel's reception.

We've seen this everywhere, even in our own lives. Sometimes a truth told just does not register. Our habitual ways of thinking do not give it room. The challenge then is for us to stay with it, to cling to it and not let it quickly be snatched away. It is the challenge to open our hearts enough to give it the room it needs to sink in. If we stay with it, its wisdom will reveal itself when we are ready. But we have to keep it close enough not to let it be "snatched up."

We also know about hearing things that excite or inspire us, but we drop them soon after the excitement wears out, looking for the next interesting thing. This can even happen to seriously religious persons. St. John of the Cross writes about *spiritual avarice* insight-fully. "Many . . . hardly ever seem content with the spirit God gives them. They become unhappy and peevish owing to a lack of the consolation they desire to have spiritual things. Many never have enough of hearing counsels, or of learning spiritual maxims, or of keeping them and reading books about them. . . . They will now put these down, now take up others."[14] St. John's confidant, St. Teresa of Avila, describes some sisters in her convent who lose their staying power, whose "strength gives way . . . and perhaps they were no more than two steps from the fount of living water."[15] And finally, of course, our preoccupations, our attachments, and our absorption in worldly values—so ubiquitous in a consumerist culture—make integrating the Gospel troublingly difficult.

All three of these possible responses are typical in our lives and experience. And they all have to do with our receptivity, that is, the kind of soul we nurture. Being a fertile ground has to do with being available to God. It has to do with cultivating a heart that is open, spacious, and free. St. Gregory the Great notes, "Good earth . . . brings forth fruit by patience."[16] It is never too late. St. John Chrysostom, commenting on this parable, notes that "stones can change and turn into fertile soil, the beaten path can be no longer trampled down but may become a productive field; the thorns too can disappear."[17] We should not miss the end of the parable. For those who are fertile ground the word of God, the seed Jesus sows, produces fantastically: thirtyfold, sixtyfold, a hundredfold. No ac-tual wheat plants do this, of course, but the word of God does; it is a seed capable of developing into a holy life here and eternal life ultimately. The fruitfulness of our labors may not appear clearly. But we must not lose heart. Here is another parable: "The kingdom of God is as if someone would scatter seed on the ground, and would sleep and rise night and day, and the seed would sprout and grow, he does not know how. The earth produces of itself, first the stalk, then the head, then the full grain in the head. But when the grain is ripe, at once he goes in with his sickle, because the harvest has come" (4:26-29). How does God work in our lives? Fundamentally, God works mysteriously and often unbeknownst to our consciousness. A good axiom is that God *normally* works through the normal; God *usually* works through the usual. Few people have extraordinary religious experiences, and those fortunate to have had them typically experience them rarely. Spiritual transformation is a long project of staying present to God in the ordinary. The graces come—they surely come—but they usually come softly. Because God is Goodness itself and Truth itself, our pursuit of goodness and truth is necessarily a participation in the life of God. And it is all premised on grace, on God's active presence as goodness and truth. The kingdom is here; it is available and present all the time. To make it ours means to strive unreservedly to pursue it moment by moment, so often in the ordinariness of life itself. Pope Francis reflects, "The fruitfulness is often invisible, elusive, and unquantifiable. We can know quite well that our lives will be fruitful, without claiming to know how, or where, or when. We may be sure that none of our acts of love will be lost, nor any of our acts of sincere concern for others. No single act of love for God will be lost; no generous effort will have been meaningless, no painful endurance wasted. All of these encircle our world like a vital force."[18]

Confronting Chaos and Evil (4:35–5:20)

Jesus and his disciples venture from the "Jewish" side of the Sea of Galilee to its southeastern side, which marks Gentile territory. The area is that of the Decapolis, or the "ten cities." As we saw in Matthew (8:24-27), Jesus and the disciples experience a windstorm so great it was swamping the boats. Awakened by his frenzied disciples, Jesus "rebuked the wind, and said to the sea, 'Peace! Be still!' Then the wind ceased, and there was a dead calm" (4:39). As I noted in the chapter on Matthew, the sea when it was raging often represented chaos and evil, where only the power of God could save.[19] Jesus quickly confronts even more manic chaos and evil on the shore: "And when he had stepped out of the boat, immediately a man out of the tombs with an unclean spirit met him. He lived among the tombs; and no one could restrain him any more, even with a chain; for he had often been restrained with shackles and chains, but the chains he wrenched apart, and the shackles he broke in pieces; and no one had the strength to subdue him. Night and day among the tombs and on the mountains he was always howling and bruising himself with stones" (5:2-6). The man's demon, whose "name is Legion; for we are many," begs Jesus not to cast him out indiscriminately but rather to cast him into the nearby swine that were feeding. He does so, and they all rush over a cliff and drown into the sea.

> The swineherds ran off and told it in the city and in the coun-try. . . . They came to Jesus and saw the demoniac sitting there, clothed and in his right mind, the very man who had the legion; and they were afraid. . . . Then they began to beg Jesus to leave their neighborhood. . . . [And to the man Jesus said], "Go home to your friends and tell them how much the Lord has done for you, and what mercy he has shown you." And he went away and began to proclaim in the Decapolis how much Jesus had done for him; and everyone was amazed. (5:14-20)

There is much to unpack here. The sea rages uncontrollably, and the demoniac rages uncontrollably. The wind and sea overwhelm the disciples, and the man is overwhelmed with a legion of demons. Through Jesus's word the sea becomes "dead calm," and the man becomes perfectly calm. The details about the man and the legion are additionally interesting. Tombs were seen as a regular place for demons to dwell, and Legion's request not to be simply sent out would align with not wanting to be sent to their eternal place of punishment. They want to stay in the area. But, of course, they invaded pigs that drowned themselves. This certainly heightens the drama. And, for Jews pigs are unclean animals, so the Jewish mind would have no qualms about their deaths.[20] Finally, we see that the man becomes a kind disciple and apostle, spreading the good news throughout the ten cities.

Rather than seeing these two stories or *pericopes* only as Jesus's powerful confrontation with chaos and evil, we might also see them representing dynamics in our own lives. There is no shortage of challenges from the vicissitudes of life. Life is often unfair, and even when it is not it can be dauntingly challenging. Children exhaust their parents' patience (and vice versa); workloads can be overwhelming; faithfulness, love, and constancy in our relationships test our metal. Francis Fernandez wisely reflects,

> Each person has to work in his own environment, in spite of the hostility we will meet and the misunderstandings of people who cannot or do not want to understand. Walk therefore, *in nomine Domini*, with joy and security in the name of the Lord. If

> difficulties arise, then the grace of God will come more abundantly
> as well. . . . Divine help is always proportionate to the obstacles
> with which the world and the devil oppose apostolic work. . . .
> We can use this opportunity to purify our intention, to be more
> attentive to the Master, to strengthen our faith. . . . It is enough
> to be in his company to feel we are safe.[21]

It is possible to have real equanimity in dealing with the challenges
of life. But, unless this is through the power and presence of Christ,
it is more likely that we only bury our frustrations, guaranteeing that
we will see them come out sideways at a later date. Christ's grace
allows us to even lean into our suffering. "Peace! Be still," he says
to the storm. Peace, he says to our souls. I am here, I am with you.
My grace will carry you.

The Kingdom and the Power of Faith (5:21–6:13)

Mark's narrative unfolds with three pericopes that seem quite
unrelated but have a central theme, that is, the direct relationship
between faith and the kingdom of God. First, he tells of a synagogue
leader named Jarius who begged Jesus to come to his house. "My
little daughter is at the point of death. Come and lay your hands on
her, so that she may be made well, and live" (5:23). We later learn
that she is twelve years old. Surrounded by a crowd, Jesus begins the
journey to Jarius's house only to encounter a woman who for the
same twelve years had the "scourge" of hemorrhaging blood (perpetual gynecological spotting). This made her continuously unclean
and untouchable (Lev 15:19-30). She touches Jesus's cloak and is
healed. His response is to assure her, "Your faith has made you well."
Jarius's daughter dies in the meantime, and Jesus calls for a similar
faith. "Do not fear, only believe" (5:36). He comes to the bedside,
takes her hand, and says to her, " 'Talitha cum,' which means, 'Little
girl, get up!' " (5:41). By giving us the Aramaic words, Mark allows
us to experience the intimacy and affection Jesus brings to those to
whom he ministers. *Talitha cum* literally means *little lamb, arise.*[22]

The contrast between these relative strangers' experiences (and
faith!) and those in Jesus's hometown of Nazareth could not be
clearer. Mark tells us that they found his teaching in the synagogue
impressive: "What is this wisdom that has been given to him?" Nonetheless, they ultimately questioned that, since they knew him and his

family, how special could he be? " 'Is not this the carpenter, the son of Mary and brother of James and Joses and Judas and Simon, and are not his sisters here with us?' And they took offense at him. . . . And he could do no deed of power there, except that he laid his hands on a few sick people and cured them. And he was amazed at their unbelief " (6:2-6). As I once noted,

> Jesus' miracles only make sense in the context of anticipating the kingdom and in some way already participating in it. Without faith, Jesus' healings would make him more a magician than a Messiah. Failing in his hometown, Jesus remained the perfect prophet, making clear that he was not a court jester to amuse or amaze. And in witnessing to the imperative of faith, he reminds us to scrutinize our own relationship with him. Do we have the proper awe? Do we hang on his word? Do we seek merely the consolations of God; or do we, rather, pursue the God of consolations?[23]

Jesus says something else interesting in this encounter: "Prophets are not without honor, except in their hometown, and among their own kin, and in their own house" (6:4). We tend to be unimpressed with those we think we know well. I know two pastors who were friends. They had a hard time getting parishioners to come to adult education opportunities in their parishes. So they simply went to each other's parish representing a kind of "visiting expert." Parishioners now came out in high numbers. Here is someone they hadn't seen week after week at church or someone they hadn't seen buying gas, getting groceries, or getting their hair cut alongside them.

Finally, Jesus sends the Twelve "two by two, and gave them authority over the unclean spirits" (6:7). He demands that they rely on God's providence and the generosity of potential hosts in the towns they visit. The two usually go together: God's providence corresponds with our willingness and cooperation. Jesus alerts them that in some towns it may not go well: "If any place will not welcome you and they refuse to hear you, as you leave, shake off the dust that is on your feet as a testimony against them." Still, they were willing to trust Jesus and be entrusted by him to proclaim the kingdom just as Jesus had done from the beginning of his ministry: "So they went out and proclaimed that all should repent. They cast out many demons, and anointed with oil many who were sick and cured them" (6:11-13).

What is striking here is that we will find the disciples not really understanding Jesus or his kingdom. Later in chapter 6 the disciples find themselves in another squall on the Sea of Galilee and Jesus walking on water to meet them and calming the winds. "They thought it was a ghost and cried out; for they all saw him and were terrified. But immediately he spoke to them and said, 'Take heart, it is I; do not be afraid.' . . . And they were utterly astounded . . . but their hearts were hardened" (6:49-52). There will be much that they have to learn about Jesus, a Messiah who "came not to be served but to serve, and to give his life as a ransom for many" (10:45). So they continue to misunderstand both Jesus and his kingdom. And yet, to their credit they were willing to go to unknown towns with trust in God's providence.

Jesus had instructed them to take "nothing for their journey except a staff; no bread, no bag, no money in their belts" (6:8). This can be instructive for us. We do not have to wait until we understand everything about our faith to minister on behalf of Jesus. We rely on Christ, that is all. And this faith is a powerful witness in and of itself and a condition for God's grace to flow through us. Paul addresses the Corinthians with this same conviction:

> Consider your own call, brothers and sisters: not many of you were wise by human standards, not many were powerful, not many were of noble birth. . . . God chose what is low and despised in the world, things that are not, to reduce to nothing things that are, so that no one might boast in the presence of God. . . . When I came to you, brothers and sisters, I did not come proclaiming the mystery of God to you in lofty words or wisdom. For I decided to know nothing among you except Jesus Christ, and him crucified. And I came to you in weakness and in fear and in much trembling. My speech and my proclamation were not with plausible words of wisdom, but with a demonstration of the Spirit and of power, so that your faith might rest not on human wisdom but on the power of God. (1 Cor 1:26–2:5)

Herod, John, and Jesus (6:14-44)

Herod Antipas was the son of Herod the Great, and he ruled the Galilee region on behalf of Rome. He had put John the Baptist in prison for denouncing Herod's unlawful marriage to Herodias, his brother's wife. At his birthday party Herod's stepdaughter danced before the guests. Herod, so enamored by her, offered her anything she wished. "She went out and said to her mother, 'What should I ask for?' She replied, 'The head of John the baptizer'" (6:24). To avoid shame before his guests, he did just that. Hearing this, Jesus went by himself to a "deserted place" to be alone. But the crowds came—five thousand strong—and he taught them. "When it grew late, his disciples came to him and said, 'This is a deserted place, and the hour is now very late; send them away so that they may go into the surrounding country and villages and buy something for themselves to eat.' But he answered them, 'You give them something to eat'" (6:35-37). With only five loaves and two fish, the five thousand were all fed. "Taking the five loaves and the two fish, he looked up to heaven, and blessed and broke the loaves, and gave them to the disciples to set before the people" (6:41). They ended up with twelve baskets of leftovers, a symbolic number surely. In chapter 8, Mark tells us that Jesus did the same for four thousand.

Compare the two stories. Herod, in his opulent palace, provides a lavish meal for nobles. Jesus, in a "deserted place,"[24] feeds the multitude. Herod acts the fool, intoxicated presumably by both the wine and the dance. Jesus preaches the kingdom. Herod is concerned about what his guests might think of him. Jesus is concerned for what the people need. Herod takes; Jesus gives. Herod kills; Jesus feeds. There are eucharistic overtones here as well. Jesus blessed the loaves, broke them, and they were distributed. This corresponds to how Mark describes the Last Supper (14:22).

There is more: Mark tells us that Jesus had intended to simply spend time alone with his disciples, but "he saw the great crowd; and he had compassion for them, because they were like sheep without a shepherd" (6:34). Herod reminds us of so many failed leaders in Israel's history. The prophet Micaiah, challenging Israel's King Jehoshaphat, proclaims, "I saw all Israel scattered on the mountains, like sheep that have no shepherd" (1 Kgs 22:17). And Jesus fulfills Ezekiel's prophecy: "For thus says the Lord GOD: I myself will search for my sheep, and will seek them out. . . . I myself will be the shepherd of my sheep" (Ezek 34:11-15). There is still more: When the disciples come to Jesus to dismiss the crowd, he literally says, "Give to them yourselves to eat."[25] Of course, the implied meaning is that the disciples give them what they themselves *have* to eat. We should allow the literal wording to inform us as well, particularly as this episode has eucharistic connotations. In the Eucharist, we unite our self-offering to God with the original self-offering of Christ on the cross. As Christ becomes our spiritual food, we who are also the Body of Christ as a church offer spiritual food to the world. We become sacraments of God. With so little that we alone have, in God's grace our gifts and our service become multiplied. You never know; even small gestures of love can become overwhelmingly fruitful.

The Tradition of the Elders (7:1-23)

In Jesus's day, Judaism was not a single agreed-upon set of religious practices or theology. The Sadducees, for example, held that only the first five books of the Hebrew Bible were actually "biblical" or "canonical." The Pharisees held as canonical what is essentially the Hebrew Bible we have today, including the prophets, historical texts, and wisdom literature. The Sadducees did not anticipate a messiah or last judgment, nor did they believe in any possibility of a meaningful afterlife. These ideas emerged only in later writings. The Pharisees (and Jesus) held all these views.

In Deuteronomy Moses insists, "So now, Israel, give heed to the statutes and ordinances that I am teaching you to observe. . . . You must neither add anything to what I command you nor take anything away from it, but keep the commandments of the LORD your God with which I am charging you" (Deut 4:1-2). This is the Torah by which Israel could "be holy, for I the LORD your God am holy" (Lev 19:2). Yet it is not that easy. The command to "remember the sabbath day, and keep it holy" (Exod 20:8) offers little specifics beyond the demand not to work. Thus, there developed in Judaism an Oral Torah that supported and specified how to live out the Written Torah. Some four centuries after Jesus, Judaism produced the Talmud, which required 260 pages (in my English translation) to delineate how to keep the sabbath holy.

The Jewish historian Josephus says little about the Pharisees, though he does mention that "the Pharisees had passed on to the people certain regulations handed down by former generations and not recorded in the laws of Moses."[26] The common modern belief that Pharisees attempted to live out the Torah with the ritual purity of temple priests actually has little to no historical warrant. What we do know is that they were popular and respected leaders, as noted in the chapter on Matthew. We also know that some of them were among Jesus's biggest rivals, even as he shared much of their theology.

This next section of Mark depicts a confrontation between Jesus and some Pharisees and scribes that "had come from Jerusalem." According to Mark, they challenge Jesus's disciples because the disciples did not ritually purify their hands before eating. Mark then tells us, "(For the Pharisees, and all Jews, do not eat unless they thoroughly wash their hands, thus observing the tradition of the elders; and they do not eat anything from the market unless they wash it; and there are also many other traditions that they observe, the washing of cups, pots, and bronze kettles.) So the Pharisees and scribes asked him, 'Why do your disciples not live according to the tradition of the elders, but eat with defiled hands?'" (7:3-5). Not all Jews actually followed this custom, nor I think all Pharisees. But to these scribes and Pharisees before him, Jesus responds by calling them "hypocrites" and citing Isaiah: "This people honors me with their lips, but their hearts are far from me; in vain do they worship me, teaching human precepts as doctrines" (7:6-7; see Isa 29:13). Jesus points out a practice of dedicating funds to the temple (*corban*) that allows them to withhold support for their parents, thus undermining the commandment to honor father and mother for the sake of a religious custom, "thus making void the word of God through your tradition that you have handed on. And you do many things like this" (7:13). This would be an instance of both adding to and subtracting from the Torah. Then Jesus called the crowd to listen:

> There is nothing outside a person that by going in can defile, but the things that come out are what defile. . . . [And to his disciples] Do you not see that whatever goes into a person from outside cannot defile, since it enters, not the heart but the stomach, and goes out into the sewer? . . . It is what comes out of a person that defiles. For it is from within, from the human heart, that evil intentions come: fornication, theft, murder, adultery, avarice, wickedness, deceit, licentiousness, envy, slander, pride, folly. All these evil things come from within, and they defile a person. (7:18-23)

We might ask ourselves: How could washing undermine a law of God? It certainly would not. Jesus is clearly using the controversy to discuss how we can lose ourselves in traditions and rules while ignoring what really matters.

The exact historicity of this encounter is complicated, but the point is certainly not. Religious hypocrisy was rife in ancient Israel, and it is rife in our modern world. The Greek term *hypokritēs* references an actor wearing a mask for a role. Used here, it would be like calling someone a "pretender" or "two-faced." It is also clear in the Gospels that such a seemingly devout posture actually took a toll on the common people, whose ordinary lifestyle made it impossible for them to attain the Pharisees' level of observance. "Woe to you, scribes and Pharisees, hypocrites! For you lock people out of the kingdom of heaven. For you do not go in yourselves, and when others are going in, you stop them" (Matt 23:13-14). In commenting on this passage, Pope Francis writes about the journey of the heart and interior purification:

> Jesus meets people who are afraid to take up the journey and who create a "caricature" of God. But that is a false identity, because these non-restless ones have calmed the restlessness of their heart by describing God with commandments. In doing so, however, they have forgotten God and see only the tradition of men. . . . Today, too, the Lord invites us to avoid the danger of giving more importance to form than to substance. He calls us to recognize, ever anew, what is the true core of the experience of faith—that is, love of God and love of neighbor—by purifying it of the hypocrisy of legalism and ritualism.[27]

We can think of Inspector Javert, the evil (or is he tragic?) policeman in Victor Hugo's classic novel, *Les Misérables.* So committed was he to the exact specifications of the law that he became inflexible and cruel. The purpose of the law is the common good, but he really never considered this. Hugo's narrative contrast is Jean Valjean, someone who violated the law out of necessity but was devoted to compassion. The Gospels make it clear enough that Jesus did not intend to reject Torah. And he seemed fine with his fellow Jews who added pious expressions of it. But his ire emerged when these were imposed on the backs of those least able to adhere to them. A virtually constant question in my life is, what does it mean to live a holy life? Of course, such a question admits to various expressions. In such considerations we ought to embrace the often-repeated dictum: *In essentials, unity; in nonessentials, liberty; in all things, charity.* At the end of the day, "Owe no one anything, except to love one another; for the one who loves another has fulfilled the law" (Rom 13:8).[28]

Crossing Boundaries (7:24-44)

Mark portrays Jesus always seemingly on the move. In the space of four short chapters we find him and his disciples in Gerasa, southeast of the Sea of Galilee in the area of the Decapolis. Then he is back to Nazareth, then to a "deserted place" along the shores of Galilee, then, apparently alone, to the far north cities of Tyre and Sidon in the land of Phoenicia, then only to return to the shores of Galilee at Bethsaida, and finally to another far northern territory of Caesarea Philippi. Some of this is Gentile territory and some Jewish. It is dizzying, and one wonders how well Mark knows the geography. After Jesus's challenging words to the Pharisees and scribes we learn the following, and we should quote it in full:

> From there he set out and went away to the region of Tyre. He entered a house and did not want anyone to know he was there. Yet he could not escape notice, but a woman whose little daughter had an unclean spirit immediately heard about him, and she came and bowed down at his feet. Now the woman was a Gentile, of Syrophoenician origin. She begged him to cast the demon out of her daughter. He said to her, "Let the children be fed first, for it is not fair to take the children's food and throw it to the dogs." But she answered him, "Sir, even the dogs under the table eat the children's crumbs." Then he said to her, "For saying that, you may go—the demon has left your daughter." (7:24-30)

Following this episode, we immediately find Jesus in the Gentile world of the Decapolis, healing a deaf and mute man (7:31-37). And finally, we find him back on the shores of Galilee feeding four thousand, much like he did in chapter 6. What are we to make of all this, particularly the seemingly brusque way he treated the mother of a possessed daughter? Some have tried to soften Jesus's words. In using the metaphor of dogs, Jesus's term is *kunariois* (little dogs) as though "pups" is a really a friendly term. But to refer to anyone as a dog (of any kind) was rather insulting for Jews, even if used metaphorically.[29] It could be that Jesus was intentionally provoking her to a fuller expression of faith. This might be the case, if a bit odd, given that she bowed to his feet and begged him.

As we saw in Matthew's Gospel, sometimes issues in the church get reflected back into the Gospel narrative. If so, this may explain the church's realization that Gentiles are part of the saving ministry that Jesus brought. And indeed, the woman's "counter-metaphor" of referring to herself (and perhaps all Gentiles) as house pets conditions the healing. In Matthew's rendering of the same story Jesus says, "I was sent only to the lost sheep of the house of Israel" (Matt 15:24). Only after his resurrection will the Lord command, "Go therefore and make disciples of all nations" (Matt 28:19). Paul speaks about Jesus's salvation as an olive tree that is initially wholly Jewish. Gentiles are then a "wild olive shoot" being "grafted . . . to share the rich root of the olive tree" (Rom 11:17). Perhaps this is the case. On the other hand, Jesus had already exhibited divine power by exorcising "Legion" from the Gerasene demoniac in Gentile territory. The story seems to draw us to a similar account of Elijah. Elijah was sent by God to Zarephath, which is just north of Tyre. There he conditions a miraculous feeding and, at the mother's urging, brings her son back to life (1 Kgs 17:8-24). Jesus likewise cures a mother's child and soon provides a miraculous feeding—this time of four thousand. Perhaps this is the case.

For me, the message is this: we have primary duties and primary relationships. Naturally and rightly these take our principal focus, time, and concern. But life and sometimes God's direct providence often throw us a curveball. Something comes up; someone outside our primary sphere of responsibility has need. What ought we to do? In the Letter of James he writes, "If a brother or sister is naked and lacks daily food, and one of you says to them, 'Go in peace; keep warm and eat your fill,' and yet you do not supply their bodily needs, what is the good of that?" (Jas 2:15-16). And Hebrews insists, "Do not neglect to show hospitality to strangers, for by doing that some have entertained angels without knowing it" (Heb 13:2). Two days prior to my writing this, I tried to drop off my car to a friend devoted to a ministry of caring for the poor of Toledo. He needed a car for a week, and I did not. But he wasn't home. "Sorry," he later told me, "but I encountered an abused homeless woman, and it took me the rest of the day to get her in a safe facility." This was his only day off. Perhaps that woman was an angel in disguise. More likely she was a "Gentile of Syrophoenician origin."

Learning Discipleship (8:11–9:38)

Mark tells us that after Jesus fed the four thousand, Pharisees sought to test him by asking for a sign. This would not be unusual, as prophets often confirmed their words with divine signs.[30] But he just miraculously fed a crowd of four thousand! And further, much of Jesus's ministry so far has been expressions of divine power, typically rendered *dunamis* (dynamite). Further, as we have seen, they are performed in the context of faith, which is why he did little in Nazareth. Jesus refuses the Pharisees' demand. He and his disciples then take a boat and cross the Sea of Galilee. In the boat he tells his disciples to "Watch out—beware of the yeast of the Pharisees and the yeast of Herod" (8:15). The disciples take him quite literally: "They said to one another, 'It is because we have no bread'" (8:16). Leaven or yeast is a great metaphor as it is something quite small and hidden that will affect the whole loaf. As we saw in Matthew, the kingdom of God is like yeast that spreads everywhere (Matt 13:33). Obviously here it is like a hidden corrupting agent. Paul uses this latter framing to reference the effects of boasting, malice, evil (1 Cor 5:6-8), and false teaching (Gal 5:9). In failing to understand Jesus, the disciples show they are just as confused as *outsiders*. "Do you still not perceive or understand? Are your hearts hardened?" (8:17). In the Jewish mindset understanding is located in the heart; thus, their hearts were hardened. And a hardened heart is often used in the Old Testament for resisting signs of God's presence.[31]

Understanding is not a strength of the disciples, and discipleship is a long road of learning. This leads us to the next pericope, where Jesus cures a blind man. On the surface it is an unusual healing as it takes two stages. Jesus took the man from Bethsaida outside of town, "and when he had put saliva on his eyes and laid his hands on him, he asked him, 'Can you see anything?' And the man looked up and said, 'I can see people, but they look like trees, walking.'" Jesus again placed his hands on the man's eyes and "his sight was restored" (8:23-25). Why twice? Most scholars see this as a metaphor for Jesus's disciples who can only learn about who he really is and what his mission is fully about in stages.

It is here where Jesus asks his disciples, " 'Who do you say that I am?' Peter answered him, 'You are the Messiah.' And he sternly ordered them not to tell anyone about him" (8:29-30). But it cannot be so easy. "Then he began to teach them that the Son of Man must undergo great suffering, and be rejected by the elders, the chief priests, and the scribes, and be killed, and after three days rise again. He said all this quite openly. And Peter took him aside and began to rebuke him. But turning and looking at his disciples, he rebuked Peter and said, 'Get behind me, Satan! For you are setting your mind not on divine things but on human things' " (8:31-33). Peter was not wrong in calling him the Messiah. It is just that Jesus is not the Messiah he was expecting. Glory? *Yes!* Suffering? *No!* Death? *Absolutely not!* And this is the path he demands of his disciples too.

Peter and his fellow disciples are now like the blind man at Bethsaida. Their eyes are opened, but they do not fully see. Then to the disciples and the crowd: "If any want to become my followers, let them deny themselves and take up their cross and follow me. For those who want to save their life will lose it, and those who lose their life for my sake, and for the sake of the gospel, will save it. For what will it profit them to gain the whole world and forfeit their life?" (8:34-36).

We saw this paradox in Matthew's Gospel, and we will see it again in Luke. It is that central a teaching and rather perplexing. Taking up one's cross and denying oneself is complicated. What it is *not* is self-denigration. God is not glorified by half persons. Certainly, lost or abused souls who have little self-possession cannot offer themselves with full freedom. We are made in the image and likeness of God (Gen 1:26). This is the foundational truth and has to be appropriated before all else. Still, Jesus calls us to a kind of real paschal donation of ourselves to God—we follow the master here. Decentering ourselves from our own narcissism and recentering ourselves in God is a real dying to "self," at least that false self that controls so much. The paradox is that such a self-offering is really freedom and true self-possession. One finds one's true self and authentic power only in God, who holds all meaning in the universe.

It also means that we take on a kind of paschal challenge with our own suffering and trials. The imperative is to relocate one's own trials in the passion of Christ, to participate in Christ's compassionate redemption. Paul will say, "I am now rejoicing in my sufferings for your sake, and in my flesh I am completing what is lacking in Christ's afflictions for the sake of his body, that is, the church" (Col 1:24). Paul saw his own suffering as a participation in Christ's ongoing salvation. Consider it this way: The Father's plan is to embrace the entire universe in the Son's paschal love, "to gather up all things in him, things in heaven and things on earth" (Eph 1:10), "so that God may be all in all" (1 Cor 15:28). We are part of his enterprise, for we have been incorporated into Christ, into his body and his mission. This means that we are profoundly and mystically united to all people, and our suffering on behalf of the salvation of the world is also our work in Christ. Our suffering, paschally embraced, binds us in love not only to those who are acutely suffering but to all in need of Christ's salvation. "Who do you say that I am?" Each Christian's response will be unique. Yet, Jesus's message tells us that it will have to include this recognition: You are the crucified one who commands me to walk the same road. Vincent Pizzuto puts it elegantly:

> At the center of the Christian contemplative life stands the scandal of the cross, the chief witness and paradigm of Christ's posture toward the very world into which he emptied himself. . . . The scandal of his descent is the scandal of a God who has transgressed the abyss between divinity and humanity and is revealed in Christ not as emperor of the universe but as "crucified love." . . . The practice of contemplative prayer is thus a kind of death-to-self through which each of us discovers that "it is no longer I who live, but Christ in me" (Gal 2:20).[32]

On a personal note, the holiest time in my life—tragically decades ago—was when I entered a fourteen-month dark night of the soul. During this darkest period, I was never more loving, compassionate, or generous. This is Jesus's *crucified wisdom*.

The Kingdom's Imminence, the Transfiguration, and Elijah (9:1-13)

I noted in the introduction two things that I want to revisit. The first is that Matthew and Luke draw directly on Mark for their own Gospels. So we are seeing much of the same narrative material here that we addressed in Matthew, and we will see it in Luke. There are differences, and the very tone and theological slants of the evange-lists matter for interpreting each text. I will try to avoid repeating myself, but I do not want to give short shrift to Mark simply because I discussed something earlier. Such is the case with what has been traditionally called *the transfiguration*. Second, recall that biblical events are laden with history, theology, themes of identity, and so on. The evangelists often want us to see interconnections between the Old Testament and Jesus's life. We can see this here.

We begin with an astounding claim by Jesus: "Truly I tell you, there are some standing here who will not taste death until they see that the kingdom of God has come with power" (9:1). Jesus did not exactly know when the consummation of history would occur. Later in Mark, Jesus will say, "But about that day or hour no one knows, neither the angels in heaven, nor the Son, but only the Father" (13:32). According to Christian dogma, Jesus had two natures: one human and another divine. And these natures were "unconfused"; that is, they did not "mix." This ensures that Jesus Christ was fully both human and divine in an absolute, complete way. This also means that there were simply things Jesus did not know. What seems clear, reading Mark, is that Jesus believed the full expression of the king-dom, including an apocalyptic reordering of all things, would happen imminently. What he says in 9:1 he will repeat in 13:30: "Truly I tell you, this generation will not pass away until all these things have taken place." *These things* refers to seeing the "Son of Man coming in clouds with great power and glory" (13:26). The early church took this to heart, and we find Paul feeling assured that he would still be living at the time of the second coming (1 Thess 4:15). He believed it to be so soon that he advised the Corinthians who were not mar-ried to remain so. "The appointed time has grown short. . . . For the present form of this world is passing away" (1 Cor 7:29-31). In *this sense* Jesus (and Paul) were wrong. The second coming was not imminent; it did not happen in that generation.

This takes us to the event of the transfiguration. Mark begins, "Six days later, Jesus took with him Peter and James and John, and led them up a high mountain apart, by themselves. And he was trans-figured before them" (9:2). Moses too waited six days on Mount Sinai when the glory of the Lord appeared to him (Exod 24:15-17). *Transfigured* is a Latinized version of the Greek *metamorphōthē*; he "changed form" now to reflect his divine glory. Appearing with him are Elijah and Moses, two prophets who experienced God on Sinai. Elijah, who was taken up to heaven in a whirlwind (2 Kgs 2:11), was prophesied to return and precede the "day of the LORD" (Mal 4:5). God, from a cloud, speaks to the three disciples: "This is my Son, the Beloved; listen to him!" (9:7).

Consider the associations between Moses and his Sinai experience and the disciples and their transfiguration experience: they went to a high mountain (Exod 24:12); there is a special group (Exod 24:1-2); the Divine is expressed as radiance (Exod 24:17); and the divine encounter is in a cloud (Exod 24:16). As for Elijah, Jesus identifies John as the very Elijah figure to precede the Lord's coming (9:13).[33] Consider as well the extraordinary experience the disciples had: "And he was transfigured before them, and his clothes became dazzling white, such as no one on earth could bleach them. And there appeared to them Elijah with Moses, who were talking with Jesus" (9:2-4). We have seen something of the *messianic secret* in Mark, where Jesus does not want to be publicly known as the Messiah. Peter had just declared it, and "he sternly ordered them not to tell anyone about him" (8:30). This *kind* of messiah is not what they are expecting. This *kind* of messiah will suffer and die. But this is not Jesus's last word. His last word is *glory*, and now the disciples get a glimpse at the twofold reality of who Jesus is. He is the suffering servant *and* he is the glorified Lord.

The disciples will struggle to hold those two truths together. And we do the same. We want to cling to the glory part but not to that which enters the depths of suffering or the lives of those who suffer. As I noted in the chapter on Matthew, Peter wants to cling to the glory experience. In this sense, Jesus was spot on, as "the transfiguration represents *a* (if not *the*) coming of God's kingdom in power."[34] Peter wants to prolong the experience. "Let us make three dwellings, one for you, one for Moses, and one for Elijah" (9:5). This is all too common for us. We have a religiously peak experience, a taste of God's glory, and we want it to last. Pope Francis remarks, "But we cannot stay there! Encounter with God in prayer inspires us to then 'descend the mountain' and return to the plain where we meet many brothers and sisters weighed down by fatigue, sickness, injustice, ignorance, and poverty, both material and spiritual. To these brothers and sisters in difficulty we are called to bear the fruit of that experience with God by sharing the grace we have received."[35] The cross and the resurrection, humility and glory, spiritual darkness and radiant light, these are all parts of our lives and necessary parts.

Being Moonstruck (9:14-29)

Jesus and these three closest disciples return from their mountain experience only to find the other disciples in a kind of turmoil. They had already been empowered by Jesus to heal and expel demons (6:7-13) and had been successful. But they were now with a man's son whose demon "seizes him, it dashes him down; and he foams and grinds his teeth and becomes rigid" (9:18). As Matthew related this same story, he identifies it as what we would call epilepsy (Matt 17:15). Literally, it is "moonstruck" (*selēniazetai*), reflecting the belief at the time that epilepsy was related to the phases of the moon (*selēnē*). Further, in Jesus's day the lines between natural evil, such as sickness, and supernatural evil of demon possession were thin to nonexistent. The man appeals to Jesus, "If you are able to do any-thing, have pity on us and help us" (9:22). Jesus seems indignant: " 'If you are able!—All things can be done for the one who believes.' Immediately the father of the child cried out, 'I believe; help my unbelief!' " (9:23-24). Jesus casts out the demon, takes the man's son by the hand, and lifts him up. Privately to his disciples he remarks, "This kind can come out only through prayer" (9:29)

There is much to mine here. The first is the imperative of faith. Jesus, in fact, castigates the whole crowd, "You faithless genera-tion, how much longer must I be among you? How much longer must I put up with you?" (9:19). Faith in God is not blind faith—believing any- and everything without scrutiny. Nor is it a kind of faith that imagines everything will always come out well. The human condition, by definition, is one rife with challenges, illnesses, and suffering. Faith in Christ does not free us from this condition. Faith does, however, place trust in God's love, providence, and care. The man's response to Jesus, "I believe; help my unbelief," rather well sums up discipleship. We do believe in Christ, in his presence and love, but not perfectly. Discipleship, especially as we see in Mark, is a long and sometimes quite confusing road.

Saying to his disciples that "This kind can come out only through prayer" is again so important. And this is particularly true for both supernatural and moral evils. In *The Rite*, journalist Matt Baglio details the apprenticeship of Father Gary Thomas in becoming the exorcist for the Diocese of San Francisco. Father Thomas was mentored by several exorcists in Rome, and what was striking is that he discovered many of those possessed were not free of their possession immediately. Sometimes it takes years of prayer and a repetition of the ritual for the demon to leave. When so, the exorcist's practice is to *weaken* the demon, progressively emasculating it until it leaves. What is central is a deep prayer life for the exorcist and ongoing prayer for those possessed.[36] The same is said, of course, for moral evil, an affliction that possesses all of us to one degree or another. In his short primer on prayer, William Berry sensibly notes, "The longer people remain in conscious relationship with Jesus, the more like him they become . . . where before they wanted Jesus to be where they were, now they want to be where he is. Now they focus more on Jesus himself. . . . They desire to love as he loves, to forgive as he forgives."[37]

A Passion Prediction, Who's Important, and Salt (9:30-50)

Jesus is beginning his journey to Jerusalem. Some scholars have imagined Mark's Gospel as neatly broken into two parts: ministry in Galilee and its environs and his fateful last week in Jerusalem. Perhaps so. We have seen a ministry of powerful words and powerful deeds. Jerusalem will be a time of conflict and suffering. On his way, he teaches about discipleship. And it begins with a passion prediction: " 'The Son of Man is to be betrayed into human hands, and they will kill him, and three days after being killed, he will rise again.' But they did not understand what he was saying and were afraid to ask him" (9:31-32). It is almost as though the disciples are regressing. Mark then tells us that they were discussing among themselves who was the greatest. "He sat down, called the twelve, and said to them, 'Whoever wants to be first must be last of all and servant of all.' Then he took a little child and put it among them; and taking it in his arms, he said to them, 'Whoever welcomes one such child in my name welcomes me, and whoever welcomes me welcomes not me but the one who sent me'" (9:35-37).

This is about ministry and who matters. As I noted in the chapter on Matthew, children stood for powerlessness. Children were society's nobodies, those who lacked social status or legal rights. The human condition has not changed much in two thousand years. Most people want to "be somebody." Thus, there are really two things going on. The first is that all ministry is servanthood. And the second is that everyone matters, particularly those least imagined to matter in society. And there is an implicit third thing: we already *are somebody*; "We are children of God, and if children, then heirs, heirs of God and joint heirs with Christ" (Rom 8:16-17).

When I taught at the seminary, the faculty was charged with voting on candidates for the priesthood. Preparing for this, I would ask the janitor (call him Fred), who had significant mental disabilities, what he thought of each seminarian I was to vote on. Fred did not know a lot about some of these young men, but he did know who respected him and who dismissed him. To receive a child with the same dignity and value as the Lord himself is an extraordinary challenge to change our perspective. And it reflects the truth that we are all children of God. I once noted, "To receive a child as though he or she were Christ is intimately related to the Passion; for treating a social nonperson with respect requires renunciation of the grasping self that views others only with regard to one's own interests."[38] Imagine Judgment Day and God asks the Freds of our lives, "What do you think?"

Jesus then insists, "If any of you put a stumbling block before one of these little ones who believe in me, it would be better for you if a great millstone were hung around your neck and you were thrown into the sea" (9:42). This should exercise our conscience every day. And then he turns to what are stumbling blocks in our own interior lives: "If your hand causes you to stumble, cut it off; it is better for you to enter life maimed than to have two hands and to go to hell, to the unquenchable fire." The same for one's foot; cut it off. And one's eye; tear it out (9:43-48). Obviously, he is speaking figuratively. Yet, are we willing to cut out those things in our lives that cause us to stumble? Is it anger? Cut it off. Is it alcohol consumption? Cut it off. Is it pride? Tear it out. Jesus ends with an enigmatic teaching:

"For everyone will be salted with fire. Salt is good; but if salt has lost its saltiness, how can you season it? Have salt in yourselves, and be at peace with one another" (9:49). Both salt and fire are images of purification. For the world and for the sake of our own souls, Christians must be both salty and on fire.

Being One Flesh (10:1-12)

We saw the question of divorce in Matthew's Gospel (19:3-12), and Matthew was drawing on Mark. Here, the original source has some Pharisees "testing" Jesus: "Is it lawful for a man to divorce his wife?" (10:2). They already know the "biblical answer" is yes (Deut 24:1-4). Jesus takes them back to Genesis to tell them God's vision that " 'the two shall become one flesh.' So they are no longer two, but one flesh. Therefore what God has joined together let no one separate" (10:8-9). This Jesus applies to both men and women, which addresses Roman law whereby women could initiate divorces. Jesus then insists that whoever divorces and remarries commits adultery (10:11-12). Clearly, the early church struggled with this saying. Matthew will add the exception of adultery. Paul addresses the issue, knowing what Jesus taught: "I give this command—not I but the Lord" (1 Cor 7:10). But then Paul adds a pastoral exception: "The rest I say—I and not the Lord." The exception had to do with "mixed" marriages between a believer and unbeliever. If the unbeliever wants to divorce, "let it be so; in such a case the brother or sister is not bound. It is to peace that God has called you" (1 Cor 7:12-15).

What it looks like we have is that Matthew and Paul did not take Jesus to be issuing a universal, absolute law, as they modified it for the good of their communities. Today, the Catholic Church takes the indissolubility of marriage as a divine law but allows annulments for various reason, including the vague "lack of discretion." These ongoing considerations reflect efforts to take the teachings of Jesus seriously in a complex world. The ideal always remains: strive to be of one mind, one heart, and one flesh in your marriage. Divorce is clearly contrary to what we were made for in terms of marriage. This is the teaching of the Lord. No one knows this truth more deeply than earnest believers who committed their lives to a union that is now fractured by divorce. Their pain, loneliness, sense of failure, and often even shame speak loudly and clearly that this brokenness is not the flourishing God intended. Does this make them violators of the divine law? Not necessarily at all. Like Matthew, Paul, and the modern church, one is wise to take Jesus's words, the dynamic tradition, and the human condition to heart, and to consider all these when wrestling with this complex moral problem. One thing should be obvious: when we do such wrestling, we should always be sensitive to everyone's pain and the priority of conscience. Our solidarity involves entering into each other's joy and brokenness.

A Rich Man, a Blind Man, and Grasping Disciples (10:17-52)

"As Jesus was setting out on a journey, a man ran up to him, knelt before him, and asked him, 'Good Teacher, what must I do to inherit eternal life?'" (10:17). Jesus responds by reminding him of the commandments, to which he replied: " 'Teacher, I have kept all these since my youth.' Jesus, looking at him, loved him and said, 'You lack one thing: go, sell what you own, and give the money to the poor, and you will have treasure in heaven; then come, follow me.' When he heard this, he was shocked and went away grieving, for he had many possessions" (10:20-22). Soon after, Jesus tells his disciples, "How hard it is to enter the kingdom of God! It is easier for a camel to go through the eye of a needle than for someone rich to enter the kingdom of God." They then ask, "Then who can be saved?" And Jesus responds, "For mortals it is impossible, but not for God; for God all things are possible" (10:24-27).

Widely in the Old Testament wealth was considered a blessing from God and a sign of God's favor.[39] And yet, some sensitive souls recognized that it did not always work that way. "Why," Jeremiah asks, "does the way of the guilty prosper?" (Jer 12:1); "Why," Job asks, "do the wicked live on, reach old age, and grow mighty in power?" (Job 21:7). And the Psalmist realizes that "I was envious of the arrogant; I saw the prosperity of the wicked" (Ps 73:3). The terms "rich" and "poor" are used in the Bible variously. They can distinguish those with or without material resources. They can also be used to address one's inner life, and here we have to be savvy. For example, one who is "poor in spirit" is a humble person who could thereby have inner wealth. Being poor in spirit is very different from having an impoverished soul.

There are several problems with wealth, particularly significant wealth. The first is that it can insulate us from the suffering that is around us. Not only can we stop seeing those struggling, we can also stop hearing their cry. Riches can also simply replace God. At the end of the day, wealth can be what we seek. Most typically, I think, riches act as a regular competitor for our interior affections. Pope Francis observes: "Riches are not bad in themselves, but it is bad when one serves those riches. . . . The young man did not allow himself to be conquered by Jesus' loving gaze. . . . Money, pleasure, and success dazzle but then disappoint; they promise life but procure death. The Lord asks us to detach ourselves from these false riches in order to enter into true life, into full, authentic, luminous life."[40]

It is not just wealth or comfort that can seduce or blind one. On the way to Jerusalem, Jesus gives his disciples a third passion prediction. It is short and blunt, as were his former two predictions. Immediately James and John ask, "Grant us to sit, one at your right hand and one at your left, in your glory" (10:37). We saw this in Matthew's Gospel, but Matthew had their mother make the request. This is straightforward, shameless, glory seeking. "When the ten heard this, they began to be angry with James and John" (10:41). Why *angry*? Why not, *they shook their heads* or *they seemed confused*? James and John were seeking what they themselves wanted, only James and John got in first; they got the jump. This might be the biggest danger for the disciples: being thought of well, having power, being elite. Jesus reminds them, "You know that among the Gentiles those whom they recognize as their rulers lord it over them, and their great ones are tyrants over them. But it is not so among you; but whoever wishes to become great among you must be your servant, and whoever wishes to be first among you must be slave of all" (10:42-44). There's a paradox here: if you want to become great, be a servant (not great). Of course, one could interiorly imagine oneself quite great *by serving*, but this misses the point. You have to really strive to *become* a servant.

St. John of the Cross, in describing reaching union with God, uses the metaphor of ascending to the top of Mount Carmel. In his sketch of this, he writes about those seeking the goods of the earth. The aspirant taps out midway and concludes, "The more I desired to seek them, the less I had." And then he shows the stalled path of those seeking the goods of heaven with the same failure and conclusion. The only way to get to the top of Mount Carmel is "nothing, nothing, nothing, nothing, nothing, nothing, and on the Mount nothing." On the top of the mount, the soul has everything sought by the others: "Now that I no longer desire them, I have them all without desire."[41] Most important, one has union with God, and the flames of love that God has for the soul and the soul has for God fuse into a single divine flame. "Thus these movements of both God and the soul are not only splendors, but also glorifications of the soul."[42] This is quite a promotion. The paradox is that on the top of Carmel it still is *nothing*; that is, it still can only be about God. If one seeks divine union as a personal possession, one will never attain it. It is always only about God.

Just before coming to Jerusalem, Jesus and his disciples pass through Jericho. There a blind begging man, Bartimaeus, cries out emphatically and against the scolding crowd, "Jesus, Son of David, have mercy on me" (10:48). Jesus calls him and he runs up, " 'What do you want me to do for you?' The blind man said to him, 'My teacher, let me see again.' Jesus said to him, 'Go, your faith has made you well.' Immediately he regained his sight and followed him on the way" (10:51-52). This final miracle before Jesus enters Jerusalem works as a metaphor. Bartimaeus desperately wants to *see*, unlike the disciples who haven't really seen or understood what Jesus is about and perhaps don't want to see. He is desperate and undaunted by others. And upon gaining his sight, he becomes a follower of Jesus to Jerusalem. We must seek Christ with the same desperation, the same single-mindedness, if we want to really see and follow.

I would like to recommend the following spiritual exercise: read slowly and repeatedly the story (10:46-52). Imagine what the streets of Jericho look like, what the day feels like. Imagine the crowd and then Jesus and his disciples passing. Imagine that you are a beggar on the road where he passes. Imagine calling out to him. And he asks you, "What do you want me to do for you?" What is it? Stay there; ponder your inner life. Ask Jesus to reveal your deepest desire. I was assigned this meditation by my spiritual director. I spent around six weeks every morning with this meditation. I came up with a lot of possible answers, but nothing really hit the core. It *finally* came to me, and it was this I asked Jesus for. I believe that the answer that finally rang deeply true was a desire inspired by Jesus himself. The answer (I'm keeping it a secret) sustained and guided me for the next three years.

Jesus Enters Jerusalem and the Temple "Sandwich" (11:1-33)

Jesus seems to create an uproar wherever he goes. Mark shows that regularly people came to him in droves, often unexpectedly. Yet, his family did not seem to understand him and even tried to restrain him. Those in his own town of Nazareth seemed disdainful, and early on some Pharisees and Herodians began to plot his demise. Jesus's entry into Jerusalem carries the same dynamic: uproar. As I noted in Matthew, Jesus enters Jerusalem on a colt, just as the prophet Zechariah foresaw (Zech 9:9). "Many people spread their cloaks on the road, and others spread leafy branches that they had cut in the fields. Then those who went ahead and those who followed were shouting, 'Hosanna! Blessed is the one who comes in the name of the Lord! Blessed is the coming kingdom of our ancestor David! Hosanna in the highest heaven!'" (11:8-10). Here Jesus is proclaimed Messiah, the anointed one who would be king.

Hosanna is a Greek transliteration of the Hebrew *hôša ʿ-nā*, meaning "save, please!" or "save, now!"[43] The last line, "Hosanna in the highest heaven," doesn't really translate well but would be something of pure jubilation.[44] "Blessed is the one who comes in the name of the Lord" comes from Psalm 118:26. It is a psalm of victory and includes, "Bind the festal procession with branches, up to the horns of the altar" (v. 27). It will also include, "The stone that the builders rejected has become the cornerstone. This is the Lord's doing; it is marvelous in our eyes" (vv. 22-23). This is a glorious day for Jesus and his disciples, and it is the beginning of the end.

The next day Jesus returned to Jerusalem from the nearby town of Bethany. On the way, Jesus went to a fig tree when he was hungry.

> When he came to it, he found nothing but leaves, for it was not the season for figs. He said to it, "May no one ever eat fruit from you again." And his disciples heard it. Then they came to Jerusalem.

And he entered the temple and began to drive out those who were selling and those who were buying in the temple, and he overturned the tables of the money changers and the seats for those who sold doves; and he would not allow anyone to carry anything through the temple. He was teaching and saying, "Is it not written, 'My house shall be called a house of prayer for all the nations'? But you have made it a den of robbers" (11:15-17).

Here Jesus is citing both Isaiah (56:7), in which Isaiah anticipates a future of worldwide devotion to God in his temple, and Jeremiah, where the temple has become desecrated by those whose lives are sinful and hypocritical. Jeremiah begins his prophecy: "Hear the word of the LORD, all you people of Judah, you who enter these gates to worship the LORD. . . . Amend your ways and your doings. . . . Do not trust in these deceptive words: 'This is the temple of the LORD'" (7:2-4).

Now we return to the fig tree the next day. Peter says, "'Rabbi, look! The fig tree that you cursed has withered.' Jesus answered them, 'Have faith in God. Truly I tell you, if you say to this mountain, "Be taken up and thrown into the sea," and if you do not doubt in your heart, but believe that what you say will come to pass, it will be done for you. So I tell you, whatever you ask for in prayer, believe that you have received it, and it will be yours'" (11:21-24). Mark begins with the fig tree, sandwiches in the cleansing of the temple, and returns to the fig tree. Here the fig tree becomes the interpretive lens to understanding the temple incident. The cleansing of the temple is ultimately a cursing of the temple's authorities, who have made it a "den of robbers." Ultimately the temple and its sacrifices would be replaced by the one who came to "give his life as a ransom for many" (10:45). The withered tree is really the failure by so many to accept Jesus and his kingdom.

Thus, the role of faith becomes central. Jesus speaks in hyperbole about casting a mountain into the sea if one truly believed. And, of course, fully believing without doubt does not guarantee the boon one seeks from God. But it matters utterly that we have faith in Jesus, a faith he found wanting in Jerusalem, even among the crowds who sang out, "Hosanna." In Jesus's entry into Jerusalem and his "cleansing" of the temple, he sets up the very charges against him in his trial with the Sanhedrin (14:53-65). He was accused of claiming to destroy the temple and to be the Messiah. He did "curse" the temple as it was being run and he was proclaimed Messiah, a role he symbolically and publicly took.

Jesus Won't Play Their Games (11:27–12:27)

In the beginning of Mark's Gospel, we find Jesus involved in controversies with the religious authorities of his day (2:1–3:6). We now find another set of controversies, the first of which includes quite a group of contenders: "As he was walking in the temple, the chief priests, the scribes, and the elders came to him and said, 'By what authority are you doing these things? Who gave you the authority to do them?'" (11:27-28). In typical rabbinical style, Jesus answers a question with a question, promising that a real response from them will gain them a decided answer from him. "Did the baptism of John come from heaven, or was it of human origin? Answer me" (11:30). They are trapped. The people believed in John, but the leaders stayed away. If John was a real prophet, they should have heeded him. If not, they should have denounced him. But they stood aloof and now can't commit. They would look bad to the people either way. They lose.

Jesus amps up the pressure with a parable of a vineyard owner who leases his land to tenant farmers. When it was harvest time, he sent a slave who was beaten, then another slave who was beaten more severely, then another whom they killed. Finally, he sent his son, his "beloved." Him they killed, thinking they would take over his inheritance (the land) for themselves. "What then will the owner of the vineyard do? He will come and destroy the tenants and give the vineyard to others. Have you not read this scripture: 'The stone that the builders rejected has become the cornerstone; this was the Lord's doing, and it is amazing in our eyes'?" (12:9-11). The allegory is pretty obvious: the tenants are the chief priests and scribes; the servants are the prophets; Jesus is the "beloved son" whom they seek to kill. He is the "stone rejected by the builders."

The Pharisees and Herodians, whom we met plotting to destroy Jesus almost immediately in his ministry (3:6), are now back on the scene attempting to trap him. "Is it lawful to pay taxes to the emperor, or not?" (12:14). The term here for taxes is *kēnsos*, the census or poll tax. The census tax was levied on all citizens of Samaria,

Judea, and Idumea. It was both a burden and a cruel reminder that they were under direct Roman rule. The "nationalists" or Zealots would have been alienated if Jesus told them to capitulate. But to say, "No, do not pay the tax," is tantamount to a revolution. Further, the coinage had to be Roman; that is, it would have a graven image of Caesar on it, a taboo for Jews. Jesus's response is clever. " 'Bring me a denarius and let me see it. And they brought one. Then he said to them, 'Whose head is this, and whose title?' They answered, 'The emperor's.' Jesus said to them, 'Give to the emperor the things that are the emperor's, and to God the things that are God's' " (12:15-17).

Now it is time for the Sadducees to chime in. Here is a little background: The ancient historian Josephus writes that "The Pharisees . . . believe that souls have power to survive death and receive rewards or punishments. . . . The Sadducees teach that the soul dies along with the body."[45] Here the Sadducees rely on the bulk of the Old Testament tradition that did not see any real life after death. Whether one was good or bad, one ended up in Sheol, a kind of dark slumber at best. But in the two centuries before Jesus, we find the hope in a resurrection of the just.[46] Obviously Jesus shares the same claims as the Pharisees. Further, we should know that Moses commanded that if a man dies without a son, his brother should marry his dead brother's wife, so as to have children on behalf of his deceased brother (Deut 25:5-10). Thus, to test Jesus, the Sadducees pose a problem: "There were seven brothers; the first married and, when he died, left no children; and the second married the widow and died, leaving no children; and the third likewise; none of the seven left children. . . . In the resurrection whose wife will she be? For the seven had married her" (12:20-23). Jesus's response is "For when they rise from the dead, they neither marry nor are given marriage, but are like angels in heaven" (12:25).

In all these controversies, it is obvious to us (and surely to Jesus) that truth is not being sought, but traps are being laid. What's your authority? Should we pay taxes? Whose wife is she in this absurd family scenario? Jesus's responses to each of these is a version of "I'm not playing your game." There is a massive difference between trying to find wisdom in hard questions and using theology or scripture to engage in one-upmanship or worse. Paul makes a distinction between living by the spirit and living by the flesh. By "flesh" (*sarx*) Paul does not mean "body" (*sōma*) but disordered desires, which include "enmities, strife, jealousy, anger, quarrels, dissensions, factions" (Gal 5:20). "By contrast, the fruit of the Spirit is love, joy, peace, patience, kindness, generosity, faithfulness, gentleness, and self-control" (Gal 5:22-23).

In the kind of controversies Jesus encountered, and indeed the kind that we sometimes find in our own lives, we might ask ourselves: what is driving this dynamic, flesh or spirit? It is instructive that Jesus's response to the Sadducees is that the resurrection is a spiritual existence. Our future resurrected body is a mystery to us. Paul will call it a "spiritual body" (*sōma pneumatikos*; 1 Cor 15:44). But we have the Spirit now as the "first fruits" of our new life in Christ (Rom 8:23) as a pledge of our fullest inheritance to come (Eph 1:13-14). Thus, in many of our own conflicts, we ought to ask whether real truth or real wisdom is being sought, or is it simply contention for contention's sake. Is this flesh or spirit?

Another scribe, this time an earnest one, asks Jesus which of the commandments is the first of all. We saw this in Matthew, and I will only comment briefly: "Jesus answered, 'The first is, "Hear, O Israel: the Lord our God, the Lord is one; you shall love the Lord your God with all your heart, and with all your soul, and with all your mind, and with all your strength." The second is this, "You shall love your neighbor as yourself." There is no other commandment greater than these'" (12:29-31). Here Jesus is quoting Deuteronomy 6:5 and Leviticus 19:18. Love, for Jesus, is both the essence of the law and the lens through which to interpret all laws. His response is typical and similar to other famous rabbis. What is unique is that Jesus combined them, for love by its very nature has a unitive quality to it. As I noted in an earlier publication: "To love God but not others is impossible and to imagine loving others without cultivating a love for God—the very source of all love—is to make a colossal error. The First Letter of John puts both together: 'Whoever does not love does not know God, for God is love' (1 Jn 4:8). Loving another fulfills the law (Rom 13:8); love is the one thing that is eternal (1 Cor 13:8-13). . . . Love then is both the means of union with God and the principal expression of what it means to be a Christian (1 Jn 2:10)."[47]

Denouncing the Scribes, Praising the Widow (12:38-44)

Mark provides two scenarios that ought to be taken together, for they concern ways of being religious, inauthentic and authentic. He begins, "Beware of the scribes, who like to walk around in long robes, and to be greeted with respect in the marketplaces, and to have the best seats in the synagogues and places of honor at banquets! They devour widows' houses and for the sake of appearance say long prayers" (12:38-40). This is quite a collection of charges. A scribe is someone who knew how to read and write and was knowledgeable about the law. Sometimes the New Testament calls them "lawyers." Sirach praises them as uniquely important for Jewish life: "How different the one who devotes himself to the study of the law of the Most High! He seeks out the wisdom of all the ancients. . . . If the great Lord is willing, he will be filled with the spirit of understanding; he will pour forth words of wisdom of his own. . . . The Lord will direct his council and knowledge. . . . He will show the wisdom of what he has learned, and will glory in the law of the Lord's covenant" (Sir 39:1-11). But so many scribes did not look like this to Jesus. Jesus accuses them on two fronts. The first is pride. They loved and asserted their status. The ancient adage "Pride goeth before the fall" references Adam and Eve who wanted to be "like God" (Gen 3:1-6). The tradition developed the *seven deadly sins* (pride, greed, wrath, envy, lust, gluttony, and sloth) with pride consistently being the first on the list. John Cassian writes,

> The demon of pride [is] a most sinister demon, fiercer than all that have been discussed up till now. He . . . seeks to destroy those who have mounted almost to the heights of holiness. Just as a deadly plague destroys not just one member of the body, but the whole of it, so pride corrupts the whole soul, not just part of it. Each of the other passions that trouble the soul attacks and tries to overcome a single virtue which is opposed to it, so it darkens and troubles the soul only partially. But the passion of pride darkens the soul completely and leads to its utter downfall.[48]

Jesus's second critique is their "devouring widows' houses." A widow, with no legal protection and illiterate, would hire a scribe to oversee her assets. Those unscrupulous scribes could easily take advantage of the situation and enrich themselves while impoverishing the widows, thus exploiting the most vulnerable. With a public face of great piety, a scribe would look particularly trustworthy, even when he was not. The Old Testament is filled with God's concern for the widow and the orphan, those most in need, the weakest.[49] Yet, even those who were honest in their profession still could live ego-inflated lives, feasting on the honors given them in public.

This takes us to a poor widow Jesus sees at the temple who gives two copper coins to the treasury. Jesus observes "Truly I tell you, this poor widow has put in more than all those who are contributing to the treasury. For all of them have contributed out of their abundance; but she out of her poverty put in everything she had, all she had to live on" (12:43-44). Many commentators assert that the receptacle in the temple would have been trumpet-shaped and the noise this made when they threw in many coins would have reverberated. It would act like a version of, "Look at me, everybody." This is like those scribes Jesus saw, even the "honest" ones; "Look at me." And then, of course, she "put in everything that she had."

Should one contribute everything that one has, making oneself destitute? Probably not. When St. Paul was gathering a collection for the Jerusalem church, he cautioned them, "For if the eagerness is there, the gift is acceptable according to what one has—not according to what one does not have. I do not mean that there should be relief for others and pressure on you, but it is a question of a fair balance between your present abundance and their need" (2 Cor 8:12-14). Still, discipleship ought to have a cost that is a real cost to oneself. Pope Leo XIII (d. 1903) argued that one may live according to the norms of one's culture and state of life and in that context live comparatively simply. Any excess belongs to the poor. This is comforting to me—I can do this! Pope Francis, on the other hand, teaches regularly that we ought to live with actual expressions of poverty and literally (not just *spiritually*) live in solidarity with the poor. This is extremely uncomfortable for me to hear. And it should be.

Jesus's Apocalypse (13:1-37)

During Jesus's final days in Jerusalem he predicts the destruction of Jerusalem to his disciples. Soon after, while sitting on the Mount of Olives and looking at the great city, Peter, James, John, and Andrew question him more. Thus begins Jesus's apocalyptic predictions. As noted in the chapter on Matthew, apocalyptic literature was rife in Israel and had been for the past two centuries.[50] Much of what Jesus says echoes images and prophecies coming from these sources. The only biblical material comes from Daniel (7:9–12:13). Daniel was narratively placed during the time of the first exile in the sixth century BCE but is widely believed to have been written during the time of persecution by the Seleucid king Antiochus IV Epiphanes, who outlawed the Jewish religion and set up an image of Zeus in the temple in 167 BCE. This sparked the Maccabean war. Here are two salient selections:

> I saw one like a Son of Man[51] coming with the clouds of heaven. And he came to the Ancient One and was presented before him. To him was given dominion and glory and kingship, that all peoples, nations, and languages should serve him. His dominion is an everlasting dominion that shall not pass away, and his kingship is one that shall never be destroyed. (Dan 7:13-14)

> At that time Michael, the great prince, the protector of your people shall arise. There shall be a time of anguish such as has never occurred since nations first came into existence. . . . Many of those who sleep in the dust of the earth shall awake, some to everlasting life, and some to shame and everlasting contempt. Those who are wise shall shine like the brightness of the sky, and those who lead many to righteousness, like the stars forever and ever. (Dan 12:1-3)

Jesus tells his disciples, "Beware that no one leads you astray. Many will come in my name and say, 'I am he!' And they will lead many astray. When you hear of wars and rumors of wars, do not be alarmed; this must take place, but the end is still to come. . . . For nation will rise against nation, and kingdom against kingdom; there will be earthquakes in various places; there will be famines. This is but the beginning of the birth pangs" (13:5-8). This will be a time of persecution: "When they bring you to trial and hand you over, do not worry beforehand what you are to say; but say whatever is given you at that time, for it is not you who speak, but the Holy Spirit. . . . But the one who endures to the end will be saved" (13:11-13). This is the first part.

The second part is marked by the "desolating sacrilege set up where it ought not to be" (13:14). We might consider this aligned to what Antiochus IV did. People will have to flee and "false messiahs and false prophets will appear and produce signs and omens, to lead astray" (13:22). The third part becomes cosmic: "But in those days, after that suffering, the sun will be darkened, and the moon will not give its light, and the stars will be falling from heaven, and the powers in the heavens will be shaken. Then they will see 'the Son of Man coming in clouds' with great power and glory. Then he will send out the angels, and gather his elect from the four winds, from the ends of the earth to the ends of heaven" (13:24-27). The fourth part is a word of caution. "But about that day or hour no one knows, neither the angels in heaven, nor the Son, but only the Father. Beware, keep alert; for you do not know when the time will come" (13:32-33).

As I noted in Matthew, Jesus drew on a number of references of the Old Testament and the current texts of his day to describe the kingdom and its coming. An apocalyptic framing is just one of them. They do not adhere systematically to each other, nor should they. Ultimately, the kingdom of God is a transcendent reality, one that goes beyond human conceptions. These varieties of images, themes, and frameworks invite us to an array of access points to the divine mystery. And further, they ground different spiritualities or spiritual resources that can collectively guide us. Considering this heady text, I wrote some years ago:

> The biblical reflections on the sacredness of creation heighten my experiences of awe and wonder, and they inspire me to look for God's presence there. When I take life too seriously, I am challenged and freed by thinking of a universe that is passing away. I think my heart is big enough to realize that I am both a resident alien in this world (1 Pet 2:11) and commissioned to "promote the welfare of the city to which I have exiled you" (Jer 29:7). In another vein, I can recognize as Paul did that I am nothing (2 Cor 12:11)—what freedom!—and that I am loved deeply as a child of God and heir with Christ himself (Rom 8:16-17)—what dignity!
>
> The images help us engage the mystery but should not be identified with it. It would be a mistake to imagine apocalyptic texts as if they were newspaper headlines from the future. Instead of thinking that Jesus erred in his prediction—he said it would happen in

his generation—we might realize that not only Mark's generation needed to hear it, but ours as well. An apocalyptic vision helps us recognize that God's forces are fighting for us. It inspires us not to give up when we are overwhelmed and tempted to quit. It helps us yearn for Christ with the ancient plea, *Maranatha*, "Come, Lord Jesus."[52]

A Prophetess and a Betrayer (14:1-11)

"It was two days before the Passover and the festival of Unleavened Bread" (14:1). We need to pause here for some background. Passover commemorates the exodus when God "passed over" the Israelite houses that were marked by the blood of the Passover lamb, as God took the lives of the firstborn among the Egyptians (Exod 12:1-28). It was joined with the festival of Unleavened Bread and extended eight days. The final day included the sacrifice of lambs and the Passover meal, later called a *Seder*. In Jesus's day, Jerusalem swelled fourfold during this week. This would have been a time of celebration and devotion. Given the theme, freedom from slavery, it was also a very tense time when riots and revolts occurred. The Roman prefect, Pontius Pilate, typically resided in the harbor city of Caesarea Maritima, but during Passover he resided in Jerusalem with increased troops to make sure a disturbance did not happen. Earlier that week, Jesus entered the city and was proclaimed by the crowds a Messiah, an anointed king. Over the next two days, Jesus disrupted the temple and contended with every religious authority. "The chief priests and the scribes were looking for a way to arrest Jesus by stealth and kill him; for they said, 'Not during the festival, or there may be a riot among the people'" (14:1-2).

Mark then tells us that Jesus was in Bethany, about two miles from Jerusalem, sitting at table. "A woman came with an alabaster jar of very costly ointment of nard, and she broke open the jar and poured the ointment on his head" (14:3). Mark tells us that the ointment, nard, was worth three hundred denarii, or a laborer's yearly wage. To the scolding of the crowd at such an extravagant waste, Jesus defends her: "She has done what she could; she has anointed my body beforehand for its burial" (14:8). One might think here of the Psalmist: "You prepare a table before me in the presence of my enemies; you anoint my head with oil; my cup overflows" (Ps

23:5). This remarkable woman and Jesus's response to her brings to high relief the paradox. She anoints Jesus, thus formally making him the *Messiah*—literally anointed—and he describes the anointing as a preparation for his death. "The Son of Man came not to be served but to serve, and to give his life as a ransom for many" (10:45). His kingship is a self-offering.

The prophetess anticipates Jesus's death. Now Judas prepares it: "Then Judas Iscariot, who was one of the twelve, went to the chief priests in order to betray him to them" (14:10). Everything will follow from this incident.

The Last Supper and Peter's Confidence (14:12-25)

At the end of Jesus's final week in Jerusalem he celebrates Passover with his disciples. So much here is both inspiring and disturbing at the same time. During this supper that commemorates God's cove-nantal love and fidelity, Jesus announces, " 'Truly I tell you, one of you will betray me, one who is eating with me.' They began to be distressed and to say to him one after another, 'Surely, not I?' He said to them, 'It is one of the twelve, one who is dipping bread into the bowl with me' " (14:18-20). How distressing!

"While they were eating, he took a loaf of bread, and after bless-ing it he broke it, gave it to them, and said, 'Take; this is by body.' Then he took a cup, and after giving thanks he gave it to them, and all of them drank from it. He said to them, 'This is my blood of the covenant, which is poured out for many' " (14:22-24). As we saw in Matthew's Gospel, covenants were ratified by sacrifice. In the case of the Sinai covenant, Moses sprinkled the blood—the life force—of the sacrifice on the people; it implicated them (Exod 24:8). This new covenant of the kingdom of God now must implicate the dis-ciples. Now it is deeply part of them, Christ is deeply part of them. But this is not the glorified Christ or the fullness of the kingdom. Jesus will then say, "Truly I tell you, I will never again drink of the fruit of the vine until that day when I drink it new in the kingdom of God" (Mark 14:25). The prelude is self-offering, a "ransom for many." They are implicated. And so are we.

The disciples may actually now start to understand this kind of messiah. As Jesus takes them to the Mount of Olives he predicts,

"You will all become deserters; for it is written, 'I will strike the shepherd, and the sheep will be scattered'" (14:27). Jesus even predicts Peter's denial: "Before the cock crows twice, you will deny me three times" (14:30). As we know, Peter will reject this as even possible, and Peter will fail that very night. But they are beginning to understand the cost of discipleship: "'Even though I must die with you, I will not deny you.' And all of them said the same" (14:31).

As disturbing as much of this scene is, it is all the more inspiring. The Last Supper interprets so much of the paradox of our salvation and conditions our participation in it. One ancient Latin hymn captures much of the mystery: *O sacrum convivium in quo Christus sumitur, memoria passionis ejus recolitur, et nobis datur pignus aeternae gloriae* (O sacred banquet in which Christ is received, the memory of his passion is brought to life, and to us is granted a pledge of eternal glory).[53]

The Ransom Becomes a Captive: The Passion of the Christ (14:32–15:32)

Gethsemane

Jesus leads his disciples from the upper room in Jerusalem to the Mount of Olives and into the Garden of Gethsemane. He then took Peter, James, and John apart from the rest. These are the three who experienced the transfiguration. Soon they will experience the other side of the coin. "And he said to them, 'I am deeply grieved, even to death; remain here, and keep awake.' And going a little farther, he threw himself on the ground and prayed that, if it were possible, the hour might pass from him. He said, 'Abba, Father, for you all things are possible; remove this cup from me; yet, not what I want, but what you want'" (14:34-36).

Jesus had been predicting this very night and told his disciples three times it would come. But the weight of it all is overwhelming, even to him. This is the very human Jesus experiencing literally the weight of the world. The "cup" he anticipates was the "cup" James and John assured him they could drink (10:38-39). The Psalmist proclaims, "For in the hand of the LORD there is a cup with foaming wine, well mixed; he will pour a draught from it, and all the wicked of the earth shall drain it down to the dregs (Ps 75:8).[54] This is the cup that Jesus will drink from, absorbing the guilt of the sins of the world. In one of Isaiah's *suffering servant songs*, he proclaims,

> Yet it was the will of the LORD to crush him with pain. When you make his life an offering for sin . . . through him the will of the LORD shall prosper. . . . The righteous one, my servant, shall make many righteous, and he shall bear their iniquities. Therefore I will allot him a portion with the great, and he shall divide the spoil with the strong; because he poured out himself to death, and was numbered with the transgressors; yet he bore the sin of many, and made intercession for the transgressors. (Isa 53:10-12)

"He poured out himself to death," Isaiah writes. Interestingly, Gethsemane literally means "oil press" in Hebrew. In this garden, Jesus was being pressed with unimagined weight. It may seem strange to think about sacrifice in this way, but it would not have been odd in the Jewish mind of the ancient world. As Gerhard Lohfink observes, "Sacrifice in the biblical sense . . . signifies self-surrender, listening with one's whole existence to what God wills. Then it is no longer about one's own cause but about God's."[55] Our modern culture is highly individualistic. Thus, imagining someone as a representative of anything but oneself, much less a whole people or even the world, does not resonate. But the biblical worldview sees representative substitution and atonement as almost normative. Lohfink again: "The questions might be asked: how can another do for me what I must do for myself? How can I be redeemed by another? But we are all dependent on other people. We rely on an endless number of surrogates, representatives. In all this, representation or substitution never means dispensing the other from her or his own action, faith, and repentance. Rather, substitution is intended to make one's own actions possible."[56] Atonement is not about appeasing an angry God or a God who demands a price in blood for sin's debt. Rather, it frees us to be rescued by God's own self from the death we deserve.[57]

And what of his disciples? They had fallen asleep—twice! Jesus chastises Peter, who had just promised so much: "Simon are you asleep? Could you not keep awake one hour?" (14:37). He literally asks Simon if he is not "strong enough" (*ischusas*) to stay awake. Recall that Jesus describes Satan as "the strong one" (3:27) and John the Baptist refers to Christ as "the stronger one" (1:7-8).

Discipleship will necessarily depend on the power of God's grace and not merely on our own powers. Reflecting on Jesus's prayer to the Father, Patrick Hartin notes, "Jesus illustrates the spiritual attitude all believers should adopt in their own prayer life. While it is important to make known our needs and desires to God, we must also recognize that God has a plan. Our requests to God must always be tempered, as Jesus shows, by an openness to God's will. . . . [W]e show our trust and dependence on God. At the same time, we acknowledge that all prayer needs to be expressed 'according to God's will.' "[58]

Now Judas comes with an armed crowd. A sign of respect was to kiss the cheek of the master, and this is now the sign Judas uses to identify and betray the master.[59] "So when he came, he went up to him at once and said, 'Rabbi!' and kissed him. Then they laid hands on him and arrested him. . . . All of them deserted him and fled" (14:45-46, 50).

Two Trials and Two Humiliations

Jesus's first trial was before the high priest, "and all the chief priests, the elders, and the scribes" (14:53), that is, virtually all his enemies. The trial was rigged: they were "looking for testimony against Jesus to put him to death" (14:55). Mark tells us that some gave "false testimony" and yet his accusers' testimony was so hackneyed that they did not even agree with themselves. Jesus was silent, as the suffering servant was silent (Isa 53:7), and the trial was off track. "Again the high priest asked him, 'Are you the Messiah, the Son of the Blessed One?' Jesus said, 'I am; and "you will see the Son of Man seated at the right hand of the Power," and "coming with the clouds of heaven" ' " (14:61-62).[60] While the "messianic secret" was necessary during his ministry, Jesus now saw that it was time to reveal himself. He is Son of God, Son of Man, and the Messiah. "Then the high priest tore his clothes and said, 'Why do we still need witnesses? You have heard his blasphemy! What is your decision?' All of them condemned him as deserving death" (14:63-64).

The humiliation continues. "Some began to spit on him, to blindfold him, and to strike him. . . . The guards also took him over and beat him" (14:65). In the courtyard, there is more humiliation. Peter—the rock—denies him with increasing vigor. At first, his response is "I do not know or understand what you are talking about." And then he outright denies being a disciple. And finally, "He began to curse, and he swore an oath, 'I do not now that man you are talking about'" (14:68-71).

Early the next morning they bring him to Pilate, not as a blasphemer, but as a messiah—king of the Jews. Jesus remains silent. Pilate finds no real case against Jesus, but the crowds egg him on. "Crucify him!" "So Pilate, wishing to satisfy the crowd, released Barabbas for them; and after flogging Jesus, he handed him over to be crucified" (15:14-15). The soldiers then likewise humiliated him, putting on him a purple cloak as if he were royalty and a crown of thorns. "And they began saluting him, 'Hail, King of the Jews!' They struck his head with a reed, spat upon him, and knelt down in homage to him. After mocking him, they stripped him of the purple cloak and put his own clothes on him. Then they led him out to crucify him" (15:17-20). Compare this scene to the treatment of the righteous man in the book of Wisdom:

> Let us lie in wait for the righteous man, because he is inconvenient to us and opposes our actions; he reproaches us for sins against the law, and accuses us of sins against our training. He professes to have knowledge of God, and calls himself a child of the Lord . . . and boasts that God is his father. . . . Let us test him with insult and torture, so that we may find out how gentle he is, and make trial of his forbearance. Let us condemn him to a shameful death, for according to what he says, he will be protected. (Wis 2:12-20)

Crucifixion: The Ultimate Humiliation

Jesus is crucified with the mock designation that is ironically true: The King of the Jews. "Those who passed by derided him, shaking their heads and saying, 'Aha! You who would destroy the temple and build it in three days, save yourself, and come down from the cross!' In the same way the chief priests, along with the scribes were also mocking him. . . . Those who were crucified with him also taunted him" (15:29-32). The humiliation is complete. John Donahue and Daniel Harrington note, "The physical sufferings of a crucified person were intense, and indeed gruesome. . . . But Mark also helps us to move beyond the physical sufferings of Jesus to recognize what was perhaps an even greater suffering that Jesus endured: misunderstanding and rejection by practically everyone."[61] Jesus is plotted against immediately by the Pharisees and Herodians. The people of his own hometown reject him. His disciples are habitually obtuse. He is rejected by the leadership in Jerusalem and finally abandoned by his disciples. "On the cross, Jesus has no friends, he is a solitary righteous man surrounded on all sides by enemies."[62]

The Death and Resurrection of the Suffering Messiah (15:33–16:8)

I noted in the introduction that Mark's original readers are widely believed to have been Christians in Rome shortly after Caesar Nero's persecution of Christians. Mark's Gospel is a meditation on suffering, and discipleship will necessarily include it. Discipleship is the way of the cross. The historian Tacitus describes some of the torture these Christians faced: "Dressed in wild animals' skins, they were torn to pieces by dogs, or crucified, or made into torches to be ignited after dark as substitutes for daylight."[63] Mark's Christian community was confronted with a terrible choice: faithfulness in suffering like Jesus or cowardice like Peter.[64] Thus Mark's language is sober and stripped down, even in the resurrection.

Jesus had been on the cross from nine to noon, and then "darkness came over the whole land until three in the afternoon. At three o'clock Jesus cried out with a loud voice, 'Eloi, Eloi, lema sabachthani?' which means, 'My God, My God, why have your forsaken me?'" (15:33-34). Jesus's own agony takes us to Psalm 22:

> My God, my God, why have you forsaken me? Why are you so far from helping me, from the words of my groaning. . . . But I am a worm, and not human; scorned by others, and despised by the people. All who see me mock at me; they make mouths at me, they shake their heads; "Commit your cause to the LORD; let him deliver—let him rescue the one in whom he delights!" . . . For dogs are all around me; a company of evildoers encircles me. My hands and feet have shriveled; I can count all my bones. They stare and gloat over me; they divide my clothes among themselves, and for my clothing they cast lots. (Ps 22:1-8, 16-18)

Psalm 22 is both a psalm of lament and one of hope and praise for God who will deliver the Psalmist. But for Jesus on the cross, it is all lament. "Then Jesus gave a loud cry and breathed his last.

And the curtain of the temple was torn in two, from top to bottom. Now when the centurion, who stood facing him, saw that in this way he breathed his last, he said, 'Truly this man was God's Son!'" (15:37-39).

The curtain of the sanctuary was rent (*eschisthē*). Mark's only other time using a form of this word is at Jesus's baptism when the heavens were rent. Barriers between heaven and earth were rent before Jesus and now are rent before the world. And still it is a Gentile, the centurion surely in charge of the crucifixion, who recognizes Jesus as God's Son. No one else seemed to understand it. This sixth-century hymn by Saint Venantius Fortunatus could be our meditation now:

> Sing, my tongue, the glorious battle; tell the triumph far and wide;
> tell aloud the wondrous story of the cross, the Crucified;
> tell how Christ, the world's redeemer, vanquished death the day
>   he died.
> God in mercy saw us fallen, sunk in shame and misery,
> felled to death in Eden's garden, where in pride we claimed the tree;
> then another tree was chosen, which the world from death would free.
> Tell how, when at length the fullness of the appointed time was come,
> Christ, the Word, was born of woman, left for us the heavenly home,
> blazed the path of true obedience, shone as light amidst the gloom.
> Thirty years among us dwelling, Jesus went from Nazareth,
> destined, dedicated, willing, did his work and met his death;
> like a lamb he humbly yielded on the cross his dying breath.
> Faithful cross, true sign of triumph, be for all the noblest tree;
> none in foliage, none in blossom, none in fruit your equal be;
> symbol of the world's redemption, for your burden makes us free.[65]

Mark tells us that Joseph of Arimathea, a member of the Sanhedrin, took Jesus's body and laid it in a tomb, rolling a stone against its entrance. Mary Magdalene and Mary the mother of Joses saw where the body was laid.

When the sabbath was over, Mary Magdalene, and Mary the mother of James, and Salome bought spices, so that they might go and anoint him. . . . When they looked up, they saw that the stone, which was very large, had already been rolled back. As they entered the tomb, they saw a young man, dressed in a white robe, sitting on the right side; and they were alarmed. But he said to them, "Do not be alarmed; you are looking for Jesus of Nazareth, who was crucified. He has been raised; he is not here. Look, there is the place they laid him. But go, tell his disciples and Peter that he is going ahead of you to Galilee; there you will see him, just as he told you." (16:1-7)

Matthew tells us that the messenger of the resurrection was an angel. For Mark, it is a "young man, dressed in a white robe." Matthew's account is dramatic, with an earthquake and a divine being "like lightning" (Matt 28:2-3). But Mark's Gospel is far more sober. As readers may see in their own Bibles, there are two (possibly three) endings for Mark, and they compete with each other. The general consensus is that Mark's Gospel ends at verse 8: "So they went out and fled from the tomb, for terror and amazement had seized them; and they said nothing to anyone, for they were afraid."

To a suffering community, to be assured that the Lord had risen is, of course, crucial. As Paul says, "If Christ has not been raised, then our proclamation has been in vain and your faith has been in vain" (1 Cor 15:14). But it is a Christ whose glorious victory can feel distant and muted to a community shattered. We live in him, we wait for him. He is our strength, especially in darkness. My last meditation is St. Ignatius of Loyola's *Anima Christi* (Soul of Christ).

> Soul of Christ, sanctify me;
> Body of Christ, save me;
> Blood of Christ, inebriate me;
> Water from the side of Christ, wash me;
> Passion of Christ, strengthen me;
> O good Jesus, hear me;
> Within your wounds hide me;
> Separated from you, let me never be;
> From the evil one protect me;
> At the hour of my death, call me;
> And close to you bid me; that with your saints,
> I may be praising you forever and ever.

The Gospel of Luke

The Prophet's Visitation

Each of the Gospels interprets Jesus differently and envisions his ministry variously. Of course, since they are writing about the same historical person, the same ministry, and are using some of the same sources, there is going to be a lot of overlap. All the evangelists think Jesus is the Son of God, the Messiah, and the Savior or the world. But their emphases are crucial if we are going to get into the heart of their individual visions. In Matthew, we saw in Jesus an embodiment of faithful Israel, an ultimate and perfect expression of true Torah fidelity. In Mark, we saw a suffering servant who will become "ransom for the many" (Mark 10:45). Matthew uses this same term (Matt 20:28). Not Luke. Jesus's ministry is seen through the lens of a prophet. Often, we think of prophets principally as divinely inspired predictors of the future. Sometimes this was the case. But more typical to their ministry was reading the signs of the times in light of God's covenant and challenging the people to greater fidelity to that covenant. Sometimes they offered hope and consolation, but more often they challenged with divine threats. So they were also often persecuted. Jeremiah was thrown into a cistern and lived for a time knee-deep in mud. Elijah had to flee for his life as Queen Jezebel vowed to kill him. Zechariah was stoned to death in Jerusalem. Now consider the following saying of Jesus in Luke: "Yet today, tomorrow, and the next day I must be on my way, because it is impossible for a prophet to be killed outside of Jerusalem. Jerusalem,

121

Jerusalem, the city that kills the prophets and stones those who are sent to it!" (13:33-34).

Luke, who also wrote Acts of the Apostles, interprets Jesus's ministry exactly this way. Consider Stephen's speech in Acts 7:2-53. In describing Israel's salvation history, he focuses on Moses, who was the quintessential prophet; Moses promised, "The LORD your God will raise up for you a prophet like me from among your own people; you shall heed such a prophet" (Deut 18:15). Stephen describes Moses's life and call to return to his people and liberate them. But they initially refused: "It was this Moses whom they rejected when they said, 'Who made you a ruler and a judge?'" (Acts 7:35). Stephen goes on: "Our ancestors were unwilling to obey him, they pushed him aside. . . . At that time they made a calf, offered a sacrifice to the idol, and reveled in the works of their hands" (Acts 7:39-41). Stephen finally ends his speech with, "You stiff-necked people, uncircumcised in heart and ears, you are forever opposing the Holy Spirit, just as your ancestors used to do. Which of the prophets did your ancestors not persecute? They killed those who foretold the coming of the Righteous One, and now you have become his betrayers and murderers" (Acts 7:51-52). In Luke, think of Jesus less as the "lamb of God" whose sacrifice atoned for the sins of the world and more as a righteous prophet, a blameless martyr. Instead of the centurion at the cross proclaiming, "Truly this man was God's Son" (Matt 27:54; Mark 15:39), in Luke, he says, "Certainly this man was innocent" (23:47).[1]

Old Testament prophets were particularly obsessed with two things: authentic worship and justice for those most marginalized. And it was not unusual for them to conflate them. Speaking for God, Isaiah proclaims, "I cannot endure solemn assemblies with iniquity. Your new moons and your appointed festivals my soul hates. . . . Even though you make many prayers, I will not listen. . . . Learn to do good; seek justice, rescue the oppressed, defend the orphan, plead for the widow" (Isa 1:13-17). "Look," he declares, "you serve your own interest on your fast day, and oppress all your workers. . . . Is not this the fast that I choose: to loose the bonds of injustice, to undo the thongs of the yoke, to let the oppressed go free, and to break every yoke? Is it not to share your bread with the hungry, and bring the homeless poor into your house; when you see the naked, to cover them. . . . Then your light shall break forth like the dawn" (Isa 58:3-8). Jeremiah declared that the temple would be forever defiled unless oppression was reversed (Jer 7:3-11), and Amos taught that Israel's temple sacrifices acted as a blasphemy when justice was not pursued in the land (Amos 2:6-7; 5:21-24). Here in Luke, Jesus—his values, his ministry, and his salvation—needs to be read with these eyes.

One Angel, Two Pregnancies, Two Songs, and Two Infants (1:1–2:52)

The first two chapters of Luke's Gospel provide almost everything we will need to know to understand the ministry of Jesus. These are among the richest chapters in all four Gospels. They center around two unlikely pregnancies, which themselves have a significant background. In Genesis, we find Abraham at ninety-nine years old and married to Sarah who had yet to have a child. God (or is it three angels?) visited Abraham and announced that by the next year Sarah would have a son. Sarah laughed, to which God replied, "Is anything too wonderful for the LORD?" (Gen 18:1-14). Their son was Isaac. Then there is Manoah, whose wife was barren. "And the angel of the LORD appeared to the woman and said to her, 'Although you are barren, having borne no children, you shall conceive and bear a son.'" This son would be Samson, a *nazarite* dedicated to God from birth (Judg 13:1-25). Then there was Hannah who had no children and vowed to the Lord that if she had a son, he would be a *nazarite*. The high priest Eli promised her, "Go in peace; the God of Israel grant the petition you have made to him" (1 Sam 1:17). This would be Samuel, the high priest and last and greatest of the judges. After Hannah weaned Samuel, she delivered him to Eli and then prayed a song of praise to God:

> My heart exults in the LORD; my strength is exalted in my God. . . .
> The bows of the mighty are broken, but the feeble gird on strength.
> Those who were full have hired themselves out for bread, but those
> who are hungry are fat with spoil. The barren has borne seven,
> but she who has many children is forlorn. . . . The LORD makes
> poor and makes rich; he brings low, he also exalts. He raises up the
> poor from the dust; he lifts the needy from the ash heap. . . . He

will guard the feet of his faithful ones, but the wicked shall be cut off in darkness; for not by might does one prevail. (1 Sam 2:1-10)

Now in Luke we have another priest, Zechariah, whose wife "Elizabeth was barren, and both were getting on in years" (1:7). The archangel Gabriel appears to him at the altar of incense and proclaims they will have a son, also a *nazarite*, "for he will be great in the sight of the Lord. . . . He will turn many of the people of Israel to the Lord their God" (1:15-16). Challenging the angel for a sign, Zechariah is left mute until the day John (the Baptist) is circumcised. In the middle of Elizabeth's pregnancy, Gabriel then appears to one of her relatives, a virgin in Nazareth, and proclaims: "Greetings, favored one! The Lord is with you. . . . And now, you will conceive in your womb and bear a son, and you will name him Jesus. He will be great, and will be called the Son of the Most High" (1:31-32). How? she wonders. "The Holy Spirit will come upon you, and the power of the Most High will overshadow you; therefore the child to be born will be holy; he will be called Son of God" (1:35). Unlike Zechariah's challenge to Gabriel, Mary's response is "Here am I, the servant of the Lord; let it be with me according to your word" (1:38).

When Mary visits Elizabeth, John leaps in Elizabeth's womb "and Elizabeth was filled with the Holy Spirit and exclaimed with a loud cry, 'Blessed are you among women, and blessed is the fruit of your womb. . . . And blessed is she who believed that there would be a fulfillment of what was spoken to her by the Lord'" (1:41-45). Mary's Magnificat is her response:

My soul magnifies the Lord, and my spirit rejoices in God my Savior, for he has looked with favor on the lowliness of his servant. Surely, from now on all generations will call me blessed; for the Mighty One has done great things for me, and holy is his name. His mercy is for those who fear him from generation to generation. He has shown strength with his arm; he has scattered the proud in the thoughts of their hearts. He has brought down the powerful from their thrones, and lifted up the lowly; he has filled the hungry with good things, and sent the rich away empty. He has helped his servant Israel, in remembrance of his mercy, according to the promise he made to our ancestors, to Abraham and to his descendants forever. (1:46-55)

When John was circumcised, and Zechariah regained his voice, he
spoke this prophecy:

> Blessed be the Lord God of Israel, for he has looked favorably
> on his people and redeemed them. . . . Thus he has shown the
> mercy promised to our ancestors, and has remembered his holy
> covenant. . . . And you, child, will be called the prophet of the
> Most High; for you will go before the Lord to prepare his ways,
> to give knowledge of salvation to his people by the forgiveness
> of their sins. By the tender mercy of our God, the dawn from on
> high will break upon us, to give light to those who sit in darkness
> and in the shadow of death, and guide our feet into the way of
> peace. (1:67-79)

Consider all this: not only do we have two of the greatest canticles
in the Bible (back-to-back), but we see that God is the God who is
merciful and keeps his promises. Second Timothy notes that even
"if we are faithless, he remains faithful—for he cannot deny himself"
(2 Tim 2:13). Israel was not always faithful, nor has the church been,
nor have we been personally. But God simply will not and cannot
forget his promises or his mercy. Even in our most desperate times
or perhaps our most shameful moments we must know that God
will not and cannot abandon us.

We also see that God and his kingdom reverse fortunes, and this
will be one of the great themes in Luke's Gospel. Both Hannah and
Mary recognize that in God the mighty are broken, the proud are
scattered, but the hungry are fed, the poor and needy are lifted. We
will see these reversals most clearly in Luke's version of the Beatitudes
(6:20-26). Mary herself is a superb example of this. Luke Timothy
Johnson notes, "She is among the most powerless people in society:
she is young in a world that values age; female in a world ruled by
men; poor in a stratified economy. Furthermore, she has neither
husband nor child to validate her existence."[2] Mary is exalted and
favored in the context of "the lowliness of his servant," a lowliness
that is both an expression of humility and her concrete life in society.

Finally, we see how central the Holy Spirit is. "Even before his
birth he [John] will be filled with the Holy Spirit" (1:15); the Holy
Spirit comes upon Mary, overshadowing her (1:35); Elizabeth is
"filled with the Holy Spirit" when she greets Mary (1:41). And in

Jesus's presentation in the temple, we find Simeon, who is described thusly: "This man was righteous and devout, looking forward to the consolation of Israel, and the Holy Spirit rested on him. It has been revealed to him by the Holy Spirit that he would not see death before he had seen the Lord's Messiah. Guided by the Spirit, Simeon came into the temple" (2:25-27). After Jesus's baptism, Luke says that he was "full of the Holy Spirit . . . and was led by the Spirit in the wilderness" (4:1). Jesus will later promise the Holy Spirit to all who ask (11:13), and the Holy Spirit will clothe the disciples with power from on high (24:49). All this anticipates Acts, Luke's second volume, where the Holy Spirit dominates the life of the early church.[3]

Jesus's birth in Bethlehem is very different from what we saw in Matthew. Here we find a poor Mary and Joseph who have to travel from Nazareth to Bethlehem to enroll in an empire-wide census. Joseph traces his lineage to King David, and this is David's city. There are no Magi, and Herod is not killing infants. But there is no room in the inn, and Mary is forced to deliver her child in an animal stall. What Gabriel had foretold was true. He would be "Son of the Most High, and the Lord God will give to him the throne of his ancestor David" (1:32). And yet, what did this glory look like? "And she gave birth to her firstborn son and wrapped him in bands of cloth, and laid him in a manger" (2:7). Jesus's glorious birth is in the humblest circumstances. Further, the good news of Jesus's birth is given to shepherds, among the lowest professions. "Then an angel of the Lord stood before them, and the glory of the Lord shone around them. . . . 'Do not be afraid; for see—I am bringing you good news of great joy for all the people: to you is born this day in the city of David a Savior, who is the Messiah, the Lord.' . . . And suddenly there was with the angel a multitude of heavenly host, praising God and saying 'Glory to God in the highest heaven, and on earth peace among those whom he favors!'" (2:9-14).

After giving birth, a mother has just over a month for purification according to the law of Moses (Lev 12:1-8), after which Jesus was presented in the temple. It is here that we find Simeon, mentioned above. "Simeon took him in his arms and praised God, saying, 'Master, now you are dismissing your servant in peace, according to your word; for my eyes have seen your salvation, which you have prepared in the presence of all peoples, a light for revelation to the Gentiles and for glory to your people Israel'" (2:28-32). Simeon also predicts, "This child is destined for the falling and the rising of many in Israel, and a sign that will be opposed so that the inner thoughts of many will be revealed—and a sword will pierce your own soul too" (2:34-35). All this foreshadows Jesus's ministry.

Finally, the whole world is implicated in Jesus's birth. Luke situates his narrative with Herod as king (1:5), with the emperor as Augustus, with the governor of Syria as Quirinius (2:1-2), and with Simeon proclaiming he will be "a light for revelation to the Gentiles," all as a way of expressing the full breadth of this event. This Messiah, fully Jewish, is a universal savior. And Mary must give him up to this colossal task. Traditionally, the sword that would pierce her heart has been understood as watching her son crucified. But Luke does not place Mary at Golgotha. She will have to surrender him much earlier. Luke tells us that at twelve years old, he stayed at the temple while his parents were there for Passover. They lost him for three days, and his only response was, "Why were you searching for me? Did you not know that I must be in my Father's house?" (2:49). Jesus's mission will take him away from them, particularly Mary. As favored as she is in Gabriel's annunciation, she also ever remains Mother of Sorrows.

John and Jesus (3:1–4:15)

The infancy narratives have John and Jesus paralleled and intimately tied. Gabriel comes to Zechariah, then to Mary, and both are overwhelmed. Mary praises God in a canticle, then Zechariah praises God in a canticle. There is the birth of John, then the birth of Jesus. It is obvious that John is important, but his importance is second to Jesus's and meant to support the Prophet's visitation and his inauguration of the kingdom of God. The preparation is a baptism of repentance and a life that evinces "fruits worthy of repentance" (3:8). John's style is abrasive: "You brood of vipers! Who warned you to flee from the wrath to come?" (3:7). "What then should we do?" the crowds ask (3:10). John demands that those who have more than they need (clothing and food) share with those without. To tax collectors, "Collect no more that the amount prescribed" (3:13). To soldiers, "Do not extort" (3:14). While this may seem a bit arbitrary, the theme is set: share what you have and do not abuse power.

This is not an insignificant start and can reflect the life of discipleship today. John's prophetic life is a model for the church. We too prepare for the Messiah. We too can and must lead others to Jesus. Further, we too are challenged to repent and open ourselves to Jesus's divine visitation.[4] And without sharing what we have, we show no real repentance. Pope Francis reflects, "We feel that this question—'what should we do?'—is also ours. . . . It is necessary to repent, to change direction, and to take the path of justice, solidarity, sobriety: these are the essential values of a fully human and genuinely Christian life."[5]

As we know from Matthew and Mark, Jesus is also baptized. Luke tells us that he then was at prayer when "the Holy Spirit descended upon him in bodily form like a dove. And a voice came from heaven, 'You are my Son, the Beloved; with you I am well pleased'" (3:22). Like Mark, but even more privately, Jesus hears the Father speak directly to him. Luke then provides, as Matthew did, a genealogy of Jesus. Recall that, for Matthew, this expresses the line of Jewish salvation history starting with Abraham. It is about God's providential grace now coming to full fruition. Luke's genealogy is different. Not only are many of the names hopelessly different, but Luke traces Jesus back to Adam (seventy-six generations). Luke's audience is principally Gentile Christians, and in the ancient Greco-Roman world genealogies establish the pedigree of the hero. Luke ends his genealogy with "son of Adam, son of God" (3:38). This is who Jesus is: "my Son, the Beloved." We also see more of Luke's universality. It is the whole of humanity that Jesus has come for.

All three Synoptic Gospels tell us that the Spirit guided Jesus in the desert to fast for forty days and then be tempted by Satan. These forty days align with Elijah's forty days in the wilderness without food (1 Kgs 19:8), with Moses's forty-day fast before writing down the Torah (Exod 34:28), and with Israel's forty years in the Sinai wilderness. It is also clear in this last case that this was God's way of "testing you to know what was in your heart, whether or not you would keep his commandments" (Deut 8:2). Here, the testing is by the Enemy. "The three temptations try to lure Jesus to leave the way of the servant and to assert his Sonship in a different way."[6] Stone to bread misuses his status. Jumping off the temple pinnacle forces God's hand. And to seek worldly power is to undermine his whole being. What is most interesting is that Satan promises what he clearly cannot deliver. His is not the world's power to give. "The heavens are yours," the Psalmist proclaims, "the earth also is yours; the world and all that is in it" (Ps 89:11).[7] St. Gregory Nazianzen notes, "If the tempter tries to overthrow us through our greed, showing us at one glance all the kingdoms of the world—as if they belonged to him—and demanding that we fall down and worship him, we should despise him, for we know him to be a penniless imposter. Strong in our baptism, each of us can say: 'I too am made in the image of God, but unlike you, I have not yet become an outcast from heaven through my pride.' "[8] Satan does have power and does have authority. It is not, however, over the world itself but over those who have allowed themselves to be seduced by his empty promises. Johnson describes Satan's realm: "His shadow-kingdom parodies that of God, enabling him in his challenges to this Messiah to counterfeit the coinage of God's realm."[9]

Jesus's Early Ministry (4:16–6:11)

Matthew and Mark have Jesus visiting his hometown of Nazareth around halfway through their Gospels. Luke places this incident at the start, and for a very good reason: he is announcing his prophetic agenda, one that Simeon predicted would be for the "falling and rising of many in Israel, and a sign that will be opposed" (2:34). In the synagogue on the sabbath, he unrolled the scroll and found the place where it was written: " 'The Spirit of the Lord is upon me, because he has anointed me to bring good news to the poor. He has sent me to proclaim release to captives and recovery of sight to the blind, to let the oppressed go free, to proclaim the year of the Lord's favor.' . . . Today this scripture is fulfilled in your hearing" (4:18-21).

This short citation is dense with meaning. In quoting Isaiah, Jesus is drawing on Isaiah's announcement of a jubilee year. Leviticus 25:8-55 calls for every fiftieth year to be a jubilee year where debts are released, slavery is commuted, and ancestral lands are returned to their original owners. The repeated term in the Septuagint (Greek version of the Hebrew Bible) is *aphesis* (release). This same term, *aphesis*, is used here for *release* of the captives and *freedom* for the oppressed. This likewise is the term Luke uses to describe forgiveness of sin.[10] What we see about the kingdom of God is that Jesus is calling for a radical jubilee year, one of full release from all oppression, all slaveries, all debts. Brendan Byrne notes, "The heart of that liberation is freedom from the bond of sin. But spiritual 'release' is, in Luke's perspective, a beachhead and pledge of a liberation that will encompass the totality of human life, including the socio-economic structures of society. Such a vision has already appeared in Mary's Magnificat (1:46-55); we will see it more powerfully restated in the Beatitudes (6:20-23)."[11] The Nazareth crowd was not interested in that kind of liberation but was antagonistic to it and to him. Jesus expected this: "Truly I tell you, no prophet is accepted in the prophet's hometown" (4:24).

Jesus begins his ministry in earnest at Capernaum, preaching in synagogues, expelling unclean spirits, and curing those who were sick. Along the shore of Galilee he finds the crowd pressing him and so asks a fisherman named Simon to take him a short distance from the shore, so he could preach from there. After his sermon he told Simon to pull out into deep water to lower his nets again. Simon and his companions "caught so many fish that their nets were beginning to break. . . . But when Simon Peter saw it, he fell down at Jesus' knees, saying, 'Go away from me, Lord, for I am a sinful man!' . . . Then Jesus said to Simon, 'Do not be afraid; from now on you will be catching people.' When they had brought their boats to shore, they left everything and followed him" (5:6-11).

Peter was overwhelmed; who wouldn't be? We might think of Isaiah's vision of heaven with God on his throne and Seraphim attending him and proclaiming, "Holy, holy, holy is the Lord of hosts; the whole earth is full of his glory." Isaiah's response is "Woe is me! I am lost, for I am a man of unclean lips, and I live among a people of unclean lips; yet my eyes have seen the King, the Lord of hosts!" (Isa 6:3-5). Or, on a less dramatic scene, we find Jeremiah's call: "Now the word of the Lord came to me saying, 'Before I formed you in the womb I knew you, and before you were born I consecrated you; I appointed you a prophet to the nations.' Then I said, 'Ah, Lord God! Truly I do not know how to speak, for I am only a boy'" (Jer 1:4-6). Or, finally, Moses's fear of being called: "'Oh my Lord, I have never been eloquent, neither in the past nor even now that you have spoken to your servant; but I am slow of speech and slow of tongue.' Then the Lord said to him, . . . 'I will be with your mouth and teach you what you are to speak.' But he said, 'O my Lord, please send someone else'" (Exod 4:10-13).

All of these can likely be our response to being called by God. It can feel overwhelming. It can feel weighty, even a burden too exhausting to consider. And it can simply be that we feel unworthy, simply too sinful or ashamed of ourselves to respond to the call. What we need to know is that responding to the call itself changes us. Pope John Paul II wisely reflected, "The awareness of God's holiness and of our condition as sinners does not separate persons from God, but rather brings them closer to him. Moreover, once a person has been converted, they declare their faith openly and become an apostle. They feel that God's intentions are now within their reach, and they become lovable to him. Their lives then take on their deepest meaning and value."[12]

Sometimes the sense of overwhelm comes from too wild an imagination. I recall one of my closest high school friends telling me that he was afraid of becoming a Christian, though in fact he believed in Jesus. Why? I asked him. His response: "God might tell me to become a missionary and go to Yugoslavia!" True story. While it is possible that God would call one to an extraordinarily dramatic life, most of our calls are relatively mundane. And yet, even these are filled with grace. Pope John Paul reminds us that only in God do our lives take on its truest meaning. Consider it an honor as well. In John Henry Newman's *Meditations* he writes, "God has created me to do him some definite service; he has committed some work to me which he has not committed to another. . . . If indeed, I fail, he can raise another, as he could make the stone children of Abraham. Yet, I have a part in this great work; I am a link in a chain. . . . He has not created me for naught."[13]

Thus far, Jesus has been greeted by the crowds enthusiastically, so much so that he had to "withdraw to deserted places and pray" (5:16). But starting now his ministry attracts religious leaders who begin to oppose him. To the paralyzed man lowered from the roof, he proclaims the man healed and forgiven, which makes "Pharisees and teachers of the law" appalled: "Who is this who is speaking blasphemies?" (5:21). He calls the tax collector Levi, who "got up, left everything, and followed him" (5:28). Levi's banquet for Jesus then included other tax collectors and the like, only to have the Pharisees and scribes complaining that Jesus eats with sinners. And then, why do Jesus's disciples not fast like the Pharisees and John's disciples? To these challenges Jesus responded skillfully. "Those who are well have no need of a physician, but those who are sick; I have come to call not the righteous but sinners to repentance" (5:31-32). What his antagonists do not see—and it is right before their eyes—is that Levi and his friends were celebrating the hospitality of God. Byrne notes, "Repentance is certainly required (v. 32). But repentance is not a precondition for God's acceptance. Rather, it is something that a sense of God's acceptance makes possible, joy-filled and transformative in human lives."[14]

To those wondering why Jesus and his disciples do not fast: "You cannot make wedding guests fast while the bridegroom is with them, can you? . . . No one tears a piece from a new garment and sews it on an old garment; otherwise the new will be torn, and the piece from the new will not match the old. And no one puts new wine into old wineskins; otherwise the new wine will burst the skins and will be spilled, and the skins will be destroyed. But new wine must be put into fresh wineskins" (5:34-38). Jesus is the groom to his bride, that is, those wed to the kingdom of God. His kingdom constitutes a new order, a new way of thinking and being. It is useless to cling to old forms of some "separatist" piety. This new situation, this inauguration of the kingdom of God, is the new garment—a wedding garment at that—and new wine. This is going to challenge all his hearers to a new way of being, a new solidarity, a new repentance (*metanoia*—change of mind and heart).

And finally, there are two sabbath challenges, one is his disciples plucking grain and the other healing a man with a withered hand, both on the sabbath. By telling the Pharisees that "the Son of Man is lord of the sabbath" (6:5), Jesus is not only asserting his authority but also *interpreting* the sabbath customs, particularly that the sabbath rules must give latitude to saving a life rather than destroying it, that is, not refusing to heal the man (6:9). The sabbath is about life. "But they were filled with fury and discussed with one another what they might do to Jesus" (6:11).

Calling Apostles and the Sermon on the Plain (6:12-49)

Opposition to Jesus's ministry is beginning now in earnest. It is in this context that he chooses the Twelve from among his many disciples. For Matthew and Mark, naming "apostles" (those sent)

his sending them out to towns to witness to Jesus's
ee their importance as pillars of the restored Is-
thing like what Moses did on Sinai: "Then he
Come up to the LORD, you and Aaron, Nadab,
y of the elders of Israel" (Exod 24:1). Jesus
mountain to pray; and he spent the night in
en day came, he called his disciples and chose
-13). Coming down from the mountain with
t multitude with many seeking healing. "And
rying to touch him, for power came out from
them" (6:19). Looking at his disciples, Jesus
ous Sermon on the Plain in Luke compares
on on the Mount. But recall that in Matthew,
interpret authentic Torah fidelity and challenge
n. There Jesus proclaimed *blessed* the "poor in
unger and thirst for righteousness," and so on.
ualizing here:

no are poor, for yours is the kingdom of God.
o are hungry now, for you will be filled. Blessed
now, for you will laugh. Blessed are you when
nd when they exclude you, revile you, and de-
unt of the Son of Man. Rejoice in that day and
rely your reward is great in heaven; for that is
rs did to the prophets. But woe to you who are
received your consolation. Woe to you who are
will be hungry. Woe to you who are laughing
mourn and weep. Woe to you when all speak well
s what their ancestors did to the false prophets.

Here we see vestiges of Mary's Magnificat where the poor are
raised, the hungry are fed, and the lowly are raised, while proud are
scattered and the powerful are brought down. We must be clear,
Jesus is not romanticizing poverty, nor is having financial means itself
damnable. "Luke is not declaring a social class blessed. The blessed
condition comes from . . . the kingdom which Jesus is effecting.
Moreover, membership in the Israel being reconstituted by Jesus
depends on one's becoming a disciple of Jesus."[15]

We must realize that in Jesus's day *the poor* reflected, first, virtually everyone. So, the crowd before him was made up of those in great need of healing and release from unclean spirits. In favoring the poor, Jesus was essentially expressing God's universal love and mercy. Second, in his society the poor—almost everyone—didn't matter to most of those who were rich. In the Bible at large and in Luke's Gospel specifically *the poor* represented those marginalized.[16] And finally, *the poor* represents those who acknowledge their need for God's salvation. The Psalmist prays, "Incline your ear, O LORD, and answer me, for I am poor and needy. Preserve my life, for I am devoted to you; save your servant who trusts in you" (Ps 86:1-2). Gustavo Gutierrez wisely reflects, "Beyond any possible doubt, the life of the poor is one of hunger and exploitation, inadequate health care and lack of suitable housing, difficulty in obtaining an education, inadequate wages and unemployment, struggles for their rights, and repression. But that is not all. Being poor is also a way of feeling, knowing, reasoning, making friends, loving, believing, suffering, celebrating, and praying. The poor constitute a world of their own. Commitment to the poor means entering, and in some cases remaining in, that universe."[17]

And *the rich*? The rich represent those who are content, who are comfortable, who do not need Jesus or his kingdom because they are, in their minds, already set. If we do not feel deep longing and real interior poverty, we are far from knowing the status of our souls. Solidarity with the poor is real solidarity, both interiorly and exteriorly. Paul writes beautifully, "As servants of God we have commended ourselves in every way. . . . As sorrowful yet always rejoicing; as poor, yet making many rich; as having nothing, and yet possessing everything" (2 Cor 6:4, 10). There were people of means around Jesus regularly. Some gave banquets in his honor, such as Levi (Luke 5:29). The tax collector Zacchaeus promised half his wealth to the poor, but this would not have meant that he still wasn't well off. To him, Jesus proclaimed, "Salvation has come to his house" (19:9). And we learn that wealthy women supported Jesus's ministry (8:2-3). What is clear in Luke, however, is that unless one takes on the plight of those marginalized, and identifies it as one's own plight too, one has rejected Jesus and the kingdom.

Jesus's sermon is demanding and goes far beyond the *blessed* and the *woes*. "Love your enemies, do good to those who hate you, bless those who curse you, pray for those who abuse you. . . . Be merciful, just as your Father is merciful. Do not judge, and you will not be judged; do not condemn, and you will not be condemned. Forgive, and you will be forgiven" (6:27, 36-37). The reason to love, to be merciful, to be forgiving is not reciprocal—that is, so others will love us or forgive us—but because God loves us and so God will forgive us. This is the new norm of the kingdom and the only way we can honestly call Jesus "Lord" (6:46).

The Deeds of Jesus and a "Sinful" Woman (7:1-50)

The Sermon on the Plain represents the wisdom of God's Prophet. Now Luke gives us accounts of Jesus's mighty deeds. A centurion's beloved servant was deathly ill, and he sent emissaries to Jesus to heal his servant. Not considering himself worthy of Jesus to come, he showed great faith: "Lord, do not trouble yourself, for I am not worthy to have you under my roof." But he knew, as a man of authority, that "only speak the word, and let my servant be healed" (7:6-7). This kind of faith impresses Jesus: "I tell you, not even in Israel have I found such faith" (7:9). More dramatically, he and his disciples were in the town of Nain only to witness a funeral of a mother's only son. Like Elijah in Zerephath, where he raised a widow's only son (1 Kgs 17:17-24), Jesus raised this widow's son. The response was great: "Fear seized all of them; and they glorified God, saying, 'A great prophet has risen among us!' " (7:16).

Following this, there is an interesting vignette whereby John the Baptist's disciples are sent by John, who was imprisoned, to ask Jesus if he is the Messiah. One might have thought that John would surely know, especially as they were relatives. But John had been in the desert a long time, and he had been arrested early in Luke's account.[18] John might also have been a bit surprised in learning about Jesus's prophetic style. John and his disciples were ascetical and his message was severe, while Jesus and his disciples often feasted. "Go and tell John what you have seen and heard: the blind receive their sight, the lame walk, the lepers are cleansed, the deaf hear, the dead are raised, the poor have good news brought to them" (7:22). Jesus was alluding not only to his actual ministry but also to the prophecies of Isaiah regarding the messianic age.[19] Jesus identifies John as a kind of Elijah, but then says something striking: "I tell you, among those born of women no one is greater than John; yet the least in the kingdom of God is greater than he" (7:28). John was a precursor, a preparer for the Messiah. But he belonged to the age before the kingdom was inaugurated in Jesus's ministry. John is one of the greatest prophets, but the kingdom of God is something new. Byrne writes of Jesus's style: "The holding of celebratory meals is essential to his ministry because, as tax collectors and sinners are discovering, there is a great deal to celebrate: the love and acceptance of God."[20]

This love and acceptance overflows in Luke's next reported incident. Jesus is dining at Simon the Pharisee's house when "a woman in the city, who was a sinner," enters the house, anoints Jesus's feet, and washes them with her kisses and grateful tears. If Jesus is a prophet, he would have known and not allowed this, Simon thinks. But Jesus *is* a prophet who knows her heart as well as what Simon is thinking. Jesus points out that Simon has failed at every turn to show him hospitality—with no ointment, no water for his feet, no greeting of a kiss. In contrast this "sinner" has done all that. She got it; Simon did not. She expresses great faith; Simon has none. Pope Francis notes,

> Wherever there is a person who suffers, Jesus takes on their burden. . . . Jesus feels mercy in the face of human suffering. . . . How many people even today persist in an ill-chosen life because they have found no one to look at them in a different way, with the eyes, or better, with the heart of God—that is, to look at them with hope. . . . Brothers and sisters, we are all poor sinners in need of God's mercy, which has the power to transform us and to give us back hope, day after day. And he does! And to the people who understand this fundamental truth, God gives the most beautiful mission in the world, namely, love for brothers and sisters, and the message of a mercy which he does not deny anyone.[21]

Visions of Discipleship (8:1–9:50)

As I have noted before, Mathew and Luke use Mark as one of their sources, and the following accounts here are also in Mark and thus Matthew. The danger for the Christian reader, then, is to scan through the narratives because they are familiar—we've seen all this before. But where the evangelists place these vignettes and how they frame them matters. For example, in Mark we learn that Jesus's family members were trying to see him, to which he replied, "Here are my mother and my brothers! Whoever does the will of God is my brother and sister and mother" (Mark 3:34-35). Mark puts this early in his Gospel. Jesus is in Nazareth, and the context is one of various confrontations. In fact, Mark tells us that earlier his family "went out to restrain him, for people were saying, 'He has gone out of his mind'" (Mark 3:21). This current section of Luke also contains the story, but it is in the context of Jesus teaching about what true discipleship looks like. "My mother and my brothers are those who hear the word of God and do it" (Luke 8:21). Here Luke includes the importance of hearing the word as well as doing it.

Luke begins Jesus's teachings on discipleship by telling us that women, such as Mary Magdalene, Joanna, and Susanna, were followers of Jesus and financially supported his ministry. These are among the women who stayed through Jesus's crucifixion and were the first witnesses of his resurrection (23:55). Following this, Jesus tells the parable of the sower and the seeds. I commented on this parable at length in the chapter on Mark. Recall that some seeds of the word fall on the trampled path, some on rock, some in the thorns, and, happily, some on good soil that produces a hundredfold. Regarding the latter, "But as for that in the good soil, these are the ones who, when they hear the word, hold it fast in an honest and good heart, and bear fruit with patient endurance" (8:15).

All of this corresponds to Jesus's listeners, some of whom rejected his message. Others accepted it with joy but did not persevere in faith. For these, the kingdom of God is too demanding, "and their fruit does not mature" (8:14). Here we see the big contrast between inauthentic and authentic discipleship. It is the real disciple who perseveres. The word has to be "held fast" in a heart that is true and faithful. This is about a Christian spirituality that stays on point. The Christian life is the "long game" of endurance, of not dropping the ball: in our prayer lives, we've got to stay with it; in our generosity, it has to be consistent; in our daily small sacrifices, we cannot decide "well, that's enough." Compared to Mark, Luke's Gospel plays down the apocalyptic feel of Jesus's preaching. Holiness is a lifelong project, and Jesus promises that God will succeed far more spectacularly than we might guess. Indeed, a hundredfold!

Jesus then reminds his listeners that "No one after lighting a lamp hides it under a jar, or puts it under a bed, but puts it on a lightstand, so that those who enter may see the light" (8:16). The Christian witness must be a perpetual light. Gerhard Lohfink observes, "For whom and in what situation did Jesus create this parable? . . . Our parable fits best within the body of instructions for disciples. They are to let their light shine before everyone."[22] He adds, regarding Jesus's sending of the Twelve two by two: "Many New Testament scholars rightly hold that Jesus at one time sent the Twelve out two by two to preach the reign of God and heal the sick (Mark 6:6-13). It could not have been easy for the Twelve to be suddenly on their own, commissioned to give witness in Israel. It is not only possible but probable that they raised objections and pled not to have to do it."[23] So, who are my mother and my brothers? "Those who hear the word of God and do it" (8:21).

This is the life of faith, the life that receives God's salvation. Thus, Luke includes in this section of his Gospel the twofold story of Jarius's daughter who had died and the woman who was hemorrhaging for twelve years. To the woman, "Daughter, your faith has made you well; go in peace (8:48). And to Jarius's household, "Do not fear. Only believe and she will be saved" (8:50). Our faith has to be robust, or not at all. It is immediately following these teachings on discipleship and faith that Jesus sends out the Twelve to preach the kingdom, exorcize demons, and cure the sick (9:1-6).

Luke tells us that the Twelve return from their mission enthusiastically, and Jesus brings them to Bethsaida to be alone with him. "When the crowds found out about it, they followed him; and he welcomed them, and spoke to them about the kingdom of God, and he healed those who needed to be cured" (9:11). The needs continue and the core of the kingdom is to respond to those needs. This occasions, as we saw in Matthew and Mark, the feeding of the five thousand. As I noted earlier, the evangelists align this miracle with the Eucharist. Jesus, taking the loaves and fish, "blessed and broke them, and gave them to the disciples to set before the crowd" (9:16). Notice here how this event fulfills Mary's Magnificat, "He has filled the hungry with good things" (1:53), and Jesus's beatitude, "Blessed are you who are hungry now, for you will be filled" (6:21). Also notice the abundance in the event: "And all ate and were filled.

What was left over was gathered up, twelve baskets of broken pieces" (9:17). Clearly the twelve baskets align with the twelve tribes of Israel whom the Twelve are to serve. Even more, Jesus had been talking about abundance in his Sermon on the Plain: "Give, and it will be given you. A good measure, pressed down, shaken together, running over, will be put into your lap" (6:38). Here we are to imagine a "measure basket filled with grain, which is pressed down (to make more room), shaken up (to make the grain settle and create more room), and still 'overflowing.'"[24] The feeding of the five thousand anticipates the end-times banquet of the just (13:29). This is the result of a hundredfold harvest of authentic discipleship.

This next section on discipleship is among the most difficult to understand and bear. It begins with Jesus praying alone. Luke tells us that just before important moments in Jesus's ministry he prayed. We see this after his baptism (3:21), before naming the Twelve (6:12), before he is transfigured (9:28), before he teaches his disciples how to pray (11:1), before his arrest (22:41), and finally on the cross (23:46). And sometimes, Luke simply tells us, "he would withdraw to deserted places and pray" (5:16). Now after having spent time in prayer he asked his disciples, " 'Who do the crowds say that I am?' They answered, 'John the Baptist; but others, Elijah; and still others, that one of the ancient prophets has arisen.' He said to them, 'But who do you say that I am?' Peter answered, 'The Messiah of God' " (9:18-20). Gone from this narrative is Jesus's praise of Peter as well as Peter's rebuke and the Lord's rebuke of Peter. Luke wants us to stay on point here, for while Peter was exactly right, his understanding of what he said was severely limited. Indeed, "the LORD has anointed me; he has sent me to bring good news to the oppressed, to bind up the brokenhearted, to proclaim liberty to the captives" (Isa 61:1). But his anointing also includes, "He was despised and rejected by others; a man of suffering and acquainted with infirmity" (Isa 53:3). And so, Jesus tells them plainly,

> "The Son of Man must undergo great suffering, and be rejected by the elders, chief priests, and scribes, and be killed, and on the third day be raised." Then he said to them all, "If any want to become my followers, let them deny themselves and take up their cross daily and follow me. For those who want to save their life will lose it, and those who lose their life for my sake will save it.

What does it profit them if they gain the whole world, but lose or forfeit themselves?" (9:22-25)

Prior to this teaching Jesus's only self-reference as the Son of Man was in terms of authority: the Son of Man has the authority to forgive sins (5:24); the Son of Man is Lord of the sabbath (6:5). Now it is a reference to his rejection and humiliation to come.

We have seen this demand of the Lord to "lose their life to save it" repeatedly in both Matthew and Mark. And it stayed deeply in the early church's conscience. Paul speaks personally, "I have been crucified with Christ; and it is no longer I who live, but it is Christ who lives in me" (Gal 2:20). And in Paul's description of the meaning of baptism he writes, "Do you not know that all of us who have been baptized into Christ Jesus were baptized into his death?" (Rom 6:3). Of course, this is not the whole story or it would be masochistic. Paul explains, "But if we have died with Christ, we believe that we will also live with him" (Rom 6:8). Paul is looking not just at our eternal life but at this concrete life we currently live: "So you also must consider yourselves dead to sin and alive to God in Christ Jesus" (Rom 6:11). This new life in Christ is life in the Spirit, one beautifully transformed to "love, joy, peace, patience, kindness, generosity, faithfulness, gentleness, and self-control" (Gal 5:22-23).

In the chapter on Matthew's Gospel, I contrasted "false self" with "true self." Jesus is not saying discipleship is self-hating misery. The kingdom of God is meant for flourishing souls. But we should not imagine that ridding ourselves from pride, ego-attachments, greed, and the like is easy. It *feels* like death, and that is because it *is* a real kind of death. Luke makes sure to tell us that Jesus was not just speaking here to the Twelve. Rather, "he said to them all" (9:23). The pascal mystery, death and new life, is not for the faint of heart for sure, but it is not only the way of the virtuoso Christian hero. "Here is the essential pattern for Christian identity."[25] St. John of the Cross describes some of the dynamic of the "purgative way" that seeks to rid ourselves from the narcissistic self: "The divine fire . . . which is the Holy Spirit, wounds the soul by destroying and consuming the imperfections of its bad habits. . . . For this flame is extremely oppressive. . . . It is not gentle but afflictive. Even though it sometimes imports the warmth of love, it does so with torment and pain. And it is not delightful, but dry."[26]

Luke places the scene of Jesus's transfiguration here, which we have also seen in both Matthew and Mark. Here on this mountain Peter, James, and John discover the presence of Moses and Elijah: "They appeared in glory and were speaking of his departure, which he was about to accomplish at Jerusalem" (9:31). The Greek term he uses for "departure" is *exodos*, which draws us to the exodus event where Moses led Israel to liberation from slavery. But now it refers to the divine exodus of Jesus's death and resurrection that will lead the world to liberation from sin and death. And just as God on Sinai appeared in a cloud of glory to speak to Moses, now God appears in a cloud to speak to the disciples: "This is my Son, my Chosen; listen to him" (9:35). Take the three scenes together: Peter's confession and the first passion prediction, Jesus's teaching on the cost of discipleship, and the transfiguration. Collectively, they are meant to lead both the disciples and us deeper into the mystery of Jesus's identity and our own call.

The disciples are not excellent learners; nor are we. Returning to the crowd we find a man's only son who has an unclean spirit that the other disciples have not been able to exorcize. Recall in Mark that Jesus tells them that "This kind can come out only through prayer" (Mark 9:29). Luke omits this so that it simply points to the disciples' failure. They had just been given the "power and authority over all demons" (Luke 9:1) but still seemed to fail. On the spot, then, Jesus not only heals the man's son but gives them a second passion prediction: " 'Let these words sink into your ears: The Son of Man is going to be betrayed into human hands.' But they did not understand this saying. . . . And they were afraid to ask him about this saying" (9:44-45).

The disciples' failure to understand is expressed in the very next verses as they are arguing about who among them is the greatest. Jesus takes up a child: "Whoever welcomes this child in my name welcomes me . . . for the least among all of you is the greatest" (9:48). Now they've got it! No, not yet. Immediately John complains that someone was casting out demons in Jesus's name, "and we tried to stop him, because he does not follow with us" (9:49). Translation: there's somebody who's not in our clique doing something extraordinary, and we tried to get in his way. "But Jesus said to him, 'Do not stop him, for whoever is not against you is for you' " (9:50).

Clearly more discipleship training is going to be necessary. But we should not simply shake our heads, as we know the outcome of this story. All of this is also meant to help us scrutinize our own lives. To be a disciple of Jesus turns the tables on much of what and how we think. I recently heard an Evangelical theologian interviewed about racism in the South, particularly among Christians. His honest response was revealing: "In terms of identity, a white southern Christian is typically white first of all, southern second of all, and Christian only third. And the third is understood through the eyes of the first two." There is much to learn and much to rethink.

Jesus "Sets His Face" toward Jerusalem (9:51–10:42)

We have a decided transition in the ministry of Jesus. Thus far, he has concentrated all his mission in the Galilee region. But as he will soon tell his disciples, "It is impossible for a prophet to be killed outside of Jerusalem. Jerusalem, Jerusalem, the city that kills the prophets and stones those who are sent to it!" (13:33-34). So Luke begins here, "When the days drew near for him to be taken up, he set his face to go to Jerusalem" (9:51). We might think here of Ezekiel being commanded by God to "set your face toward Jerusalem and preach against the sanctuaries" (Ezek 21:2) or Isaiah's suffering servant who has "set my face like flint" (Isa 50:7). The "taken up" draws us to the transfiguration where Moses and Elijah (both of whom tradition says were taken up into heaven) discuss with Jesus his coming "exodus."

Until his arrival in Jerusalem, we have something of a travelogue, where Jesus's teaching takes center stage.[27] Notice the different audiences in the narratives and how Jesus deals with them. Luke often mentions Jesus's disciples. To them, he gives instructions and encouragement. Then there is the "crowd" (*ochlos*) or the "people" (*laos*). To them, Jesus calls for conversion and warns them of God's judgment. Some receive his message gladly and his parables reference their rewards, while others resist his call and hear parables of rejection. Finally, there are the Pharisees and lawyers who act increasingly antagonistic to his ministry. They receive the strongest censures.[28]

As we saw in Matthew's Gospel, some would-be followers approached Jesus. It is worthwhile, I think, to quote the whole episode:

As they were going along the road, someone said to him, "I will follow you wherever you go." And Jesus said to him, "Foxes have holes, and birds of the air have nests; but the Son of Man has nowhere to lay his head." To another he said, "Follow me." But he said, "Lord, first let me go and bury my father." But Jesus said to him, "Let the dead bury their own dead; but as for you, go and proclaim the kingdom of God." Another said, "I will follow you, Lord; but let me first say farewell to those at my home." Jesus said to him, "No one who puts a hand to the plow and looks back is fit for the kingdom of God." (9:57-62)

We simply must feel the urgency in Jesus's proclamation. This is not normal time (*chronos*) but elevated time, crucial time, an imperative moment (*kairos*). If you want to follow me, Jesus implies, know that I'm on the move and so must you be. In Matthew's Gospel, I suggested "let the dead bury the dead" was probably *literary hyperbole*. This is especially clear in that Jews bury their dead within a day, so this man would have done this essentially on the spot. But it could mean something else. The young man could have meant that he would follow Jesus only after his father had died and he was then "free" to follow Jesus unreservedly. For Jesus, discipleship is all in, right now. And this leads to the one who wished to bid his family farewell. One would think that this needn't take any time. This is an obvious allusion to Elijah's calling of Elisha, who would replace him. Elisha accepted, but only asked, "Let me kiss my father and my mother, and then I will follow you" (1 Kgs 19:20). Elijah will have none of this. The time is now. If your hand is on the plow, there's no looking back.

New in Luke's account is that Jesus appointed seventy disciples to preach the kingdom and prepare for his visitation in their respective towns. Again, listen to the echoes of Moses here who chose seventy elders to share his work and the spirit of prophecy (Num 11:16-17, 25). These are the elders who also accompanied Moses on Sinai when he received the Torah. Like the Twelve, they were to go on trust: "Carry no purse, no bag, no sandals" (Luke 10:4). They are Jesus's envoys, and he empowers them to cure those who are ill—a sign of the kingdom emerging in their midst. These are real envoys of Jesus. He reminds them that there will be towns that accept the message and those that do not, but that is on the people of those towns. "Whoever listens to you listens to me, and whoever rejects you rejects me, and whoever rejects me rejects the one who sent me" (10:16). Luke tells us that "The seventy returned with joy, saying, 'Lord, in your name even the demons submit to us!' He said to them, 'I watched Satan fall from heaven like a flash of lightning. . . . Nevertheless, do not rejoice at this, that the spirits submit to you, but rejoice that your names are written in heaven'" (10:17-20).

Jesus is clearly pleased and praises the Father for it all. But we should not miss that, for them, it isn't their success that is important. One typically cannot control what others do and many of our efforts, from the point of view of concretely changing the situation, seem to come to nothing. A disciple does what the Master bids. That is enough. We cannot be attached to the outcome. The following is adapted from a sign on the wall of Shishu Bhavan, Mother Teresa's children's home in Calcutta. It is titled *ANYWAY*:

People are often self-centered, and loving them can hurt you.
LOVE THEM ANYWAY
If you care, you will be exploited or even accused of selfish motives.
CARE ANYWAY
The good you do may be forgotten tomorrow.
DO GOOD ANYWAY
Honesty and frankness make you vulnerable.
BE HONEST AND FRANK ANYWAY
What you spent years building may be destroyed overnight.
BUILD ANYWAY
People who need help may not thank you.
HELP THEM ANYWAY
Give the world the best and it may not care.
GIVE THE WORLD YOUR BEST ANYWAY
For all that you do is ultimately done for God,
And this makes everything you are and do eternally meaningful.
IT'S REALLY ABOUT GOD ANYWAY

Brendan Byrne observes: "Christian joy does not ultimately rest upon achievement. It rests upon a deep sense of relationship with God and a knowledge of the destiny to which that relationship leads."[29]

"Just then a lawyer stood up to test Jesus. 'Teacher,' he said, 'what must I do to inherit eternal life?'" (10:25). Since a "lawyer" is equivalent to a theologian, Jesus asks him how he interprets the law (Torah). "You shall love the Lord your God with all your heart, and with all your soul, and with all your strength, and with all your mind; and your neighbor as yourself" (10:27). We have seen versions of this same dialogue in Matthew and Mark, but Luke's version is what is famous: "But wanting to justify himself, he asked Jesus, 'And who is my neighbor?' " (10:29). Jesus's response is the famous parable of the *Good Samaritan*. A man traveling from Jerusalem to Jericho is beaten, robbed, stripped, and left half-dead. A priest and later a Levite are also going down from Jerusalem to Jericho. Upon seeing the man, they move to the other side of the road and pass by. Later a Samaritan sees the man. "He went to him and bandaged his wounds, having poured oil and wine on them. Then he put him on his own animal, brought him to an inn, and took care of him" (10:34). He even pays the innkeeper to care for him and promises to repay any additional costs. Jesus asks the lawyer which was the neighbor. "He said, 'The one who showed him mercy.' Jesus said to him, 'Go and do likewise' " (10:37).

The land of Samaria had been conquered eight centuries earlier by the Assyrian dynasty, and much of its citizenry was replaced by non-Jews. Ultimately, a Jewish priest was sent to regularize their collective faiths. They eventually built a temple on Mount Gerizim that intended to rival worship at the temple in Jerusalem. Thus, there were regular conflicts and typical tensions between *Samaritan* Judaism and *orthodox* Judaism. There was even an incident in Jesus's lifetime where a group of Samaritans scattered human bones throughout parts of the Jerusalem temple during the Passover feast, thus making it "unclean" for Passover.[30] The Samaritans did not like Judean Jews, and Judean Jews did not like the Samaritans.

What ought we to make of this parable? The most obvious point is that the "neighbor" is one who is merciful. Surely, we can say more here. Leviticus addresses the issue of whom one must love, that is, "sons of your own people," which is translated in English as "neighbor" (Lev 19:18). Just a few verses later (vv. 33-34) it also includes the "resident alien," that is, non-Jew. Still, who's in and who's out remains a question. It is a question that would be on the Samaritan's mind too. They also read from Leviticus. From his point of view, was the half-dead Jew his neighbor? Neither camp considered each other as co-religionists or as resident aliens. Is the term "good

Samaritan" even helpful here? Amy-Jill Levine reflects that in today's climate, using the term "good Samaritan" is something like saying, "He's a good Muslim" (in contrast to other possible terrorists), or, "She's a good immigrant" (as opposed to those who are trying to scam our welfare system).[31]

Jesus was surely intentional in choosing a priest and Levite. These would not be aristocratic Jews, like most of the Sadducees, but they did represent institutional leadership. Some have argued that, since the man probably looked dead, they had reason to stay away so as not to be ritually unclean, given their temple duties. But Jesus tells us that they were "going down that road." The key is "down." No matter where you are, Jerusalem is always "up." Thus, they had fulfilled their temple duties and were presumably returning home. Perhaps this is a prophetic critique on the institutional leadership of the day. As I noted in the beginning of this chapter, prophets regularly united authentic worship with care for those most in need.

I have three insights that I think are useful in digging deeper here. The first is that Jesus wanted to prepare *all* the children of Israel for the kingdom of God. The city of Samaria was the historical center of the Northern Kingdom of Israel, just as Jerusalem was the historical center of the Southern Kingdom of Judah. But they all belonged to God as his people. Jesus's parable served, among other purposes, to announce that Judah and Samaria were one (whether they liked it or not). Second, this parable is not about who deserves or has a right to be cared for. Rather, the parable is about becoming the person who has no boundaries and who treats everyone with mercy regardless of how unnerving that might make one feel. "Be merciful, just as your Father is merciful" (6:36). The great church father Origen saw the Samaritan as a Christ figure and the model for how we might imitate the Lord:

> This guardian of souls *who showed mercy to the man who fell into the hands of brigands* was a better neighbor to him than were either the law or the prophets, and he proved this more by deeds than by words. Now the saying: *Be imitators of me as I am of Christ* [1 Cor 11:1] makes it clear that we can imitate Christ. . . . We can go out to them, bandage their wounds after pouring in oil and wine, place them on our own mount, and bear their burdens. And so the Son of God exhorts us to do these things. . . . *Go and do likewise.*[32]

My third point is borrowed from the insights of Emerson Powery who asks, "In our discourse, do we ever include conversations, teaching, or words of wisdom from people unlike us? Do we include Muslims, Jews, transgender people, queer people, or immigrants? Must our heroes always look like us, love like us, and share our values? Is it possible to conceive of the dignity of another who is most unlike us?"[33]

The last pericope in this section is denser than it seems on the surface. Jesus and his disciples were welcomed by Martha into her home. Her sister Mary sat at Jesus's feet attentive to what he was saying. Martha complained that she had to do all the work and begged Jesus to tell Mary to help her. Jesus's response: "Martha, Martha, you are worried and distracted by many things; there is need of only one thing. Mary has chosen the better part, which will not be taken away from her" (10:41-42). Traditionally, this has been interpreted as the difference between the active apostolate and the contemplative monastic life. That isn't it. Martha is "worried" (*merimnas*), the very term in Jesus's sower parable about those whose seed is choked by *anxieties*. And Martha is "distracted," which is an unfortunate translation of *thorubazā*, as it means more like "putting yourself in an uproar." Here Martha has so lost her sense of proportion for hospitality that she has even asked her guest to intervene in a family matter, which is a serious violation of hospitality. But there's more. Obviously on the surface guests have to be fed, and this takes preparation of which Mary is opting out of (how fair is that?). Read more deeply, we see that Mary recognizes Jesus as God's Prophet and a prophet is defined by his words. She hangs on them. She knows more of what Jesus is about than Martha. Jesus plays on words here: Mary has "chosen the better part." The "part" is *merida*, which literally means "portion," as in "portion of a plate." It turns out that what Jesus shares is the real meal, and *he* has become the host. Mary has the best portion, and it will not be taken away. This ought to be a lesson for us all. St. Elizabeth of the Trinity, in one of her letters, shared a prayer that is apropos:

O Lord, give me a passion for listening to you. Sometimes this desire to be silent is so strong that the only thing I long to do is to remain like Magdalen at your feet, O my adored Master, eager to hear everything and to penetrate deeper and deeper into the mystery of charity that you came to reveal to us. Grant that in action, even when I seem to be fulfilling the office of Martha, my soul may remain buried like Madgalen in her contemplation, remaining at the source like one athirst.[34]

Throwing One's Lot with Jesus: Praying and Committing (11:1-36)

In the last section, as Jesus praised the Father for the success of his seventy emissaries, he says something interesting: "All things have been handed over to me by my Father, and no one knows who the Son is except the Father, or who the Father is except the Son and anyone to whom the Son chooses to reveal him" (10:22). The disciples get this; they are learning that Jesus is their access to God. This is the context for Luke's rendition of the Lord's Prayer:

> He was praying in a certain place, and after he had finished, one of his disciples said to him, "Lord, teach us to pray, as John taught his disciples." He said to them, "When you pray, say: Father, hallowed be your name. Your kingdom come. Give us each day our daily bread. And forgive us our sins, for we ourselves forgive everyone indebted to us. And do not bring us to the time of trial." (11:1-4)

I gave an extended reflection on the Lord's Prayer in the chapter on Matthew, but I think we can say even more here. Jesus begins by teaching us to call God "Father." This intimacy is the start. Pope John Paul II reflected in a homily, "To learn to pray means 'to learn the Father.' If we learn the 'Father' really in the full sense of the word, in its full dimension, we have learned everything. . . . To learn who the Father is means learning what absolute trust is."[35] Jesus, so thoroughly Jewish, then teaches them to proclaim, "hallowed by your name." The Jewish Prayer, the *Kaddish*, begins, "Exalted and sanctified be His great name." And the third of the famous daily Eighteen Benedictions that Jews have prayed since the ancient period, we find, "We will sanctify Your Name in the world even as they sanctify it in the highest heaven, as it is written by the hand of Your prophet: And they call to one another and said, 'Holy, holy, holy is the Lord of Hosts: The whole earth is full of his glory.'" Prayer begins by sanctifying God's great name.

Your kingdom come: Luke in particular understands that the kingdom has in fact arrived, as he will make clear later in this section: "the kingdom of God has come to you" (11:20). But, of course, it hasn't come in its fulness, in its completeness. Jesus has not entered into his *exodus*, and the experience of the early church is still one of anticipation in the midst of suffering, as Luke makes abundantly clear in Acts. The anticipation of the fullness of the kingdom, both in our own lives—real holiness—and in the world, is something we must yearn for. *Give us each day our daily bread*: I noted in Matthew that "daily" is the English translation of an odd term (*epiousion*). Given that Jesus had sent both the Twelve and then the seventy disciples out with no provisions, but rather utter reliance on God's providence and the hospitality of those they missioned to, "daily" is a good translation here. It is something like: as we are sojourners for the kingdom, give us what we need. *And forgive us our sins*: "Jesus' community, composed of sinners, prays in confidence to its gracious Father-God for forgiveness. Disciples who are closed to forgiving each and every person who has sinned against them do not have a proper view of Jesus' God, who is merciful to all (6:35-36)."[36] Finally, *And do not bring us to the time of trial*: This final petition reflects how deeply fragile we are and how powerful anti-kingdom enemies can be. Later Jesus will describe the apocalyptic final days as, "People will faint from fear and foreboding of what is coming upon the world, for the powers of the heavens will be shaken" (21:26). Here is Pope Francis's gloss on the whole prayer:

> Jesus' prayer, and therefore the Christian prayer, first and fore-most, makes room for God, allowing him to show his holiness in us and to advance his kingdom, beginning with the possibility of exercising his Lordship of love in our lives. Three other supplica-tions . . . relate to our basic needs: bread, forgiveness, and help in temptation. One cannot live without bread, one cannot live without forgiveness, and one cannot live without God's help in times of temptation. The bread that Jesus teaches us to ask for is what is necessary, not superfluous. It is the bread of pilgrims, the righteous; a bread that is neither accumulated nor wasted, and that does not weigh us down as we walk. Forgiveness is above all what we ourselves receive from God. Only the awareness that we are sinners forgiven by God's infinite mercy can enable us to carry

out concrete gestures of fraternal reconciliation. . . . The last supplication, "lead us not into temptation," expresses awareness of our condition, which is always exposed to the snares of evil and corruption. We all know what temptation is![37]

Jesus continues to speak of prayer in terms of confidence and trust in God. Imagine, he has us consider, a friend who comes in the middle of the night banging on our door for a loaf of bread to feed his guest. But his friend initially resists him; his family is settled in. Jesus tells them that, if not friendship, then persistence will ensure he gets that loaf. "So I say to you, Ask, and it will be given you; search, and you will find; knock, and the door will be opened for you" (11:9). Or consider how a good father will give his children what they need. "If you then, who are evil, know how to give good gifts to your children, how much more will the heavenly Father give the Holy Spirit to those who ask him!" (11:13). There is some humor here. The term "persistence" (*anaideia*) literally means "shamelessness." There is a shameless bothering of his friend to get the loaf he needs. Staying with God, even when God seems silent to our longings, requires a kind of shamelessness. We must be unrelenting in our prayer. How and when God responds is up to God.

Many years ago I went through a fourteen-month period of spiritual darkness (a dark night of the soul). At that time I regularly referred to Jesus in prayer as "Mr. Stone Face." I think I was trying to egg him on. I also remember telling Jesus that my life was his and he could do anything he wanted with it, but "You're going to have to stand there and watch me suffer, and if that's fine with you, then that's fine with me!" What I recall about that time was that, paradoxically, I was more compassionate, generous, and loving than any time of my life, before or since. And, indeed, when the darkness abated the next three years marked a period of luminous experiences of God's indwelling in my soul.

We might also remember how Jesus finishes this short discourse on trust: "How much more will the heavenly Father give the Holy Spirit to those who ask him!" Our lives will suffer the challenges and often calamities that mark all human existence. Prayer does not exempt us from the human condition, but it changes the human condition. In the same homily by Pope John Paul II, cited earlier, he describes meeting a wounded man in a hospital during the Warsaw Uprising.

The man, despite his injuries, was filled with interior joy. "This man achieved happiness by some other way because visibly, judging his physical state from the medical point of view, there was no reason to be so happy, to feel so well, and to consider himself heard by God. Yet he was heard in another aspect of his humanity."[38]

Following this lesson in prayer, Luke relates a challenge to Jesus that he casts out demons by Satan's power, not God's. I commented on this in both Matthew and Mark, but Luke's language is a little different, and this matters. Jesus says, "Every kingdom divided against itself becomes a desert, and house falls on house. If Satan also is divided against himself, how will his kingdom stand? . . . But if it is by the finger of God that I cast out the demons, then the kingdom of God has come to you. . . . Whoever is not with me is against me, and whoever does not gather with me scatters" (11:17-20, 23). The *finger of God*: this is an allusion to Moses and Aaron besting Pharaoh's magicians who announce to Pharaoh, "This is the finger of God!" (Exod 8:19). There was a real and deadly conflict between Israel and her Egyptian oppressors, and Israel was far outnumbered. But they had God on their side who was strong enough to drown Egypt's army and bring Israel ultimately to the Promised Land. In Jesus's case, there is an even greater war, that between Satan and God, between forces of the anti-kingdom and forces of the kingdom. Jesus will start demanding that his listeners choose sides. Recall earlier Jesus had said, "Whoever is not against you is for you" (9:50). Now, he flips this: "Whoever is not with me is against me." You have to choose a side. Jesus is not contradicting himself. Then, someone was doing God's work in the name of Jesus. This is something to affirm, as they are working for the kingdom. Now, Jesus is challenging his hearers to decide what side they are on.

To fail to decide is itself a decision. To wonder, should I weed that garden or not? And then to continue to muse on this indefinitely is to have tacitly decided; the garden will get overrun with weeds. It is this failure to decisively opt for Jesus and his kingdom that ultimately leads Jesus to announce: "This generation is an evil generation; it asks for a sign, but no sign will be given to it except the sign of Jonah. . . . The people of Nineveh will rise up at the judgment with this generation and condemn it, because they repented at the proclamation of Jonah, and see, something greater than Jonah is here!" (11:29-32).

Jesus then offers the crowd several enigmatic images of lighting a lamp, including, "Your eye is the lamp of your body. If your eye is healthy, your whole body is full of light; but if it is not healthy your body is full of darkness. Therefore consider whether the light in you is not darkness" (11:34-35). Byrne notes, "God has placed Jesus in the world to be its light. But to benefit from the light the organ of reception—the eye—must be healthy. If Jesus' hearers are not benefitting from the light, they must ask themselves whether it is not because their organ of reception—their readiness to hear the word—is faulty. If, on the other hand, they do receive the light, they will themselves be light bearers."[39]

Jesus and Bad Table Manners (11:37–12:3)

Jesus was invited to a dinner party by a Pharisee. We find out soon enough that there were a number of other Pharisees as well as "lawyers," that is, experts on Torah or the law of Moses. Soon, Jesus becomes the dinner guest from hell. Luke tells us that he did not wash before dinner, which was standard practice both ritually and in terms of hygiene. Knowing his host's thoughts—he is God's Prophet after all—he takes the opportunity to insult virtually everyone. "Now you Pharisees clean the outside of the cup and dish, but inside you are full of greed and wickedness. You fools! Did not the one who made the outside make the inside also? So give for alms those things that are within; and see, everything will be clean for you" (11:39-41). He continues to excoriate them for paying tithes on the least minutiae but neglecting justice and love of God. And, on top of this, they love public respect. "Woe to you! For you are like unmarked graves, and people walk over them without realizing it" (11:44).

Recall that Jesus had been "tested" a number of times by Pharisees and lawyers, always trying to trip him up. Now, it seems, is the time to let them have it. There is a little play on words here: the outside of the cup, the inside of the cup, the outside of the Pharisee (appearance), the inside of the Pharisee (essence). Your outside looks good, but your inside (your soul) does not. It's the inside that matters. Thus, giving alms from the inside is to be free from greed, to have a pure heart. What matters? Minutiae? God hardly cares. Justice and love of God matters utterly. By calling them "unmarked graves" that people unaware walk over, he is going after their obsession for issues of exterior purity. These holier-than-thou leaders are actually *causing* ritual impurity as people inadvertently walk on their graves. "One of the lawyers answered him, 'Teacher, when you say these things, you insult us too.'" Now Jesus attacks them for loading on an oral tradition that overwhelms the average layman, "and you yourselves do not lift a finger to ease them" (11:45-46). Then Jesus insists that they are colluders with those before them who killed the prophets of old. And finally, "Woe to you lawyers! For you have taken away the key of knowledge; you did not enter yourselves, and you hindered those who were entering" (11:52).

I know a woman, call her Gladys, who is deeply faithful. She had been married to a very angry, very controlling man whom she divorced. She eventually remarried, this time to a wonderful man who has played a great part in her own healing as well as the raising of her children. Gladys applied for an annulment but was denied. She cannot receive communion as she is imagined by church law to be in a state of grave sin. She does not think she is, nor should we. To insist on laws that harm souls rather than guide souls is to misunderstand the essential concern. More recently, I had a conversation with a canon lawyer who worked at his diocesan chancery. At one point I posed a question to him: "If someone was in dissent, even privately, with a church teaching or disagreed with a canon law, is that person de facto in bad faith?" "Yes," he answered, "on some level that person is objectively in bad faith." I had two thoughts after that conversation. First, never consult that priest again. Second, Jesus's "woes" do not stop with this dinner party; they are intended for us too.

Here is the upshot: "When he went outside, the scribes and Pharisees began to be very hostile toward him and to cross-examine him about many things, lying in wait for him, to catch him in something he might say" (11:53-54). And here is Jesus's response: "Beware of the yeast of the Pharisees, that is, their hypocrisy. Nothing is covered up that will not be uncovered, and nothing secret that will not become known" (12:1-2). Some are great at holding up a façade, even carrying this throughout the whole of their lives. But *they will be exposed!* Perhaps that exposure will only come on judgment day, and wouldn't that be the worst time for it?

Another personal story: In college, I went to a play put on by the drama department, *Waiting for Godot* by Samuel Beckett. At the time I was taking a philosophy course in Existentialism, and I believe it fit this category. After the play several friends and I went to the student union to get a cup of coffee and talk about it. I praised the play and talked some nonsense about the "theater of the absurd" and how so much of the play reflected the depths of the human condition. My principle aim was to impress an acquaintance, a very attractive fellow student who was with us. She asked me several questions as I was opining freely, and it was obvious she was not impressed. Realizing this, I simply kept laying it on. I desperately wanted her to think of me as an *intellectual.* The term *persona* is Latin for "mask," something actors put on to play a part. I had put on a *persona.* Few wear no masks in life. Most put on a "face" that we think will be a little more charming or intelligent or interesting than we believe ourselves to be. Some wear masks so thick and so often that they've lost touch with what they actually look like. I wanted this woman to be impressed by me, and perhaps want to date me, but I made sure that she never could. The best-case scenario that I allowed was that she would like my mask, my *persona,* and some part of me would be haunted: what if she knew the *real* me?

Jesus was not so interested in romantic posturing as he was in religious posturing. It works the same way. Those Pharisees, scribes, and lawyers whom Jesus excoriated were all wearing masks and getting gratified by the honor and loftiness of their supposed holiness and social position. Deep down they must have been terrified at being exposed. Their egos must have been utterly fragile, and thus the protection they needed would have to be quite a rigid, thick mask. Jesus saw through their masks, and they hated him for it.

Trusting Possessions or Trusting God: Being Ready (12:4-48)

If religious hypocrisy was the number one sin in Jesus's mind, then attachment to possessions was a close second. Luke tells us that someone from the crowd asks Jesus to demand that he get his rightful inheritance. Jesus says to the crowd, "Take care! Be on your guard against all kinds of greed; for one's life does not consist in the abundance of possessions" (12:15). He tells a short parable of a man whose wealth ensured security for him. "But God said to him, 'You fool! This very night your life is being demanded of you. . . . So it is with those who store up treasures for themselves but are not rich toward God" (12:20-21). Greed (*pleonexia*) shows up throughout the New Testament. It is part of an unreformed heart (Mark 7:22), associated with those who fail to acknowledge God (Rom 1:29), the energy that drives impurity (Eph 4:19), utterly foreign to true children of God (Eph 5:3), and a decided form of idolatry (Col 3:5). Above all, it makes us anxious. Jesus tells his disciples, "Therefore I tell you, do not worry about your life . . . what you will eat, or about your body, what you will wear" (12:22). He has us consider how God cares for ravens, so how much more for us? And God has clothed lilies with beauty. How much more with us? "Do not be afraid, little flock, for it is your Father's good pleasure to give you the kingdom. Sell your possessions, and give alms. Make purses for yourselves that do not wear out, and unfailing treasure in heaven, where no thief comes near and no moth destroys. For where your treasure is, there your heart will be also" (12:32-34).

Luke Timothy Johnson observes that Jesus has "grasped the symbolic function of possessions in human existence. It is out of deep fear that the acquisitive instinct grows monstrous. Life seems so frail and contingent that many possessions are required to secure it, even though the possessions are frailer still than life."[40] Today's consumer society makes Jesus's challenge particularly urgent. In Pope Francis's encyclical *Laudato Si'*, he calls us to a truly rich life. He says that it begins with gratitude, a recognition that the world is God's loving gift. Once freed from our obsession with consumption and the compulsion to dominate, we are spiritually available to appreciate the beauty of creation. "This is not a lesser life or one lived with less intensity; on the contrary we enjoy more, live better, shedding unsatisfied needs, reducing our obsessiveness and weariness."[41]

Jesus and indeed the whole of the New Testament are ambivalent about holding many possessions. One may say that, even though I have many possessions, my trust is in God. While this could be theoretically true, possessions are seductive. They provide a kind of comfort zone that one rarely really steps out of. One can also reverse Jesus's words in our minds, from "where your treasure is, there your heart will be also" to "where your heart is, there is where your treasure is." This gives one an "out," where we can think, "My heart is with God—that's where my *real* treasure is." These aren't Jesus's words at all! Clearly, some possessions can enhance our lives, and not even in Luke's Gospel are they somehow banned, as if authentic discipleship is de facto abject poverty. So, how much is enough? This perennial question holds no easy answer, particularly as one cannot easily transfer the apocalyptic quality of Jesus's preaching with the fact that the apocalypse did not occur as the early church anticipated. The church needed to settle in for the long haul. One way we might want to consider the issue is this: If possessions can enhance my life, how few of them can I have and still have that enhanced life? It turns the tables a bit.

At the end of the day, we are accountable. Jesus tells his disciples about being ready. If slaves are ready for their master's return, *he will serve them*! "You also must be ready, for the Son of Man is coming at an unexpected hour" (12:40). Peter asks if Jesus is addressing the disciples with these words. Jesus then offers an image of a head slave who manages the household. The master is delayed in returning. If the master comes and sees all is well, that slave will be promoted even further. But if that slave lords his authority over the other slaves, he will receive a well-deserved beating. "From everyone to whom much has been given, much will be required" (12:48). That Peter asked the question, and that Jesus ended his teaching with more being required of those who have been given more, one cannot but reflect on Luke's Christian community and the expectations that Jesus would have on its leadership. Is it servant leadership or lording-over leadership? The more authority, the more God demands; this is how it must be.

The Divisive Jesus (12:49–13:21)

"I came to bring fire to the earth, and how I wish it were already kindled! I have a baptism with which to be baptized, and what stress I am under until it is completed! Do you think that I have come to bring peace to the earth? No, I tell you, but rather division!" (12:49-51). Fire is associated in the Old Testament with divine judgment and destruction. Elijah called down fire from God against the prophets of Baal (1 Kgs 18:36-40) and, later, on King Ahaziah's soldiers (twice!) when they came to apprehend him (2 Kgs 1:10-12). Further, John the Baptist demanded repentance and threatened that those who would not repent and "bear good fruit" would be like failed trees "cut down and thrown into the fire" (3:9). John also predicted that the Messiah "will baptize with the Holy Spirit and fire," and it is clear this fire would burn all the chaff (3:16-17). Jesus also references judgment day as like what happened in Sodom where "it rained fire and sulfur from heaven and destroyed all of them—it will be like that one the day that the Son of Man is revealed" (17:29-30). Is Jesus not the *Prince of Peace* (Isa 9:6)? Did not Zechariah prophesy, "By the tender mercy of our God, the dawn from on high will break upon us, to give light to those who sit in darkness and in the shadow of death, to guide our feet into the way of peace"? (Luke 1:78-79). Yes, and as we have seen, Jesus encouraged his disciples to trust in his Father's providence and love. But Simeon prophesied that Jesus will also be "destined for the falling and the rising of many in Israel, and to be a sign that will be opposed" (2:34).

As Jesus's ministry heats up, so does his message: You must decide. He gives three examples. Say you are on your way to court. You'd better settle the conflict first, or you could end up in prison. Regarding Jesus's listeners, Luke Timothy Johnson writes, "If they do not 'settle things' now with their adversary—in this instance the Prophet himself who calls them to conversion—then it will be harder for them in the judgment to come."[42] Or consider the gory deaths of those Galileans whose blood Pilate mixed in pagan sacrifices or those construction workers in Jerusalem who had a tower fall on them. Were they particularly cursed or sinful? "No, I tell you; but unless you repent, you will all perish just as they did" (13:5). Or imagine the owner of a garden whose fig tree is not producing fruit. He's going to cut it down. His gardener pleads for one more year to give it special care. "If it bears fruit next year, well and good; but if not, you can cut it down" (13:9).

Time is running out. You must decide. Luke provides us with another healing story on the sabbath. " 'And ought not this woman, a daughter of Abraham whom Satan bound for eighteen long years, be set free from this bondage on the sabbath day?' When he said this, all his opponents were put to shame" (13:16-17). And he concludes with two brief parables of the kingdom, both of which are in Matthew and Mark but placed very differently. The kingdom is like a mustard seed: it grew in the garden and became a tree. It is like yeast that a woman mixed with flour until all of it was leavened. Why are these parables here? It refers to something small that has become large, or something virtually hidden that affects the whole batch. I imagine Jesus's intention to be something like this: So, you think this isn't urgent? That you've got time to decide? The kingdom may look like a small movement, but its consequences are nothing less than salvation for those who enter it and damnation for those who do not. You must take a stand. According to Pope Francis:

> Faith is not a decoration or an ornament; living faith does not mean decorating life with a little religion, as if we were decorating a cake with cream. No, this is not faith. Faith means choosing God as the criterion and basis of life. . . . God is mercy; God is faithfulness. He is life which is given to us all. For this reason, Jesus says, "I came to bring division." It is not that Jesus wishes to divide people. On the contrary, Jesus is our peace, he is our reconciliation! But this peace is not the peace of a tomb. . . . Following Jesus entails giving up selfishness and choosing good—truth and justice—even when this demands sacrifice and the renunciation of our own interests. . . . He establishes the criterion: whether to live for ourselves or to live for God and for others. . . . It is in this sense that Jesus is a "sign that will be opposed."[43]

Getting into the Heavenly Banquet (13:22–14:35)

Luke reminds us again that Jesus is on his way to Jerusalem, and he is asked, "Lord, will only a few be saved?" (13:22-23). This was a highly debated question in the first century. Some believed that on the last day only the righteous would be resurrected while everyone else would continue in a kind of dark, murky sleep of Sheol. This seems to have been the position the separatist Essene community had as well as many Pharisees. Others believed that all of Israel, as well as righteous Gentiles, would be saved in the end. St. Paul seems to reflect this. "I ask, then, has God rejected his people? By no means!" (Rom 11:1). Paul argues here that Jews who "stumbled" in not accepting Jesus have allowed salvation to come to the Gentiles. "Now if their stumbling means riches for the world, and if their defeat means riches for Gentiles, how much more will their full inclusion mean! . . . A hardening has come upon part of Israel, until the full number of the Gentiles has come in. And so all Israel will be saved" (Rom

11:12, 25-26). In other Pauline writings, he seems to anticipate that ultimately Christ's victory will include all.[44] If Jesus himself had a decided opinion on this, it appears he saw a final resurrection of all where some would end up in heaven and others cast to eternal death. That the latter would entail a *conscious eternal torment* goes beyond the New Testament, where typically Jesus predicts weeping and gnashing of teeth but also simply the soul's ultimate destruction.[45]

Jesus's response to this question is "Strive to enter through the narrow door; for many, I tell you will try to enter and not be able. When once the owner of the house has got up and shut the door, and you begin to knock at the door, saying, 'Lord, open to us,' then in reply he will say to you, 'I do not know where you come from' " (13:24-25). Jesus's bleakness gets even darker when some Pharisees try to dissuade him from going to Jerusalem, but for Jesus "it is impossible for a prophet to be killed outside of Jerusalem. Jerusalem, Jerusalem, the city that kills the prophets and stones those who are sent to it! How often have I desired to gather your children together as a hen gathers her brood under her wings, and you were not willing!" (13:33-34). This is Jesus's fate awaiting, and he mourns his anticipated rejection and Jerusalem's fall because of it. Jesus goes beyond the question—will only a few be saved?—to the main point: salvation is offered to all, the kingdom belongs to all, but to attain it, to enter through that door, requires conversion and faith. And many will be found lacking.

Luke tells us that on a sabbath day, Jesus was at a Pharisee's house for a meal that also included other Pharisees and lawyers. "They were watching him closely" (14:1). This occasions four rather important teachings. The first, as we have seen before, is a healing of a man who apparently just shows up. He had "dropsy," or what today we would call "edema," the accumulation of body fluid. Jesus asks, " 'Is it lawful to cure people on the sabbath, or not?' But they were silent" (14:3-4). Again, another disappointing showing by his opponents. Jesus cured the man and then offered what rabbis call the "lesser to greater," or the *a fortiori* argument. "If one of you has a child or an ox that has fallen into a well, will you not immediately pull it out on a sabbath day?" (14:5). Obviously, you would. You wouldn't let them suffer (or drown!) until tomorrow. If you would do this, *how much more* ought you to heal someone who is suffering? "And they could not reply to this" (14:6). There is great irony here. The man with dropsy has fluid that he cannot expel, swelling his limbs and causing great pain. He is healed. The Pharisees and lawyers at dinner have pride, swelling their soul, and causing great pain to themselves and everyone around them. But they do not want to be healed.

Seeing people jockeying for places of honor, Jesus offers a parable where one ought not to go to those high seats or else be demoted and ashamed when a more honorable person comes. Rather, he suggests, go to the lowest place, and this will cause the host to publicly advance you. On the surface this is pretty banal stuff and even sounds like Jesus's advice is how to look good publicly and not bad. But this is a *parable* after all. The kingdom of God is a place of reversal, as we saw in Mary's Magnificat and Jesus's Sermon on the Plain (1:51-53; 6:20-26), and we must realize that the context is a culture where honor and shame are dominating concerns. Brendan Byrne notes, "If everything is going to be reversed when the kingdom of God is established . . . those who choose now to sit with the poor and lowly are destined for promotion, while those who sit now with the rich and powerful will find themselves ordered down to the lowest places. . . . Think how much more painful it will be to experience that at the end of the age, when all is decided forever!"[46]

I think there is more to all of this. The authentic spiritual life must be grounded in humility. At the end of the day, the reason we should not strive to advance or lord over others is that the very idea of doing so must become odious to us. This "false self" is a tyrant, a schemer, and an exhausting tormentor. The soul's deepest "true self" wants none of it. We might consider humility through several lenses. The first is self-awareness. The more clearly we see ourselves, including all the petty clinging that goes on in the psyche, the less enamored we become with ourselves and the more grateful we can be for every good gift—and it's all gift! St. Francis de Sales writes, "What good do we possess that we have not received? And if we have received it, why do we glory in it? On the contrary, a lively consideration of graces received makes us humble because knowledge of them begets gratitude for them."[47] The second is deepening knowledge of God. It includes God's overwhelming love for us, which itself is utterly humbling, and it involves recognizing the contrast between God's grandeur and our smallness. And finally, humility works as a kind of door for greater intimacy with God. The great desert father Peter of Damascus describes humility as "the dwelling place of the Holy Spirit, the gateway to the kingdom of heaven. . . . He who passes through this gateway comes to God; but without humility his road is full of pain and his effort useless. Humility bestows complete repose upon whoever possesses it in his heart, because he has Christ dwelling within him."[48] If all this seems a bit unreachable, Francis Fernandez offers some sensible advice:

> True humility is not opposed to the legitimate desire for personal advancement in social life, to enjoying the necessary professional prestige, to receiving honor which is due to every human being. All this is compatible with a deep humility. . . . The virtue of humility has nothing to do with being shy, timid or mediocre. It causes us to be fully aware of the talents Our Lord has given us and, without losing a right intention, want to make them fruitful in our lives.[49]

Jesus's third teaching at this dinner party is that instead of inviting our friends and "rich neighbors" to a meal, we should "invite the poor, the crippled, the lame, and the blind. And you will be blessed, because they cannot repay you, for you will be repaid at the resurrection of the righteous" (14:13-14). Jesus's culture was one of reciprocity. If you dine at my house, I expect to be invited to dine at yours. The poor and needy cannot reciprocate. As we have seen, Jesus leans toward those most in need, most marginalized. The kingdom is especially for them. Why shouldn't we prefer them if the kingdom prefers them? In doing so, we are acting as God acts, preferring as God prefers, caring as God cares. This isn't a "salvation insurance policy" so much as a way of being a sacrament of God and his kingdom. This is the thirteenth time Luke uses the word *makarios* (blessed or happy). It is a blessing and honor to be a sacrament of God. We should be happy to be it. Jesus's fourth teaching is a parable of a host of a dinner party who sent his slave to gather those invited. Those invited begged off for various insignificant reasons. So the master had his slave find anyone and everyone to come. "For I tell you, none of those who were invited will taste my dinner" (14:24). More reversals, and those who would not come now cannot come. The moral: Those who have rejected Jesus will not come to the heavenly banquet, even if they end up regretting it.

Then later, to a large crowd Jesus declares something stunning: "Whoever comes to me and does not hate father and mother, wife and children, brothers and sisters, yes, and even life itself, cannot be my disciple. Whoever does not carry the cross and follow me cannot be my disciple" (14:26-27). We found this saying in Matthew's Gospel (10:37-38), but there Jesus says, "Whoever *loves* [*philōn*] father or mother more *than me* [*upper eme*]." Now we have *hates* (*misei*). What are we to make of this? It could be that "*hate* is a Semitic exaggeration,"[50] or a "Semitic way of expressing total detachment."[51] This must be so. Surely, Jesus does not want us to hate anyone, particularly our parents, spouses, or children. But Jesus does want to align this "hard saying" to the cross that disciples also must carry. So we must "hate" our own lives too, that is, reject and die to our former selves. Paradoxically, we rise to a happy and blessed life (*makarios*). But this is no longer exactly *ours*; it now belongs to God. All relations, even our relationship with ourself, now are in and through God. To die to our narcissism, to renounce our attachments, to cease to be slaves to them: there is a cross there even as it is also a new life.

Very Different Parables (15:1–16:31)

Losing and Finding

In the context of public sinners coming to Jesus and religious leaders grumbling about it, Jesus tells three parables. The first is that of a shepherd of one hundred sheep who loses one that strays. He abandons the ninety-nine to search for the lost one. Having found it, he returns it to the fold and announces to his neighbors, "Rejoice with me, for I have found my sheep that was lost" (15:6). Then there is a woman who has ten silver coins but loses one. Upon finding it, she also wants to rejoice with her neighbors. And finally, Jesus provides the famous Prodigal Son parable; this is much longer. The story is well known: a son demands his inheritance early, squanders it, lives in destitution, decides to return home as a servant and no longer a son, and meets his father who embraces him, kisses him, and throws a party for him. All the while his older brother is angry at the sight of it all, and the father pleads for him to join the celebration. We do not learn whether the older son returns, but the father's plea is this: "But we had to celebrate and rejoice, because this brother of yours was dead and has come to life; he was lost and has been found" (15:32).

Parables often have a shock value, and they ought not to be taken at face value. We shouldn't ask, what about the ninety-nine sheep, now subject to wolves or getting lost themselves? We shouldn't ask, how could that woman be so careless with her money? And we shouldn't ask, what good parent would give his reckless son an early inheritance? Are all three about repentance? Jesus seems to say so in the first two parables. But the real focus in the parables themselves is joy at regaining what was lost. The protagonists—shepherd, woman, and father—represent God. God searches madly for the stray and delights in finding it. God lights lamps, sweeps, and looks for the lost and relishes its recovery. The son was doubly lost. Not only was he destitute, but in working for the Gentile feeding his pigs, he had lost his Jewish life. Gerhard Lohfink remarks, "This young man was absolutely finished. He had not only squandered the portion of the estate allotted to him; he also had lost his faith. . . . No Jew in the employ of a Gentile could live his faith. Among the Gentiles there was no kosher food, no sabbath, no way of keeping the law. So Jesus' hearers understood that this man no longer had any respect for the law or for God. He is at an end in every respect."[52] In this parable, the father acts out of radical love and joy. The son's guilt is no longer part of the story. "We *had* to celebrate and rejoice," he says to the older son.

What is God like? Jesus shows in this final parable that God is absolute compassion and love. "Those who love forget themselves, they go beyond reason for 'love' is not about rational motivation but about 'foolishness' that goes beyond reasonable expectations. This does not make one irrational, but it does make one act according to a different vision of life, one that is life-giving and recreative."[53] We never find out what happens to the younger son or the older son. Jesus leaves this as an open question. What we do find is a father's utter love. To the older son: "Son, you are always with me, and all that is mine is yours." And regarding the younger son, "But we had to celebrate and rejoice, because this brother of yours was dead and has come to life; he was lost and has been found" (15:31-32).

Commending Dishonesty?

Jesus's next parable was for his disciples alone, and it is a preacher's nightmare. Here we find an estate manager who appears to be credibly accused of squandering his wealthy landowner's property. The landowner informs him he is about to be fired, so he has his master's debtors come to him one by one and reduces their debt before he is ousted. The debts are huge. One owes a hundred measures (*batous*) of olive oil (around nine hundred gallons), and he reduces it to fifty. Another owes the same outrageous amount in grain, and his debt is reduced from a hundred to eighty measures (*korous*). Now they will owe him a "right to hospitality," and he will no longer be destitute. One would expect that this manager would ultimately get his comeuppance and that this would be the point of the story. But the wealthy landowner, learning of it, praises his shrewdness.

The narrative gets odder still with several linked sayings of Jesus about immoral people being shrewder in their own interests than faithful people are in theirs and making friends through "dishonest wealth" so that, when this fails, "they may welcome you into eternal homes" (16:8-9), and so on. Finally, Jesus asserts that one cannot serve God and wealth (16:13). It appears as though the historical Jesus told this parable, and so Luke includes it. These later sayings seem a bit contorted and may be either Luke's glosses in trying to make sense of the parable or other sayings of Jesus applied as some kind of interpretation of what otherwise appears to commend immorality for some later good end.

If we take the parable on its own, we actually do better. Jesus is *not* commending the manager's theft. What the manager is praised for is his determination to get out of his predicament. The kingdom of God is Jesus's message, and you have to act fast. "The behavior of smart crooks . . . can serve to challenge those faced with God's final offer to us. . . . Can't you let the smart decision of the dishonest manager inspire you?"[54] Lohfink frames it this way: "You must act in just the same way . . . in light of the kingdom of God. It is offered to you: now, today. But it will come to you only if you apply your minds, your *smarts*, your imagination, your passion—your whole existence."[55] Now, Jesus's final saying can make some sense: "No slave can serve two masters; for a slave will either hate the one and love the other, or be devoted to the one and despise the other. You cannot serve God and wealth" (16:13). You have to utterly apply yourself, and you have to be all in.

The Rich Man and Lazarus

Jesus tells yet another parable of a "rich man who was dressed in purple and fine linen and who feasted sumptuously every day. And at his gate lay a poor man named Lazarus, covered with sores, who longed to satisfy his hunger with what fell from the rich man's table" (16:19-21). Both men die, one to be received in Abraham's bosom and the other the torment of Hades. The rich man asks Abraham to send Lazarus to wet his tongue, but alas the chasm between would not allow it. He said, "Then, father, I beg you to send him to my father's house—for I have five brothers—that he may warn them" (16:27-28). This reversal is much like what we saw in Mary's Magnificat (1:53) and Jesus's Sermon on the Plain (6:20-26). It also echoes Jesus's parable of the rich fool (12:16-21).

Besides having brothers that need to be warned, we only know three things about the rich man: he lived by monstrous extravagance, he knew who the beggar was since he knew his name, and he never "got it," even when he was in hell. Lazarus was still imagined an inferior whom he wanted to come over and quench his thirst and to be sent as a messenger to his family. We are given no reason to believe that the rich man did anything actively immoral to deserve hell. His sin was that of omission. But it was an *enormous* omission, particularly as the Old Testament is rife with the demand to care for those most in need. The clearest expression of his rejection of Torah was his neglect of Lazarus.

Here in Toledo, there is a ministry called Food for Thought, where lunches are made on Friday night and then shared Saturday with the homeless. The key here is *shared*: those who make the lunches, along with others, hang out and eat with the homeless and the hungry. Connections are made, friendships happen, and the homeless are not just statistics. Every Friday night we hear the same speech by the leader of the enterprise that includes, "When most see a homeless person, they cross the street or get fascinated with the cracks in the sidewalk." When we do this we are making choices, not just whether to look at a homeless person in the eye, but also whether we think this person is worthy of our interest or care. We may choose an enormous sin of omission. Like we saw in Matthew 25:31-46, closing ourselves to those in need is also closing ourselves to Jesus.

And this is a real choice. In a noted general audience, Pope John Paul II taught that rather than think of God as actively damning us, we ought to think of damnation as our own choice. John Paul said, " 'Eternal damnation,' therefore, is not attributed to God's initiative because in his merciful love he can only desire the salvation of the beings he created. In reality, it is the creature who closes himself to his love. Damnation consists precisely in definitive separation from God, freely chosen by the human person and confirmed with death that seals his choice forever."[56]

Jesus on Discipleship (17:1–19:27)

We are almost at Jerusalem, and this next part of Luke's Gospel seems like a disparate grouping of incidents and teachings having little to do with each other. But on closer scrutiny, they all seem to be about discipleship and the kingdom of God. Jesus begins by telling his disciples, "Occasions for stumbling are bound to come, but woe to anyone by whom they come!" (17:1). The noun form of "stumble" is *skandalon* or scandal. To scandalize is to harm another's faith. But when this happens and the disciples repent, they must be forgiven, even seven times a day. Jesus is imaging a community of disciples that ought not to sin but certainly will, and thus we must forgive again and again. This is challenging material for sure, and his disciples beg Jesus, "Increase our faith!" (17:5). Jesus has them imagine a slave working hard for his master. Is this not normal? "Do you thank the slave for doing what was commanded? So you also, when you have done all that you were ordered to do, say 'We are worthless slaves; we have done only what we ought to have done!' " (17:9-10). So, what we have here is just the minimum requirements of the kingdom.

Then Jesus is asked about the coming kingdom. As I noted in the chapter on Matthew, Christianity holds what is called an *eschatological tension*. The end time is now, but its climax is in the future. Jesus tells his hearers, "For, in fact, the kingdom of God is among you" (17:21), but then immediately speaks apocalyptically about its future glory on the Last Day. "For as the lightning flashes and lights up the sky from one side to the other, so will the Son of Man be in his day" (17:24). As we have seen, first-century Judaism was filled with apocalyptic writings. The only biblical text is from the book of Daniel: "I saw one like a Son of Man coming with the clouds of heaven. And he came to the Ancient One and was presented before him. To him was given dominion and glory and kingship, that all peoples, nations, and languages should serve him. His dominion is an everlasting dominion that shall not pass away, and his kingship is one that shall never be destroyed" (Dan 7:13-14).[57]

While this vision reflects the glory of the last day, disciples need to remember three things. First, it will come when least expected, like the people in the days of Noah or Sodom experienced before God's catastrophe (17:26-30). Second, "Those who try to make their life secure will lose it, but those who lose their life will keep it" (17:33). We've seen versions of this in both Matthew and Mark and already in Luke 9:23-25. What makes this different is the wording: "make their life secure." Jesus's revelation in Luke is one of casting out every false security, be it wealth, honor, or any other superficiality. And finally, they have to "pray always and not to lose heart" (18:1).

This leads him to a fantastic parable of a shameless judge who does not want to vindicate a widow's claim. She is relentless, and he thinks to himself, "Though I have no fear of God and no respect for anyone, yet because this widow keeps bothering me, I will grant her justice, so that she may not wear me out by continually coming" (18:4-5). This is a gentle translation. The Greek uses a form of the verb *koptein*, to punch. He's afraid she might end up giving him a black eye. Jesus's point is another *a fortiori*: if the corrupt judge will secure her justice claim, how much more will God. So, be like her, unrelenting in prayer. This kind of necessary endurance is what Jesus was referring to in his parable of the sower and the seeds (8:11-15). Don't drop the ball and "in a time of testing fall away" (8:13). Jesus ends this parable with a shocking question: "And yet, when the Son of Man comes, will he find faith on earth?" (18:8). This is the challenge: Will we persevere unrelenting or will we fall away? If one's faith is little more than an expression of spiritual mediocrity, then for us the answer would be "no, no, you probably won't."

Jesus then tells another parable: "Two men went up to the temple to pray, one a Pharisee and the other a tax collector" (18:10). The Pharisee's prayer was little more than bragging: "God, I thank you that I am not like other people, thieves, rogues, adulterers, or even this tax collector" (18:11). And he goes on to boast of his piety. It wasn't really a prayer at all. The tax collector just beat his breast, saying, " 'God, be merciful to me, a sinner!' I tell you, this man went down to his home justified rather than the other; for all who exalt themselves will be humbled, but all who humble themselves will be exalted" (18:13-14). This parable is not about works righteousness versus God's grace. It is about one's posture before God and others. And yet, we might want to ask ourselves, upon imagining the Pharisee's prayer, isn't it likely that we think something like, "I can't stand arrogant people (and I'm glad I'm not one of them)"? And now I see that I've just become one. Meditating on this passage, St. Augustine prays: "Lord, do not go far; stay near me. To whom do you stay near? You stay close to those with a contrite heart. You keep your distance from the proud, but draw near to the humble. . . . [The tax collector] showed his wounds. He had come to the physician, he knew he was sick, and needed to be cured."[58]

This section concludes with two scenarios that are meant to contrast with each other, one an encounter with a ruler (*archōn*) and one with a "chief" (also *arch*) tax collector Zacchaeus. The ruler wants to know what he must do to attain eternal life. He assures Jesus he has kept the commandments faithfully. " 'There is still one thing lacking. Sell all that you own and distribute the money to the poor, and you will have treasure in heaven; then come, follow me.' But when he heard this, he became sad; for he was very rich" (18:22-23). Contrast this now to Zacchaeus who climbed a sycamore tree to see Jesus. Jesus tells him to come down because he wanted to stay at Zacchaeus's house that day. The people grumble that he is a *sinner*. "Zacchaeus stood there and said to the Lord, 'Look, half my possessions, Lord, I will give to the poor; and if I have defrauded anyone anything, I will pay back four times as much.' Then Jesus said to him, 'Today salvation has come to this house, because he too is a son of Abraham' " (19:8-9).

The issue is not necessarily selling everything and giving to the poor. Zacchaeus is wealthy, and by offering half his wealth he still might be quite rich. The issue is how both of these men received Jesus, one still relying on his wealth for security and the other demonstrating his enthusiasm for Jesus by his generosity. And he also commits himself to rigorous self-scrutiny. If he defrauded anyone, they get back fourfold. The Torah commands that restitution for theft be full, plus one-fifth. Zacchaeus will repay fourfold. What Zacchaeus was saying was that he would look back at what he assessed to see if any of it was unfair. If so, he would reimburse his fellow citizens 400 percent. Zacchaeus, the "sinner," welcomed Jesus, gave massive alms to the poor, and repented. This makes him a "son of Abraham."

The Controversial Prophet Enters Jerusalem (19:28–21:38)

Luke describes Jesus's entrance to Jerusalem as both glorious and controversial. His ministry started small with the Twelve and those who provided for their needs (8:1-3). It grew large enough for him to send out seventy disciples to prepare for his preaching in the towns he was to visit (10:1-12). By this time we find: "As he was now approaching the path down from the Mount of Olives, the whole multitude of the disciples began to praise God joyfully with a loud voice for all the deeds of power that they had seen, saying, 'Blessed is the king who comes in the name of the Lord! Peace in heaven and glory in the highest heaven'" (19:37-38). Even though this is a moment of great celebration, Jesus also mourns: "As he came near and saw the city, he wept over it, saying 'If you, even you, had only recognized on this day the things that make for peace!'" (19:41-42). Jesus prophesies the destruction of the city for having failed to recognize God's visitation. Until the Holocaust, the greatest pain in Jewish memory was the first destruction of Jerusalem in the sixth century BCE. Nehemiah "wept, and mourned for days, fasting and praying before the God of heaven" (Neh 1:4), and Jeremiah prays "O that my head were a spring of water, and my eyes a fountain of tears, so that I might weep day and night for the slain of my poor people!" (Jer 9:1).

As we saw in Matthew and Mark, Jesus then cleansed the temple by driving out the merchants. Jerusalem and the temple symbolized God's presence among his people. This was literally the center of the universe for all good Jews. Thus, it is all the more tragic that it became sullied. Again, one hears the voices of prophets past. Malachi declares, "I am sending my messenger to prepare the way before me, and the Lord whom you seek will suddenly come to his temple.

The messenger of the covenant in whom you delight—indeed, he is coming, says the LORD of hosts. But who can endure the day of his coming, and who can stand when he appears?" (Mal 3:1-2). And Jeremiah proclaims,

> Hear the word of the LORD, all you people of Judah, you that enter these gates to worship the LORD. Thus says the LORD of hosts, the God of Israel: Amend your ways and your doings, and let me dwell with you in this place. Do not trust in these deceptive words: "This is the temple of the LORD, the temple of the LORD, the temple of the LORD." . . . Here you are, trusting in deceptive words to no avail. Will you steal, murder, commit adultery, swear falsely . . . and then come and stand before me in this house, which is called by my name, and say, "We are safe!" . . . Has this house, which is called by my name, become a den of robbers in your sight? (Jer 7:2-4, 8-11)

Jerusalem and the temple did not stand in Jeremiah's day, nor will it withstand the Roman siege from the revolt just a few decades after Jesus's death and resurrection. He then told a parable about those who would reject him. A man leased his vineyard to tenants and sent his servant to receive his fair due. They beat him. He sends a second and third, both also beaten and thrown out. "What shall I do? I will send my beloved son; perhaps they will respect him." But they slayed the son. "What then will the owner of the vineyard do to them? He will come and destroy those tenants and give the vineyard to others" (20:13, 15-16). "When the scribes and chief priests realized that he had told this parable against them, they wanted to lay hands on him at that very hour, but they feared the people" (20:19). We are harkened to Isaiah's Song of the Unfruitful Vineyard (Isa 5:1-7). Because it yielded wild grapes, "I will make it a waste. . . . For the vineyard of the LORD of hosts is the house of Israel, and the people of Judah are his pleasant planting; he expected justice, but saw bloodshed; righteousness, but heard a cry!" It is interesting that Jesus's term for the owner of the vineyard is *kurios*, Lord. As we saw before, this is not a parable about Jews rejecting Jesus but about the leaders who have rejected God's Prophet.

And we see now that the die is cast. This is the beginning of the end. "So they watched for him and sent spies who pretended to be honest, in order to trap him by what he said" (20:20). The first test was the question as to whether to pay taxes to Rome or not. I commented on this in both Matthew and Mark. Not only does Jesus get out of it—"Then give to the emperor the things that are the emperor's, and to God the things that are God's" (20:25)—but he shows their bad faith. He asks them to produce a coin: "Whose head and whose title does it bear?" (20:24). Its head was Tiberius's and the inscription would have read *Tiberius Caesar, Son of the Divine Augustus, Augustus;*[59] this is idolatry on two levels; and they readily had this idol in their pockets to show him. He was then posed with the problem of a woman whose husband died without a son. She marries each of his brothers who all die childless. At the resurrection, whose husband is hers now? Jesus's response is that there is no marriage in heaven. "They are like angels and are children of God, being children of the resurrection" (20:36). Jesus then marveled at and commended a poor widow who gave to the treasury two copper coins, all she had to live on.

Collectively, these scenarios hit hard on a single point: there is a wide difference between the kingdom of God that Jesus envisioned and the kind of messianic kingdom his opponents anticipated. They could only see a kind of earthly kingdom of borders and prosperity, and one where they remain in charge, seeking public honor and parading public piety. For Jesus, the kingdom transcends every border. As Johnson points out, "No king, not even a Jewish King, not even David's son, can receive the devotion of 'all the heart and soul and strength and mind' (10:27), but only God."[60] It is a kingdom symbolized by the widow who gave everything.

I have already written at length in both Matthew and Mark about Jesus's apocalyptic message, and Luke's version is very similar. There will be "wars and insurrections," "earthquakes," "famines and plagues," and so on (21:9-11). The key is that "before all this occurs, they will arrest you and persecute you," but a true disciple will rely on Jesus, whose words and wisdom will guide them. Ultimately, "By your endurance you will gain your souls" (21:19). This theme has come up regularly: a true disciple hangs in there. It is only after the very cosmos becomes in distress will they see "the Son of Man coming in a cloud with power and great glory." So, Jesus teaches, you are not going to be free from harm, but I will be with you and ultimately, "Now when these things begin to take place, stand up and raise your heads, because your redemption is drawing near" (21:28). For Jesus's disciples, this will not be a moment of horror or confusion but rather a moment of triumph and liberation.

Here at the University of Toledo there are a number of Christian campus organizations, some more "evangelical" than others. One witnessing strategy that I've encountered several times has to do with imaging the last day when we are either saved and go to heaven or damned and go to hell. The question posed is "Why should you enter?" The answer this strategy seeks—apparently the only *right* answer—is that we must say, "Jesus Christ died for my sins." Certainly this is a good answer. Here is perhaps a better answer: "I am a child of the resurrection; I belong there."

The Prophet's Passion (22:1–23:56)

As with Matthew and Mark, Luke reports that after Jesus's baptism he went into the desert and was tempted by Satan. Jesus confidently repels him. Luke ends this with, "When the devil had finished every test, he departed from him until an opportune time" (4:13). Now is that opportune time. "The chief priests and the scribes were looking for a way to put Jesus to death, for they were afraid of the people. Then Satan entered into Judas called Iscariot, who was one of the Twelve; he went away and conferred with the chief priests and officers of the temple police about how he might betray him" (22:2-4). At the Last Supper, Jesus proclaims, "Satan has demanded to sift all of you like wheat" (22:31). And when Jesus is arrested in Gethsemane, his response is "When I was with you day after day in the temple, you did not lay hands on me. But this is your hour, and the power of darkness" (22:53).

The struggle Jesus has is, in a sense, all too human. Some religious leaders refuse the kingdom and will not recognize God's visitation of his Prophet. He publicly humiliated them and exposed their pride and thirst for power. His kingdom did not look like their kingdom, so they had to figure out a way to get rid of him. On the other hand, this is also a cosmic contest between Satan and Jesus. Even Jesus's torment in the garden speaks of this. Luke says that "in his anguish he prayed more earnestly, and his sweat became like great drops of blood falling down on the ground" (22:44). Luke's term for "anguish" is *agōn*, a term used to describe a gladiator's struggle. This is a cosmic battle royale between the forces of the anti-kingdom and Jesus, the bringer of the kingdom.

The Last Supper is a Passover meal, and this fact is so crucial that Luke references this thirteen times, including "Then came the day of Unleavened Bread, on which the Passover lamb had to be sacrificed" (22:7). Jesus is this lamb to be sacrificed for our liberation (cf. Exod 12:1-14). Paul exhorts the church to purity and says, "For our paschal lamb, Christ, has been sacrificed" (1 Cor 5:7), and in referencing the Eucharist he says, "This cup is the new covenant in my blood. . . . For as often as you eat this bread and drink the cup, you proclaim the Lord's death until he comes" (1 Cor 11:23-26). The bread and wine, now identified as Christ's body and blood, are offered to the disciples. This is a multilayered mystery. Jesus will tell his disciples that this is a foretaste of the heavenly banquet, and to those who eat and drink with him: "I confer on you, just as my father has conferred on me, a kingdom, so that you may eat and drink at my table in my kingdom, and you will sit on thrones judging the twelve tribes of Israel" (22:29-30). But the breaking of the bread is their "breaking" too, and the cup signifies their sharing in the sufferings of the Messiah. In his beatitudes he proclaimed: "Blessed are you when people hate you, and when they exclude you, revile you, and defame you on account of the Son of Man" (6:22). Acts will detail this fate.

Luke's version of Jesus's trials is a bit different from that of Matthew and Mark. For them, this is an actual trial under the cloak of darkness. For Luke, the questioning of Jesus is Friday morning. There are no witnesses, and all the elders, chief priests, and scribes collectively ask him two questions: Are you the Messiah? Are you the Son of God? Jesus does not answer the first and only says, "You say that I am," to the second. They took it as a "yes" on both counts (22:66-71). They then take him to Pilate with clear lies: "We found this man perverting the nation, forbidding us to pay taxes to the emperor, and saying that he himself is the Messiah, a king" (23:2-3). Jesus was not perverting the nation, he explicitly said "give to the emperor the things that are the emperor's," and he refused to answer the question about being the Messiah. Pilate declares him innocent and sends him to Herod Antipas, coincidentally in Jerusalem, who finds him innocent. But to them, who cares, this is just another *problem* that can be easily solved. Mary's Magnificat comes to fore again: the powerful seated on their thrones reject him (1:52).

Just as Luke's "trials" are somewhat different from Matthew and Mark, so is his crucifixion. The people do not mock him; rather, women wail and beat their breasts (23:27). "But the leaders scoffed at him, saying, 'He saved others; let him save himself if he is the Messiah of God, his chosen one!'" (23:35). Jesus does not cry out here, but rather pleads to God: "Father, forgive them; for they do not know what they are doing" (23:34). Luke gives us a scene that is profoundly sad. Jesus commends his soul to the Father and dies. "And when all the crowds who had gathered there for this spectacle saw what had taken place, they returned home, beating their breasts" (23:48). While preaching on the feast of Christ the King, Pope Francis guides us in this mystery:

> The Gospel in fact presents the kingdom of Jesus as the culmination of his saving work, and it does so in a surprising way. "The Christ of God, the chosen king" appears without power or glory: he is on the cross, where he seems more to be conquered than conqueror. His kingdom is paradoxical: his throne is the cross, his crown is made of thorns, he has no scepter, but a reed put into his hand; he does not have luxurious clothing but is stripped of his tunic; he wears no shiny rings on his fingers, but his hands are pierced with nails; he has no treasure, but is sold for thirty pieces of silver. . . . The grandeur of his kingdom is not power as defined by this world, but the love of God, a love capable of encountering and healing all things. . . . He experienced death, the tomb, hell. And so our king went to the ends of the universe in order to embrace and save every living being. . . . This love alone overcame and continues to overcome our worst enemies: sin, death, fear.[61]

The Messiah's Resurrection (24:1-53)

Each of the evangelists has a different take on the resurrection. This should not surprise us. What we are dealing with here is something that has no correlation in historical existence. Jesus's most dramatic miracles were raising persons from the dead, such as Jairus's daughter. But they were resuscitated. The resurrection is not this. In raising Jesus from the dead, the Father did something that concepts cannot grasp. Paul describes it as a *soma pneumatikos*, a "spiritual body" (1 Cor 15:44), something we will gain as well. Jesus's resurrection is the "first fruits of those who have died" "so that God may be all in all" (1 Cor 15:20, 28). Add to this that Jesus is also divine. How does one speak of encountering this mystery? Luke provides three scenes: the road to Emmaus, Jesus in the upper room, and Jesus's ascension.

On the morning of the resurrection Luke tells us about two of Jesus's many disciples who were walking from Jerusalem to Emmaus and talking about the report of the empty tomb. "While they were talking and discussing, Jesus himself came near and went with them, but their eyes were kept from recognizing him" (24:15-16). He wants to know what they are talking about. "The things about Jesus of Nazareth, who was a prophet mighty in deed and word before God and all the people. . . . But we had hoped that he was the one to redeem Israel" (24:19, 21). They go on to relate the report of his resurrection. Jesus schools them: " 'Was it not necessary that the Messiah should suffer these things and then enter into his glory?' Then beginning with Moses and all the prophets, he interpreted the things about himself in all the scriptures" (24:26-27). Luke retains the theme of Jesus as God's Prophet and Messiah who *had* to go through suffering unto glory. This was proclaimed throughout the Torah, from Moses to the prophets. It has always been his fate. Arriving at Emmaus, they press him to stay. The guest then becomes the host: "He took bread, blessed and broke it, and gave it to them.[62] Then their eyes were opened and they recognized him; and he vanished from their sight" (24:30-31). They returned immediately to Jerusalem and told the apostles what they experienced "and how he had been made known to them through the breaking of the bread" (24:35). What we have is the resurrected Lord who can appear and vanish at will, who can hide his identity, and who still interprets the Torah. The Eucharist is obviously the parallel to this story. The "breaking of the bread" (*klasei tou artou*) is Luke's term for the Eucharist.[63] This is where the risen Christ is not seen but "recognized" (*epegnōsan*), that is, experienced as present.

While these two disciples were conveying all this, Jesus appears in the upper room. He eats with them, so this is no ghost, and he again interprets the scriptures, which show that "the Messiah is to

suffer and to rise from the dead on the third day, and that repentance and forgiveness of sins is to be proclaimed in his name to all
nations, beginning from Jerusalem" (24:46-47). Then Jesus took
them out to Bethany, a town two miles from Jerusalem and, "While
he was blessing them, he withdrew from them and was carried up
into heaven" (24:51). The story of Elijah's ascension prefigures all
of this (2 Kgs 2:1-18). Elijah is taken into heaven while his disciple
Elisha watches on. Elijah had promised him that he would receive the
"spirit of Elijah," in fact, a double portion. Just so here, Jesus tells
them to "stay here in the city until you have been clothed with the
power from on high" (24:49). Acts of the Apostles, Luke's "second
volume," is a narrative of the early church, empowered and led by
the Holy Spirit. These disciples too receive a portion of the spirit of
the Master. So do we.

The Gospel
of John

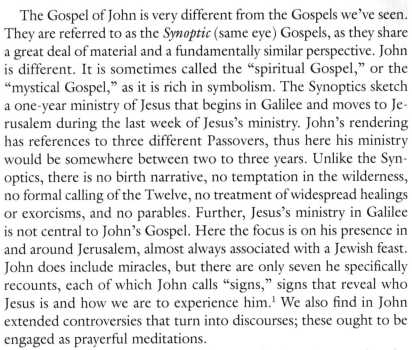

Jesus, the Face of God

The Gospel of John is very different from the Gospels we've seen. They are referred to as the *Synoptic* (same eye) Gospels, as they share a great deal of material and a fundamentally similar perspective. John is different. It is sometimes called the "spiritual Gospel," or the "mystical Gospel," as it is rich in symbolism. The Synoptics sketch a one-year ministry of Jesus that begins in Galilee and moves to Jerusalem during the last week of Jesus's ministry. John's rendering has references to three different Passovers, thus here his ministry would be somewhere between two to three years. Unlike the Synoptics, there is no birth narrative, no temptation in the wilderness, no formal calling of the Twelve, no treatment of widespread healings or exorcisms, and no parables. Further, Jesus's ministry in Galilee is not central to John's Gospel. Here the focus is on his presence in and around Jerusalem, almost always associated with a Jewish feast. John does include miracles, but there are only seven he specifically recounts, each of which John calls "signs," signs that reveal who Jesus is and how we are to experience him.[1] We also find in John extended controversies that turn into discourses; these ought to be engaged as prayerful meditations.

As I noted regarding John in the introduction, Jesus makes the Father *known*; that is, he is the interpretation (*exāgāsato*) of God.

John's *Christology*, or understanding of the nature of Jesus Christ, is the highest among the four Gospels. Jesus is the incarnate word of God, is God—in some sense—and was with God, as the Word, from eternity. God proclaims to Moses "You cannot see my face; for no one shall see me and live" (Exod 33:20). Yet, here is the revelation of God's own self. So, if we want to know the unseen God, we must look to Jesus. He shows us, paradoxically, the unseeable face of God. St. Augustine writes:

> The first three evangelists present their diverse accounts of what Christ did in human flesh during his historical life, whereas John had in view above all the Lord's divinity, in which he is equal to the Father, and strove to emphasize this in his Gospel. . . . He is therefore borne up high above the other three, so that you may consider these as remaining on this earth below in order to engage with the human Christ, but John as ascending above the clouds covering the whole earth and attaining that pure heaven.[2]

As Jesus will make abundantly clear, deciding on him is exactly deciding on God.[3] At the same time, John provides a truly robust humanity of Jesus. We see him experiencing fatigue (4:6), anguish (12:27; 13:21), deep sadness (11:33-35), contention (7:6-8; 8:25), and suspicion (2:24-25). He also has real friends and is involved in their lives (11:1–12:9).[4]

We must note something else in John that should strike the reader as odd or even disturbing. Frequently we find Jesus in conflicts with "the Jews." Obviously, Jesus is Jewish, as are his disciples and virtually everyone in the narrative, with the exception of his time in Samaria. "Messiah" is strictly a Jewish term and role. As we will see, John understands Jesus as perfecting the law of Moses, not dispatching it. John was almost certainly written from a Jewish perspective to primarily Jewish believers in Jesus. The consensus in scholarship is that its final composition was very late first century. By this time, there was great acrimony between Jewish believers in Jesus and Jews who did not believe Jesus was the Christ. By now the temple had been destroyed, as had the Zealots and the Essene community. There was no longer a priestly class or a Sadducee party. Rabbinic Judaism was emerging, and, at least in Palestine, Jews who confessed Jesus as Lord were expelled from the synagogue. We find references to this even inside John's Gospel itself (9:22; 12:42). As I mentioned in the introduction, the experience of the early church often finds its way into the narrative, and this is one poignant example. The distinction between Jesus and "the Jews" has fueled anti-Semitism for most of Christian history. Typically when John uses the term "the Jews" he has in mind Jewish leaders who opposed Jesus's ministry.

John's Prologue: Word Made Flesh (1:1-18)

In the beginning was the Word, and the Word was with God, and the Word was God. He was in the beginning with God. All things came into being through him, and without him not one thing came into being. What has come into being in him was life, and the life was the light of all people. . . . He came to what was his own, and his own people did not accept him. But to all who received him, who believed in his name, he gave power to become children of God. . . . And the Word became flesh and lived among us, and we have seen his glory, the glory as of a father's only son, full of grace and truth. . . . From his fullness we have all received, grace upon grace. The law indeed was given through Moses; grace and truth came through Jesus Christ. No one has ever seen God. It is God the only Son, who is close to the Father's heart, who has made him known. (1:1-18)

We saw in Luke's Gospel that the Canticle of Zechariah and the Magnificat of Mary set up the whole of the Gospel; so too here. John's prologue, much of which was probably initially an early Christian poem or hymn, tells us much of what we will encounter through the rest of the Gospel and how we ought to interpret Jesus's actions and words. This is one of the most celebrated and densest passages in the whole of the New Testament, a virtual synthesis of John's Christology and theology. Most scholars see three movements here: the Word's preexistence as divine and the divine outflow into creation (vv. 1-5); the incarnation of the Word (vv. 6-14); and the revealer of grace, truth, and the Father (vv. 15-18).

John opens the prologue with "In the beginning," a parallel to Genesis 1:1. But the Word existed before *the beginning*, as he was "with God and was God." There is an intentional blurring here. The Word is not exactly God, as the rest of the prologue clearly distinguishes them.

He was "with God" or, more literally, "toward God" (*pros tov theon*). But the Word was not exactly not God either. The Word speaks out of intimacy with God (vv. 1-2) and thus makes God known, both in creation and in the presence of the Word in human history. And his reality is both life and light (vv. 3-4).

In verses 6-14 we find the eternal Word anchoring itself in history in the person of Jesus. Some would not accept him, but "to all who received him, who believed in his name, he gave power to become children of God" (v. 12). These two terms: to receive (*lambanein*) and to believe (*pisteuein*) come up regularly in John's Gospel. Jesus Christ has to be "received" and "believed in." As I have noted several times earlier, to believe or have faith is not merely to intellectually assent to a claim. Rather, it means to entrust oneself. So, to have faith, one must recognize the truth that is Jesus Christ and hand oneself over to that truth—this is how we live the truth. Here, it is framed as becoming "children of God"; we undergo a change of lineage.

Verse 14 is really the high point of the prologue: "And the Word became flesh and lived among us, and we have seen his glory." Throughout the Hebrew Bible we find an overwhelm of God's presence as that of glory. Moses was not allowed to see God's face, but he did see something of God's glory (Exod 33:18-22); when Solomon dedicated the temple, God's glory filled it (1 Kgs 8:11); and the prophet Ezekiel was taken by vision to heaven and describes "the appearance of the likeness of the glory of the LORD" (Ezek 1:28). No one can see the face of God and live (Exod 33:20), but they can see his glory, itself overwhelming. Here, in Jesus, we see the divine glory. John tells us that the fruition of the appearance of God's glory in Christ is "grace upon grace," referencing the grace given to God's people in the law of Moses and now completed in the Christ event. "He is the perfection of God's gifts."[5] Francis Moloney puts it all together: "The Word preexisted creation with God; creation was through the Word; divine filiation [becoming children of God] is possible for believers; Jesus Christ is the incarnation of God, the Word become flesh; he shares in the divinity of God, yet he has taken on the human condition totally; Jesus is the unique, once-and-for-all revelation of God in the human story; the perfection of God's earlier gift of the law of Moses takes place in and through Jesus Christ."[6]

I teach religious studies here at the University of Toledo, and much of my scholarship involves interreligious dialogue and mutual exchange. There is much to learn from other religious traditions, and they can even help Christian theology to rethink its own presuppositions and even conclusions. So, in this place of mutual respect and interreligious learning, I've regularly been asked by my students why I am a Christian. My answer is always something like the following: For God to save humans who live in time, in history, it has to be a salvation that is fully integrated into our own reality for it to become real for us. But it can only come directly from God. Christianity, like no other religion, teaches that God radically did just this. The Word became flesh, entered time, entered history. God changed the world within the world. Perfect is good enough!

From John the Baptist to the First Disciples (1:19-51)

In all three Synoptic Gospels, John the Baptist is associated with Elijah. Priests and Levites come from Jerusalem to investigate John and ask him if he is exactly that, Elijah. Here John explicitly denies this and rather identifies himself as someone preparing for the Messiah. "I am the voice of one crying out in the wilderness, 'Make straight the way of the Lord'" (1:23; cf. Isa 40:3). The next day he recognizes the Lord: "Here is the Lamb of God who takes away the sin of the world! . . . I came baptizing with water for this reason, that he might be revealed to Israel. . . . I saw the Spirit descending from heaven like a dove, and it remained on him. I myself did not know him, but the one who sent me to baptize with water said to me, 'He on whom you see the Spirit descend and remain is the one who baptizes with the Holy Spirit.' And I myself have seen and have testified that this is the Son of God" (1:29-34). Two of John's disciples, one being Andrew, begin to follow Jesus. Andrew finds his brother Simon (Peter): "'We have found the Messiah' (which is translated Anointed). He brought Simon to Jesus who looked at him and said, 'You are Simon son of John. You are to be called Cephas' (which is translated Peter)" (1:42).

Jesus, as divine, knows everything here, including who Peter was. The next day in Galilee he will call Nathanael with the same kind of uncanny knowledge of who Nathanael was. Nathanael, overwhelmed by this, announces, "Rabbi, you are the Son of God! You are the King of Israel!" (1:49). This is heady language, but not as over the top as we might think. The Messiah was believed to restore David's monarchy, thus a king. Solomon himself was framed as God's son (2 Sam 7:14), and the Psalmist sees the king thus: "You are my son; today I have begotten you" (Ps 2:7). Further, a holy person can be considered a "child of the Lord" (Wis 2:13).[7] So these are large claims, but they fall short of who Jesus really is. Jesus promises Nathanael (and implicitly the other disciples) that "you will see heaven opened and the angels of God ascending and descending upon the Son of Man" (1:51). This is early faith: they see that Jesus is extraordinary, and they are ready to imagine him the Messiah. But they will discover, as we must ourselves, that Jesus is much more. Their expectations are based on what they are prepared to see or know. This will have to change.

There is an ancient dictum about the spiritual life that is utterly wise: *quidquid recipitur ad modem recipitur recipientis*; Whatever is received is received according to the mode of the receiver. Spiritually, we experience God through the subjectivity of our own minds, our own forms of thinking and being. The asset is that God can make sense to us and his presence and grace can be incorporated into our lives. The liability here is that we are restricted in what we receive and integrate by the limitations of our ways of seeing and knowing. In order to see more and be radically transformed, we are going to have to unlearn some things and be open to a mystery that takes us well beyond what we expect. This will be a running theme in the Gospel of John, and indeed it ought to be a running theme in our own lives. We have to enter the mystery.

From Cana to Cana: Five Scenes (2:1–4:54)

Scene One: Wedding at Cana

John describes a number of encounters Jesus has in the next three chapters, and collectively they express the dynamics of discipleship and the beginning of Jesus's revelation of his glory. It starts in Cana and returns to Cana. The first clue comes immediately: "*On the third day* there was a wedding in Cana of Galilee, and the mother of Jesus was there" (2:1). The language takes us to Pentecost, the Jewish celebration of the reception of the Torah on Mount Sinai. Moses tells the people that "*on the third day* the Lord will come down upon Mount Sinai in the sight of all the people" (Exod 19:11). Exodus describes the overwhelm of thunder, lightning, a thick cloud of smoke, and fire. They experienced the glory of the Lord. The Torah was the first grace, and now we have Jesus as "grace upon grace" (John 1:16).

The story is well known. Over the several days of the wedding feast, they run out of wine. Jesus's mother informs him of this, and his response seems curt: "Woman, what concern is that to you and to me? My hour has not yet come" (2:4). Jesus's mother is undaunted and tells the servants to do whatever Jesus directs them to do. Then Jesus has the servants fill purification water jars (twenty-four gallons each!) with water that then turns into wine. The steward speaks to the groom: " 'Everyone serves the good wine first, and then the inferior wine after the guests have become drunk. But you have kept the good wine until now.' Jesus did this, the first of his signs, in Cana of Galilee and revealed his glory; and his disciples believed in him" (2:10-11). The pericope gives us clues for what is to come. The setting is a marriage feast, an image of the messianic era marked by a great feast. God promises through Hosea, "I will take you for my wife forever" (Hos 2:19), and Isaiah imagines the end times where "the Lord of hosts will make for all peoples a feast of rich food, a feast of well-aged wines" (Isa 25:6).[8] Jesus's *hour* of glory is his crucifixion, where he will "draw all people to myself" (12:32). Jesus will reference this *hour* eleven more times. And through this *sign* he *revealed his glory*. We find *glory* and forms of *to glorify* fourteen more times. These two intertwining themes, his hour and his glory, become central to understanding Jesus in John's Gospel. Finally, the disciples start to recognize the glory of God in Jesus.

Scene Two: Cleansing the Temple

John then tells us that Jesus went up to Jerusalem at the time of Passover and cleansed the temple. We saw this in the Synoptic Gospels, but that was during Jesus's last week (Holy Week). John puts it here at the beginning of his ministry. Jesus needs to set things right immediately. This is not just the temple, it is "my Father's house" (2:16). One can recall Zechariah's messianic prophecy: "And there shall no longer be traders in the house of the Lord of hosts on that day" (Zech 14:21). "The Jews then said to him, 'What sign can you show us for doing this?' Jesus answered them, 'Destroy this temple, and in three days I will raise it up' " (John 2:18-19). And now we see another theme: Jesus speaks about heavenly and spiritual things, but those who have yet to *receive* and *believe* can only understand him on a human and literal level. They object to the absurdity of his claim, "But he was speaking of the temple of his body" (2:21).

Scene Three: Nicodemus

In the third scene we find a "Pharisee named Nicodemus, a leader of the Jews. He came to Jesus at night and said to him, 'Rabbi, we know that you are a teacher who has come from God; for no one can do these signs that you do apart from the presence of God.' Jesus answered him, 'Very truly, I tell you, no one can see the kingdom of God without being born from above'" (3:1-3). On the surface, it looks like Nicodemus simply doesn't want to be seen publicly with Jesus and thus comes to him at night. But Jesus is the *light* (1:4-5, 9), and Nicodemus is coming from the darkness to the light. Jesus uses the term *gennāthā anōthen* (lit. "born from on top"), which can mean either "born again" or "born from above." Nicodemus understands it as "born again" and wonders how one can reenter one's mother's womb. But to be a child of God, one has to be born from on high, from above (1:13). Jesus answers, "What is born of flesh is flesh, and what is born of the Spirit is spirit" (3:6). Jesus anticipates his *hour*: "And just as Moses lifted up the serpent in the wilderness, so must the Son of Man be lifted up, that whoever believes in him may have eternal life" (3:14-15).

What is fascinating about this dialogue is that initially it is a private conversation between Nicodemus and Jesus with singular pronouns. By verse 11 the pronouns become plural as though Jesus (and the believing community) is speaking to all of Israel about the crux of the whole issue between John's community and those fellow Jews who had not received the truth and believed in him. "For God so loved the world that he gave his only Son, so that everyone who believes in him may not perish but may have eternal life. Indeed, God did not send the Son into the world to condemn the world, but in order that the world might be saved through him. Those who believe in him are not condemned; but those who do not believe are condemned already, because they have not believed in the only Son of God" (3:16-18). The Catholic Church, the Orthodox Church, and most Protestant churches believe that when one pursues goodness and truth to the best of their ability, one is implicitly responding to God's grace and participating in God's salvation. You do not have to be a card-carrying Christian to be saved. We saw this expressed in Matthew's last judgment (25:31-46) and widely through Luke in terms of a preferential option for the poor. But this is not the language of John. You must decide; you must take a stand. Nicodemus shows early faith, but he is not there yet.

Quick, personal story: The week I was ordained, my neighbor—let's call her Agnes—who is very close to our family asked me a favor. "Would you hold my funeral?" she asked. Neither she nor her husband were religious, and she wasn't seeking the Catholic funeral rite, but she wanted me to preside over some kind of religious funeral. She wasn't old or frail, so presumably this would be sometime in the distant future. Of course, I agreed happily. Several years later, while at a dinner party, Agnes announced that "Peter here is going to have my funeral." I took that moment. "I certainly am," I said. "That reminds me, what do you want me to say at your funeral?" Agnes blushed, "Oh, if you're uncomfortable with this, you don't have to do it." I assured her I wasn't hesitating a bit, I just wanted to know what she wanted me to say. "Look, you're uncomfortable. Really, you don't have to do this." I replied, "I am not at all uncomfortable. But what do you want me to say?" Immediately, Agnes got up from the table, grabbed the salad bowl and asked, as she was bolting into the kitchen, "Does anyone want any more salad?" I was asking her, and she knew it, "What do you stand for? What are you committed to?" Maybe implicitly, "What is the status of your soul?"

Scene Four: A Woman of Samaria

Much of what we have seen so far now plays out in a conversation between Jesus and a Samaritan woman. Jesus's disciples go to buy food in the Samaritan town of Sychar, and he rests at a well outside of town. Here at noon arrives a woman whom he engages. Jesus is thirsty and asks for a drink. But he's a Jew and a man, and he's starting a dialogue with a Samaritan and a woman, and he wants a favor? That is the setup. "If you knew the gift of God, and who it is that is saying to you, 'Give me a drink,' you would have asked him, and he would have given you living water" (4:10). Like Nicodemus and many others, she takes him literally and on a human level, while he is speaking *from above.* "The water that I will give will become in them a spring of water gushing up to eternal life" (4:14). "Call your husband, and come back," he tells her. But she has no husband. "You are right in saying, 'I have no husband'; for you have had five husbands, and the one you have now is not your husband" (4:16-18). First, she saw him as a Jew. Then she refers to him as "Sir." Now she thinks he must be a prophet. Jesus assures her, "The hour is coming, and is now here, when the true worshipers will worship the Father in spirit and truth" (4:23). Now, she wonders about the Messiah, and he assures her, "I am he, the one who is speaking to you" (4:26).

On one level, the Samaritan woman *represents* Samaria itself. In 2 Kings 17:24-41 we learn that after Assyria conquered the northern country of Israel, "The king of Assyria brought people from Babylon, Cuthah, Avva, Hamath, and Sepharvaim, and placed them in the cities of Samaria in place of the people of Israel" (2 Kgs 17:24). We also find out that he sent a Jewish priest to unite them. "So these nations worshiped the Lord, but also served their carved images; to this day their children and their children's children continue to do as their ancestors did" (2 Kgs 17:41). As I noted in the chapter on Luke, *orthodox* Jews did not think much of the Judaism practiced in Samaria. The woman had five husbands, that is, five other gods from five other lands. And the man she is now with is not her legitimate husband, that is, *Samaritan Judaism.* Jesus comes to unite all of God's people (including Samaritans!), but it will be now a faithfulness "in spirit and truth," where "you will worship the Father neither on this mountain nor in Jerusalem" (John 4:21). Returning to the narrative, "The woman left her water jar and went back to the city. She said to the people, 'Come and see a man who told me everything I have ever done! He cannot be the Messiah, can he?'" (4:28-29). What we find in terms of the story itself is developing discipleship: from questioning Jesus to realizing he is a prophet to considering him the Messiah. She goes beyond Nicodemus's early faith to something substantive: a witness. "Many Samaritans from that city believed in him because of the woman's testimony, 'He told me everything I have ever done'" (4:39).[9]

Scene Five: Cana and the Royal Official

Now we have come full circle. Jesus is back in Cana, and many have heard of his ministry. A royal official (from Herod Antipas's court) begs Jesus to come and heal his dying son. "Jesus said to him, 'Go; your son will live.' The man believed in the word that Jesus spoke to him and started on his way. As he was going down, his slaves met him and told him that his child was alive" (4:50-51). The time of his son's recovery was exactly when Jesus made his proclamation. "So he himself believed, along with his whole household. Now this was the second sign that Jesus did after coming from Judea to Galilee" (4:53-54). With this sign, not only does the royal official *receive* and *believe* but his whole household becomes believers. This becomes something of a model of discipleship, and it corresponds to Jesus's first sign. Then at Cana, Jesus's mother put her full, unquestioning faith in Jesus, which itself conditioned the first sign. Now we have the royal official doing the same; the second sign.

The Controversy over the Sabbath (5:1-47)

As we have seen in previous chapters, Jesus was forever wrestling with Jewish authorities over what constitutes true sabbath observance. In the Synoptics, Jesus's responses have typically framed the issue as to whether one ought to do good on the sabbath or evil? Here *good* is obviously curing those who suffered, and *evil* is allowing them to suffer yet another day. In John, we have a very different take. A man has been ill for thirty-eight years and awaits being plunged in the pool called Bethzatha. "Jesus said to him, 'Stand up, take your mat and walk.' At once the man was made well, and he took up his mat and began to walk. . . . Therefore the Jews started persecuting Jesus, because he was doing such things on the sabbath. But Jesus answered them, 'My Father is still working, and I also am working.' For this reason the Jews were seeking all the more to kill him, because he was not only breaking the sabbath, but was also calling God his own Father, thereby making himself equal to God" (5:8-9, 16-18).

While Genesis tells us that during creation God "rested" on the seventh day (Gen 2:2), Jews did not think that God ever ceased to be actively engaged in his creation—the world would cease to exist—and all the more on the sabbath. The rabbinic tradition asserts that God particularly blesses pious Jews with *neshamah yeterah*, "additional spirit" or "increased soul," on the sabbath and that God orchestrates angels to observe and report on Torah learning among humans on the sabbath.[10] "Working" on the sabbath was a prerogative of God, but this prerogative could in no way be usurped by humans. Francis Moloney writes, "Sabbath existed for the celebration of the unique sovereignty of Israel's Deity."[11] Thus, Jesus's claim to "also be working" on the sabbath suggests he has either taken over the divine role or placed himself as an alternative sabbath deity.[12] Here is the crux of the issue: "The one acting with the authority of God comes into conflict with the human custodians and exponents of God's law."[13] Jesus makes it clear that he is not usurping God's authority or rights. "Jesus said to them, 'Very truly, I tell you, the Son can do nothing on his own, but only what he sees the Father doing; for whatever the Father does, the Son does likewise. . . . Indeed, just as the Father raises the dead and gives them life, so also the Son gives life to whomever he wishes. The Father judges no one but has given all judgment to the Son, so that all may honor the Son just as they honor the Father'" (5:19-23).

Imagine yourself observing this contest between Jesus and the authorities. Does Jesus not sound like he is blaspheming? Does he not sound like a deluded fanatic? Like a pathological narcissist with an unparalleled sense of self-importance? It is as though Jesus is on a mini-trial as "the Jews were seeking all the more to kill him" (5:18). But Jesus turns the table on them. He calls up witnesses: John the Baptist, whom they "were willing to rejoice for a while in his light" (5:35); the "very works that I am doing, testify on my behalf" (5:36); the Father himself who sent him (5:36); and finally the scriptures, "and it is they that testify on my behalf. Yet you refuse to come to me to have life. I do not accept glory from human beings. But I know that you do not have the love of God in you. . . . Do not think that I accuse you before the Father; your accuser is Moses. . . . If you believed Moses, you would believe me, for he wrote about me. But if you do not believe what he wrote, how will you believe what I say?" (5:39-47).

Now, they are on the hot spot. If they loved God and if they opened their eyes to the scriptures, they would see that Jesus reveals the Father. Jesus had been appealing to his intimacy with the Father and his absolute obedience to the Father, to John the Baptist heralding him, and to the signs/works that he does. Jesus is not a deluded narcissist; he has evidence and he has witnesses, but they have to love God and be open to God's revealing himself in Jesus. They do not, and they will not.

From Feeding the Five Thousand to the Bread from Heaven (6:1-71)

John tells us that when in Galilee a large crowd followed Jesus at the time of Passover. As we saw in the Synoptic Gospels so too we see in John: Jesus feeds five thousand from five loaves and two fish. So amazed by this, they wanted to make him king, but he withdraws from the crowd and even his disciples. The disciples then take a boat to Capernaum, where in a gale Jesus walks on water and joins them. "It is I; do not be afraid" (6:20). The next day the crowd came again. This sets up one of the most inspiring and provocative teachings in the New Testament. That John tells us it was the time of Passover is crucial, for the week of Passover is also the Feast of Unleavened Bread.[14] Recall too that John the Baptist had proclaimed Jesus the *lamb of God*, a Passover term for the lamb sacrificed and consumed and whose blood kept the people of Israel safe from God's tenth plague. Finally, recall that in their wandering for forty years in the desert of Sinai God fed them with manna. We must hold all this together.

To the crowd: "Very truly, I tell you, you are looking for me, not because you saw signs, but because you ate your fill of the loaves. Do not work for the food that perishes, but for the food that endures for eternal life, which the Son of Man will give you" (6:26-27). The crowd asks, "What sign are you going to give us then, so that we may believe you? . . . Our ancestors ate the manna in the wilderness; as it is written, 'He gave them bread from heaven to eat'" (6:30-31). This launches one of Jesus's most profound teachings. "I am the bread of life. Whoever comes to me will never be hungry, and whoever believes in me will never be thirsty. . . . For I have come down from heaven, not to do my own will, but the will of him who sent me. And this is the will of him who sent me, that I should lose nothing of all that he has given me, but raise it up on the last day" (6:35-40). The Jewish theological tradition in Jesus's day identified the exodus manna from heaven as God's gifts of wisdom and Torah.[15]

Now Jesus is contrasting the bread of life from Moses (manna, wisdom, Torah) to this ultimate bread (himself), *grace upon grace* (1:16). His listeners take his words on a human and literal level. "Is this not Jesus, the son of Joseph, whose father and mother we know? How can he now say, 'I have come down from heaven'?" (6:42). But we know from the prologue that as the preexistent Word, Jesus had come down from heaven. "Very truly, I tell you, whoever believes has eternal life.

I am the bread of life. Your ancestors ate the manna in the wilderness, and they died. This is the bread that comes down from heaven, so that one may eat of it and not die. . . . And the bread that I will give for the life of the world is my flesh" (6:47-51). Here Jesus is referencing his sacrificial death on the cross offered to the world. He is the Passover "Lamb of God who takes away the sin of the world" (1:29). "As Israel ate of the manna so now the world is summoned to accept the further revelation of God in the broken body and spilled blood of the Son of Man."[16] The symbolic levels of Jesus's teaching go deeper: "Very truly, I tell you, unless you eat the flesh of the Son of Man and drink his blood, you have no life in you. Those who eat my flesh and drink my blood have eternal life, and I will raise them up on the last day. . . . I live because of the Father, so whoever eats me will live because of me. . . . The one who eats this bread will live forever" (6:53-58).

The language is actually very concrete. Jesus moves from using a common verb, "to eat" (*phagein*), to now twice using the term *trōgein*, to chew or crunch with one's teeth; it accentuates the real experience of eating. According to renowned Johannine scholar Raymond Brown, this is "a most forceful expression of the tremendous claim that Jesus gives man a share in God's own life. . . . And so it is that, while the Synoptic Gospels record the institution of the Eucharist, it is John who explains what the Eucharist does for the Christian."[17] Putting the discourse together, Moloney writes, "The Eucharist is a place where one comes to eternal life. Encountering the broken flesh and the spilled blood of Jesus, 'lifted up' on a cross, the believer is called to make a decision for or against the revelation of God in that encounter, gaining or losing life because of it."[18]

All of this seems so outlandish, not only to the crowd but also to many of Jesus's disciples. "Because of this many of his disciples turned back and no longer went about with him. So Jesus asked the twelve, 'Do you also wish to go away?' Simon Peter answered him, 'Lord, to whom can we go? You have the words of eternal life. We have come to believe that you are the Holy One of God'" (6:66-69). This is the first time anyone in the narrative expresses faith in Jesus for the ultimate reason: Jesus's origins in the Father.

Intermezzo: Short Primer on the Eucharist[19]

The Eucharist or Lord's Supper has been essential to Christian identity from the beginning (Acts 2:42). Early Christians gathered on Sunday evening, the day commemorating the resurrection, and celebrated a rite of "thanksgiving," the translation of *eucharistia*. Each of the Synoptic Gospels describes the Last Supper as a Passover meal where Jesus inaugurated his new covenant and anticipated his sacrificial death. Jesus identified the bread and wine as his body and blood, and the disciples in eating and drinking were entering into his new covenant. Paul, in recounting the eucharistic words of the Lord, ends by claiming, "For as often as you eat this bread and drink the cup, you proclaim the Lord's death until he comes. Whoever therefore eats the bread or drinks the cup of the Lord in an unworthy manner will be answerable for the body and blood of the Lord" (1 Cor 11:26-27). Here Paul identifies the eucharistic action as a proclamation of or engagement in the sacrificial death of Jesus. From the writings of the early church fathers, we glean additional insights into what Christians thought they were doing by celebrating the Eucharist. Two themes predominate: sacrifice and communion with God through the body and blood of Jesus in the form of bread and wine. These two themes were intertwined in their minds. In his treatise *Against Heresies*, St. Irenaeus of Lyon writes the following:

Again, giving direction to His disciples to offer to God the first-fruits of His own created things . . . He took that created thing, bread, and gave thanks, and said, "This is My body." And the cup likewise, which is part of that creation to which we belong, He confessed to be his blood, and taught the new oblation of the new covenant; which the church receiving from the apostles, offers to God throughout all the world. . . . . The oblation of the church . . . [is] a pure sacrifice, and is acceptable to Him. . . . Inasmuch, then, as the church offers with single-mindedness, her gift is justly reckoned a pure sacrifice with God. . . . Then again, how can they say that the flesh, which is nourished with the body of the Lord and with His blood, goes into corruption and does not partake of life? . . . But our opinion is in accordance with the Eucharist, and the Eucharist in turn establishes our opinion. For we offer to Him His own, announcing consistently the fellowship and union of the flesh and Spirit. For as the bread, which is produced from the earth, when it receives the invocation of God, is no longer common bread, but the Eucharist, consisting of two realities, earthly and heavenly; so also our bodies, when they receive the Eucharist, are no longer corruptible, having the hope of the resurrection to eternity.[20]

In this text, Irenaeus is arguing against gnostic Christians who denied the resurrection of the body. Irenaeus uses the Eucharist as his counter-argument. If the physical bread and wine can become the actual body and blood of Jesus—something now heavenly and incorruptible—so too can the human body become spiritualized. And it is done so by participating in the Eucharist, the very ritual that conditions immortality. Further, we see that the Eucharist is regularly referred to as both the original sacrifice of Christ on the cross and a sacrifice (self-offering) made by the church.

Sacred rites intend believers to enter into the deep archetypal symbols of salvation within a given religion. The rituals become *presentations* of the reality symbolized. They are meant to transform the believer by engaging the reality of that salvation through the mediation of the symbols that engage it. The symbols access the reality itself. This is not magic or superstition. Rather, it is radical participation in the life of Christ. But it has to be done, Irenaeus says, with "single-mindedness" or a pure heart to be transforming. In effect, what Christians thought they were doing was reentering the original sacrifice of Christ, offering themselves to God through it, and communing with the actual body and blood of Jesus, now risen and glorified.

The conviction that the Eucharist was a sacrifice and literal communion with the body and blood of the risen Lord, and indeed that it created the conditions for transforming the Christian, was widely shared. St. Ignatius of Antioch reminds his readers that there is just one altar of sacrifice in the church and criticizes heretics who did not "acknowledge that the Eucharist is the flesh of our Savior Jesus Christ." He imagined the eucharistic food as the "medicine of immortality."[21] The early Christian intellectual St. Justin (100–165) describes it thus:

> And this food is called among us *Eukaristia*, of which no one is allowed to partake but the one who believes that these things we teach are true, and who has been washed with the washing that is for the remission of sins, and unto regeneration, and who is so living as Christ has enjoined. For not as common bread and common drink do we receive these; but in like manner as Jesus Christ, having been made flesh by the Word of God, had both flesh and blood for our salvation, so likewise have we been taught that the food which is blessed by the prayer of his word, and from which

our blood and flesh by transmutation are nourished, is the flesh and blood of that Jesus who was made flesh.[22]

As we will see, John's Gospel has no "institution narrative" of the Eucharist, nor is John's Last Supper a Passover meal. The *Bread of Life* discourse *is* John's own kind of institution narrative. Jesus puts much together here. In St. Augustine's *Confessions* he describes a mystical experience whereby he found God indwelling in his soul and speaking to him about this sacred mystery.

> I entered and with my soul's eye, such as it was, saw above that same eye of my soul the immutable light higher than my mind. . . . It transcended my mind. . . . It was superior because it made me, and I was inferior because I was made by it. The person who knows the truth knows it, and he who knows it knows eternity. Love knows it. . . . I trembled with love and awe . . . and I heard as it were your voice from on high: "I am the food of the fully grown; grow and you will feed on me. And you will not change me into you like the food your flesh eats, but you will be changed into me."[23]

The Feast of Tabernacles in Four Parts (Plus One) (7:1–10:42)

The Setting

John tells us that it was the time of Feast of Booths or Tabernacles. Jews call it *Sukkōt*, and it commemorates God's care of his people during the exodus time of forty years in the wilderness.[24] There they lived in *sukkōt* (impermanent dwellings), always ready to be on the move as God directed them. This was an eight-day festival in Jerusalem with three particularly important daily rituals. First, each morning for seven days priests led a procession down to the Pool of Siloam to gather water in golden vessels and splash the water along with wine on the temple's principal altar. It had eschatological associations. Ezekiel had a vision of a restored Jerusalem where water flowed from the temple, increasingly becoming a river, to the Dead Sea (Ezek 47:1-12). And Zechariah imaged an apocalyptic renewal where "living waters shall flow out from Jerusalem. . . . And the Lord will become king over all the earth" (Zech 14:8-9). Second, there was a daily ceremony of light, where four large menorahs were set up that lighted up the temple at night. Men danced under the lights while Levites sang psalms of joy (Pss 120–134). Third, just before daybreak priests would turn from facing the east (Mount of Olives) to the sanctuary of the temple. This signified that they would not worship nature spirits (or any other gods) but only the Lord of the temple.

Jesus and his disciples were in Galilee, and he sends them to Jerusalem (7:8). He then went up to Jerusalem alone and remained incognito for several days of the festival.

> About the middle of the festival Jesus went up into the temple and began to teach. The Jews were astonished at it, saying, "How does this man have such learning, when he has never been taught?" Then Jesus answered them, "My teaching is not mine but his who sent me. Anyone who resolves to do the will of God will know whether the teaching is from God or whether I am speaking on my own. Those who speak on their own seek their own glory; but the one who seeks the glory of him who sent him is true, and there is nothing false in him." (7:14-18)

Jesus continues to appeal to two interrelated criteria of authenticity. The first is that if one truly seeks and conforms oneself to the will of God, then his revelation of the Father should be obvious. Years ago I took the Spiritual Exercises of St. Ignatius. On this month-long retreat I considered my retreat director to be one of the holiest persons I had ever met. He meditated on the Gospels constantly, and his prayer life was deeply rich and intimate with God. I noticed that he regularly expressed what seemed spiritually wise or unwise by saying, "That feels like the Lord," or, "That doesn't feel like the Lord." Of course, these kinds of evaluations *can* be expressions of projection or self-delusion in naïve hands—we've all seen this—but in the hands of one intensely immersed in the Lord, they can identify what Ignatius calls "movements of the good spirit" and "movements of the evil spirit." I have also experienced the ministry of a bishop—since forced to resign in disgrace—whose leadership made me often wonder: Does he even read the Gospels or get them? Does he have any idea who Jesus is?

The second criterion has to do with whether one is seeking one's own glory or solely the glory of God. We saw this earlier when Jesus announced, "I do not accept glory from human beings. . . . How can you believe when you accept glory from one another and do not seek the glory that comes from the one who alone is God?" (5:41, 44). Michael Buckley, reflecting on this issue writes,

> In no other area is self-deception or illusion so possible, so prevalent, and so emotionally fostered as in religious fanatical belief or faith. . . . When one strips away all fatuous reassurances from what is actually disclosed, what is left? What does one find oneself really committed to? What is actually uncovered by a process of demanding and rigorously honest observation to be the actual object of religious faith? . . . Faith in the understanding of John's Gospel engages something absolute and simply nonnegotiable, the foundation of all other negotiations, a commitment to which everything else is relative. . . . Faith's final independence from anything finite or idolatrous is a demand upon the religious faithful, the demand that nothing . . . is to be preferred to the love of God.[25]

I would think that Jesus's enemies, those intent not to see the glory of God revealed in him, could pass a lie detector when asked if they loved God and loved God's Torah. But they are closed off from God and do not understand the divine trajectory that Torah points to. And they do not even know it. Buckley again: "Zeal can mask a hidden but vicious agenda. A religious commitment that begins in self-denial can slip almost imperceptibly into an abiding or even demanding sense of entitlement. . . . As time passes, one can come to rely addictively upon these signs of prestige."[26]

Living Water and Light of the World

"On the last day of the festival, the great day, while Jesus was standing there, he cried out, 'Let anyone who is thirsty come to me, and let the one who believes in me drink. As the scripture has said, 'Out of the believer's heart shall flow rivers of living water'" (7:37-39). Hearing this, some of the crowd consider Jesus the Messiah, while others merely wonder out loud. The chief priests and Pharisees send the temple police to arrest him, but these temple guards are themselves bewildered. Nicodemus, who had the beginnings of faith, defends Jesus's right to a real hearing. "Again Jesus spoke to them, saying, 'I am the light of the world. Whoever follows me will never walk in darkness but will have the light of life'" (8:12).

This "last day of the festival" was treated as a sabbath day. The rituals of water, light, and the priestly turning to the temple were performed each of the first seven days, but not on the last eighth day. Now we have Jesus the new water that refreshes to eternal life. He and his truth are in some sense contrasted to the water rituals during *Sukkōt*. That water flowed from the sanctuary, but we have a new sanctuary from which life-giving waters flow. That water pointed to God's dwelling, the ritual center of Torah faith. But the water Jesus gives flows from the living source of Torah. The water Jesus provides is the Spirit (7:39). The same can be said of the rituals of light. They lit up the temple, and this light was celebrated with great joy. But Jesus is actual light itself (*light* and *life*; 1:4), not just the light for God's people, but light for the entire world. And finally, while priests performed the turning to the temple ritual, Jesus calls them (and us!) to turn to him as the absolute center of God's presence and revelation.

But this is not merely a contrast; it is also a fulfillment. As I have noted earlier, Jesus did not come to reject Moses, Torah, or temple. He came to bring all of these to their rightful completion (*telos*), their ultimate end. "From his fullness we have all received, grace upon grace. The law indeed was given through Moses; grace and truth came through Jesus Christ. No one has ever seen God. It is God the only Son, who is close to the Father's heart, who has made him known" (1:16-18).

Some among him understand this; these are his disciples. Others see *something*, but they cannot be sure exactly what they see. And others simply refuse to look or look but refuse to see. "You are from below, I am from above; you are of this world, I am not of this world. I told you that you will die in your sins unless you believe that I am he" (8:23-24). There is one more even greater opportunity to recognize his significance: "So Jesus said, 'When you have lifted up the Son of Man, then you will realize that I am he, and that I do nothing on my own, but I speak these things as the Father instructed me'" (8:28). This will not be the last time Jesus makes this prophecy. Jesus's utter self-emptiness on the cross, his total self-giving, will become an icon of God.

Conflicts: Sight or Blindness

As we have seen from the Synoptic Gospels, even Jesus's closest disciples cannot see glory in the cross or know what to do with the paradox of "losing oneself to save oneself." Jesus encourages those who believe in him to keep going, to stay the course: "If you continue in my word, you are truly my disciples; and you will know the truth, and the truth will make you free" (8:31). His promise is conditional and future looking: abiding in his word becomes the condition for coming to know the truth and to freedom. But now his hearers become argumentative. Jesus tells them, "The slave does not have a permanent place in the household; the son has a place there forever. So if the Son makes you free, you will be free indeed" (8:35-36). Then there is a volley. They: "Abraham is our father." Jesus: "If you were Abraham's children, you would be doing what he did," that is, placing faith in God. They: "We have one father, God himself." Jesus: "If God were your Father, you would love me, for I came from God." Then Jesus gets ugly: "You are from your father the devil, and you choose to do your father's desires" (8:39-44).

What is spiritual slavery and what is spiritual freedom? Consider it philosophically for a moment. If God is the source, center, and ultimate horizon of goodness, truth, and beauty—these are Plato's useful *transcendentals*—then the only way I can express and experience my own goodness, truth, and beauty is in and through God, even if this is implicit. My goodness is *only* goodness insofar as it participates in the Good itself. My truth and my beauty are only realized by me as they engage Truth itself, Beauty itself. None of these exist outside of God, who is their absolute. Outside of God we are slaves, whether this be to our egos, our disordered desires, our neediness, and so on. But a servant of God is paradoxically utterly free. C. S. Lewis expresses it eloquently in *Mere Christianity*:

> The more we get what we now call "ourselves" out of the way and let Him take us over, the more truly ourselves we become. . . . It is no good trying to *be myself* without Him. The more I resist Him and try to live on my own, the more I become dominated by my own heredity and upbringing and surroundings and natural desires. In fact what I so proudly call "Myself" becomes merely a meeting place for trains of events which I never started and cannot stop. What I call *my wishes* become merely the desires thrown up by my physical organism or pumped into me by other men's thoughts or even suggested to me by devils. . . . It is only when I turn to Christ, when I give myself up to His Personality, that I first begin to have a real personality myself. . . . Until you have given your self to Him you will not have a real self.[27]

Now back to Abraham: "Are you greater than our father Abraham who died?" (8:53). And there is more volleying until, "Jesus said to them, 'Very truly, I tell you, before Abraham was, I am.' So they picked up stones to throw at him, but Jesus hid himself and went out of the temple" (8:58-59). They wanted to stone him because of blasphemy, not because of bad grammar. I AM is the English translation of Yahweh. In Exodus, Moses asks God his name: "God said to Moses, 'I AM WHO I AM.' He said further, 'Thus you shall say to the Israelites, 'I AM has sent me to you'" (Exod 3:14). So holy has Judaism held this divine name that when "Yahweh" appears in a public reading, they substitute *Adonai*, Lord; they do not say his name out loud. Recall that, while John regards the eternal Word as divine, he also distinguishes the Word from God absolute. In Jesus's ministry, he does the same. He works for God; he represents God. He reveals God. He is not the Father, but he does carry out the functions of God. As the Father is the source of life, so also does the Son have life in him (5:21), and he has the power and authority to give it to others (5:26; 6:40, 57). The Son is a judge as the Father is a judge (5:22), and he deserves honor just as the Father does (5:23). As he will tell his disciples later, "Whoever has seen me has seen the Father" (14:9), and, "The Father and I are one" (10:30).[28]

This section ends with a fascinating narrative of Jesus healing a blind man. Jesus makes mud, smears it on the man's eyes, and tells him to wash in the pool of Siloam, meaning "Sent," a virtual title for Jesus and the very pool where priests drew water for the Feast of Tabernacles. The Pharisees investigate, as this was done on the sabbath. They interrogate the man and then his parents. His parents are cagey, "for the Jews had already agreed that anyone who confessed Jesus to be the Messiah would be put out of the synagogue. Therefore his parents said, 'He is of age; ask him'" (9:22-23). To the Pharisees, this man concluded, "He is a prophet" (9:17), only to be ridiculed by them. "Jesus heard that they had driven him out, and when he found him, he said 'Do you believe in the Son of Man?' He answered, 'And who is he, sir? Tell me, so that I may believe in him.' Jesus said to him, 'You have seen him, and the one speaking with you is he.' He said, 'Lord, I believe.' And he worshiped him" (9:35-38). In asking the man if he *believes in* the Son of Man, Jesus does not use the typical term for "in" (*en*) but "into" (*eis*). It could be awkwardly phrased, "Do you believe *into* the Son of Man?" As I have noted earlier, believing in Christ is not merely an intellectual assent but rather an entrusting of oneself to the Lord, an entering into communion with Christ. The man starts out blind but trusts Jesus. He then concludes Jesus must be a prophet, sent by God. And then, finally, he entrusts himself fully to Jesus and worships him. Now all of a sudden it seems Pharisees are around, so Jesus proclaims, "I came into this world for judgment so that those who do not see may see, and those who do see may become blind" (9:39). They balk. "Jesus said to them, 'If you were blind, you would not have sin. But now that you say, "We see," your sin remains'" (9:41). The blind man entrusts himself to Jesus and sees. His enemies refuse to entrust themselves and become blind. And so it goes.

The Good Shepherd

As we have seen throughout the Gospels, Jesus's greatest adversaries are religious leaders, many of whom he found hypocritical and lacking authentic faith. There is a long tradition in the Hebrew Bible of unfaithful leaders who are self-serving shepherds caring little for their flock. Jeremiah, for example, proclaims: "Woe to the shepherds who destroy and scatter the sheep of my pasture!" (Jer 23:1). Many prophets presented God as the future shepherd, who will rightly take care of his flock.[29] They also looked toward a future Davidic figure, a messiah who would be the true shepherd.[30] In an agrarian society, the metaphor is most apt. It is in this context, and during this same feast, that Jesus proclaims, "I am the gate for the sheep. All who came before me are thieves and bandits. . . . I am the gate. Whoever enters by me will be saved, and will come in and go out and find pasture" (10:7-9). "I am the good shepherd. The good shepherd lays down his life for the sheep. . . . I am the good shepherd. I know my own and my own know me" (10:11-14). What we have in this double metaphor of "gate" and "shepherd" is Jesus's guarantee that he cares for us, that entering his gate is to be saved, and that passing through him brings us to flourishing. And because we share an intimacy with him, we know how to follow him. What is striking in this passage is that three times Jesus says that he will die for his sheep. And further, the Father loves him for it. In Christ's sacrifice the Father's love for his Son and for us is made manifest. The cross will become a revelation of the Father's love.

Plus One: The Feast of the Dedication

The festival of the Dedication commemorates the rededication of the temple in 164 BCE. At the time, Palestine was ruled by the Syrian dynasty and its king Antiochus IV, who added to his title *Epiphanes* (divine manifestation). He had wanted to consolidate his empire by draconian means, including forbidding the practice of Judaism on penalty of death. Some Jews capitulated, even gladly, while most were sorely oppressed. In 167 BCE, Antiochus transferred the temple to Zeus and sacrificed to Zeus on an altar built over the altar of holocausts. This was known as the "desolating sacrilege" detailed in 1 Maccabees (cf. Dan 11:31). In the Maccabean revolt, Palestine eventually returned to Jewish control, the temple and most of Jerusalem as early 164 BCE. They rededicated the temple to Yahweh. Today this festival is known as Hanukkah. The celebration attends to several things: the great liberation by the Jewish army against a powerful foe; the apostasy of those who would abandon the faith; and God's ongoing care in restoring the temple, the visible sign of God's enduring presence among his people. "The feast of the Dedication . . . summoned the people to remain steadfast to the laws of their God and, by doing so, proclaim, 'Never again!' "[31]

John tells us that "Jesus was walking in the temple, in the portico of Solomon. So the Jews gathered around him and said to him, 'How long will you keep us in suspense? If you are the Messiah, tell us plainly.' Jesus answered, 'I have told you, and you do not believe. The works that I do in my Father's name testify to me; but you do not believe, because you do not belong to my sheep. My sheep hear my voice. I know them, and they follow me. I give them eternal life, and they will never perish' " (10:23-28). And then ultimately he proclaims, "The Father and I are one" (10:30). They wanted to stone him again for this blasphemy. There are really two issues here. The first is that insofar as Jesus is reticent to simply say, "I am the Messiah," it is because they would experience his message *from below* not *from above*; that is, they would only understand it on their own terms, not his.

The second issue is that, from Jesus's point of view, he has been perfectly clear, even redundant, about who he was. His image of the good shepherd whose flock hear him and follow him characterizes the authentic faith dynamic. Consider the repetition of themes so far: the true disciple "hears" his voice (eleven times), has eternal life (twelve times), follows Jesus (five times), and will never be lost (five times). Jesus's final affirmation also concludes what he has been teaching all along. He has come from his Father, does the work of his Father, is empowered to give life and to judge from his Father, and so on. "Can you say that the one whom the Father has sanctified and sent into the world is blaspheming because I said, 'I am God's Son'? If I am not doing the works of my Father, then do not believe me. But if I do them, even though you do not believe me, believe the works, so that you may know and understand that the Father is in me and I am in the Father" (10:36-38). Consider the narrative so far: On the sabbath, Jesus works as his Father works and has the authority to give life (chap. 5). At Passover, Jesus tells them he is the bread from heaven (chap. 6). At Tabernacles, Jesus tells them he is the living water, the light of the world, and the good shepherd who gives his life for his sheep (7:1–10:21). In these Jewish feasts, he personifies, fulfills, perfects, and transcends the significance of them all. And he does so because "the Father and I are one," and, "the Father is in me and I am in the Father." Just observe the works I do, he implores; just see the signs.[32] But those who reject him are like the sadly remembered apostates at the time of the original re-dedication of the temple. They do not keep faith. "Then they tried to arrest him again, but he escaped from their hands. He went away again across the Jordan to the place where John had been baptizing earlier, and he remained there" (10:39-40).

The Hour Has Come: The End of Jesus's Public Ministry (11:1–12:50)

Raising Lazarus

John tells us that, while he and his disciples were away, they got news that Martha and Mary's brother Lazarus was deathly ill. "But when Jesus heard it, he said, 'This illness does not lead to death; rather it is for God's glory, so that the Son of God may be glorified through it'" (11:4). After two days, he announces to his disciples that "Lazarus is dead. For your sake I am glad I was not there, so that you may believe. But let us go to him" (11:14-15). Given the strife Jesus had just caused and the proximity of Bethany to Jerusalem, this is an unnerving proposition. "Thomas, who was called the Twin, said to his fellow disciples, 'Let us also go, that we may die with him'" (11:16). Death is in the air.

When he arrives, Martha goes out to meet him. Hoping against hope, she appeals to Jesus. "Jesus said to her, 'Your brother will rise again.' Martha said to him, 'I know that he will rise again in the resurrection on the last day.' Jesus said to her, 'I am the resurrection and the life. Those who believe in me, even though they die, will live, and everyone who lives and believes in me will never die'" (11:23-26). John tells us that Mary approaches Jesus with other mourners. Jesus himself wept and, coming to the tomb, was "greatly disturbed" (11:35, 38). Then Jesus says to Martha: "Did I not tell you that if you believed, you would see the glory of God?" (11:40). Then Jesus prays to God: "Father, I thank you for having heard me. I knew that you always hear me, but I have said this for the sake of the crowd standing here that they may believe that you sent me." Then at his command, "Lazarus, come out!" the dead man was revived (11:43-44).

The resuscitation of Lazarus is not the central point of the narrative. The point is to reveal the glory of God so that his disciples, Martha, Mary, and the other mourners ("the Jews," v. 31) might believe that he is the resurrection and the life. And this is true even when there is suffering and death. The Last Day, the culmination of history, the Parousia or Second Coming, is not immediate or even imminent in John's Gospel, unlike in the Synoptic Gospels. Jesus does not challenge that Martha and Mary are suffering, and indeed he also weeps. What he does teach is that, even through physical death and suffering, he is the resurrection and the life. Sandra Schneiders remarks,

> Christian spirituality is neither escape from real life nor denial of its pain but a way of living that is transfigured, even now, by the resurrection and the life which is Jesus. . . . Jesus has not abolished final eschatology (some believers will die and Lazarus must eventually die again) but has given it a new dimension of depth, the experience of union with the risen Christ in this life, which constitutes the possession, here and now, of eternal life. . . . Jesus' revelation to Martha, however, is not a presentation of eschatological propositions but a self-disclosure calling for personal response. Faith at this point is not theological assent but personal spiritual transformation. "Do *you* believe this?" (11:26).[33]

Christian spirituality is not for the faint of heart. It is not meant to free us from suffering and loss or to redefine tragedies as though they are not so. A student once came to my office to talk about a family tragedy. One of her cousins accidently shot his brother dead while hunting. At one point she said, "Everything happens for a reason." I gently tried to steer her away from imagining a good here. Countless others at funerals try to comfort the bereaved with versions of "God needed her in heaven more than on earth." None of this is Christian. For Christians, tragedies, even the ultimate tragedy of death, are transformed but not unmoored from the human condition. "We are not asked not to weep, but only not to despair, for the one in whom we believe is our resurrection because he is our life."[34]

Many came to believe in Jesus through this sign (11:45), and the authorities in Jerusalem were alarmed. "What are we to do? This man is performing many signs. If we let him go on like this, everyone will believe in him, and the Romans will come and destroy both our holy place and our nation" (11:47-48). The high priest Caiaphas responds through the lens of *realpolitik*: "It is better for you to have one man die for the people than to have the whole nation destroyed" (11:50). Here he speaks prophetically as well about Jesus's mission, which he did not understand. "So from that day on they planned to put him to death. Jesus therefore no longer walked about openly among the Jews, but went from there to a town called Ephraim in the region near the wilderness; and he remained there with his disciples" (11:53-54). Death is in the air.

The Hour Has Come

The theme of death is prominent in chapter 11. There is obviously Lazarus's death (and raising). Thomas recognizes that Jesus will die, and he urges his brothers to go and die with him. And the chapter ends with plotting to kill Jesus rather than "the whole nation destroyed." Jesus knows he must withdraw for a time because of this; his *hour* had not yet come. Now it has arrived. Jesus returns to Bethany, "six days before the Passover," to a feast given by his friends Martha, Mary, and Lazarus. All four Gospels report that a woman anoints Jesus with expensive perfumed oil. In Matthew, this is performed by a woman who comes to Simon the leper's house; in Mark, simply "a woman"; and in Luke, "a woman of the city, a sinner." Now in John, this anointing comes from Mary: "Mary took a pound of costly perfume made of pure nard, anointed Jesus' feet, and wiped them with her hair. The house was filled with the fragrance of the perfume" (12:3). Judas balks at the waste. "Jesus said, 'Leave her alone. She bought it so that she might keep it for the day of my burial'" (12:7). It is as though he is already dead, a *fait accompli*.

The next day a crowd of people welcomes Jesus into Jerusalem. This is John's version of Palm Sunday. "So they took branches of palm trees and went out to meet him, shouting, 'Hosanna! Blessed is the one who comes in the name of the Lord—the King of Israel'" (12:13; cf. Ps 118:26-27). Seeing all this, "The Pharisees then said to one another, 'You see, you can do nothing. Look, the world has gone after him!'" (12:19). Then John tells us that some Greeks had come to the festival and wanted to see Jesus. Thus, his message is going beyond Palestinian Judaism and to the larger world. Jesus's response is profound and needs to be quoted fully.

> Jesus answered them, "The hour has come for the Son of Man to be glorified. Very truly, I tell you, unless a grain of wheat falls into the earth and dies, it remains just a single grain; but if it dies, it bears much fruit. Those who love their life lose it, and those who hate their life in this world will keep it for eternal life. Whoever serves me must follow me, and where I am, there will my servant be also. Whoever serves me, the Father will honor." (12:23-26)

We have seen the paradox of losing one's life to save it in all three previous Gospels, and so it is here. But Jesus adds more. A single lowly grain is not much. But if it *dies* and gets put into the ground— that is, is buried—it produces much. On our own and through our own resources, we simply have to admit to ourselves that we are not much. But to give our lives over to Christ is to be an active participant in his glory. Paul writes, "Do you not know that all of us who have been baptized into Christ Jesus were baptized into his death? Therefore we have been buried with him by baptism into death, so that, just as Christ was raised from the dead by the glory of the Father, so we too might walk in a newness of life" (Rom 6:3-4). If there is no *dying to ourselves*, then there will be no *living in him*; we become little more than walking ghosts. "Where I am, there will my servant be." Jesus continues: "'Now my soul is troubled. And what should I say—"Father, save me from this hour"? No, it is for this reason that I have come to this hour. Father, glorify your name. . . . Now is the judgment of this world; now the ruler of this world will be driven out. And I, when I am lifted up from the earth, will draw all people to myself.' He said this to indicate the kind of death he was to die" (12:27-28, 32-33).

As Jesus approaches his passion we find "his soul is troubled." This is a very human Jesus. Despite the *high Christology* in John's Gospel, and despite his long anticipated self-offering, and despite his assurance of its outcome, he is facing the most radical submission with all its implications of suffering and self-emptying. This is the human condition. It is a universally experienced human fact that love and suffering are intimately related. Jesus is being deepened by his obedience. Michael Buckley notes that "one way love becomes successively deeper is that, as it is challenged, it gathers to itself all its resources to withstand or contradict the forces that bear against it; as it faces opposition, it grows. Hebrews 5:8 actually speaks of Jesus as 'learning obedience through his sufferings.' "[35]

Many years ago a colleague told me that a young priest I once taught was assigned to his parish. He seemed dissatisfied but couldn't put his finger on why. I asked him about this priest's preaching, his service, his generosity, and so on. And he spoke positively about it all. "Then what's your problem with him?" I asked. He didn't know. Later that afternoon he stopped me in the hall: "Now I know why I'm bothered about him. He talks a huge game, but he just hasn't bled enough." What he was saying was that this young priest's confidence was unrelated to his experience; it was abstract. But my colleague did not say, "He's not experienced enough"; he said, "He hasn't *bled* enough." There is something about suffering that deepens us. I also recall living in a parish during a summer of seminary. My pastor, who loved me and mentored me, once said, "I think that you are really idealistic and earnest, but I don't think you have enough compassion. And this is probably because you haven't suffered enough." I reacted by asking him whether it would have been better if, say, I had an abusive father or alcoholic mother, rather than the wonderful, loving family I had. "No," he said, "I'm glad you had a great upbringing. But you can't have compassion until you suffer, and suffer deeply." I was unconvinced. Now, forty years later, I am *certain* that he is right. "One must learn from Jesus the meaning and possibilities, the strengths and the trust of living in obedient suffering without wavering in a fundamental confidence in the trustworthiness of God."[36] Jesus ends his teaching, "While you have the light, believe in the light, so that you may become children of the light" (12:36).

Jesus's Final Meal and Last Discourse (13:1–17:20)

The Synoptic Gospels place the Last Supper as the Passover or Seder Meal. This culminates Passover week and celebrates God's liberation of his people in the exodus and the subsequent covenant Israel made with God. As we have seen, it is in this context that Jesus proclaims a complete liberation through his new covenant. In John's Gospel, Jesus's final meal with his disciples was not a Passover meal. It was "before the festival of the Passover" (13:1), and Good Friday was "the day of Preparation for the Passover" (19:14, 31). John tells us that it was noon on Friday when Jesus was condemned to death (19:14), the very time Passover lambs were being ritually slaughtered in the temple. Jesus is the "Lamb of God who takes away the sin of the world" (1:29). Thus, we do not see in John the proclamation of the new covenant or the institution of the Eucharist. Rather, we find a lengthy discourse by the Lord and a long prayer to the Father. The only reference to the meal is Jesus's washing of his disciples' feet during the meal and a sharing of a morsel of bread dipped into wine, which he gives to Judas. After this, we experience his last discourse.

Last Supper:
Washing the Disciples' Feet and Teaching Those He Loved

John begins the narrative profoundly: "Now before the festival of the Passover, Jesus knew that his hour had come to depart from this world and go to the Father. Having loved his own who were in the world, he loved them to the end" (13:1). John's language is deft as "to the end" (*eis telos*) can refer to the end of his ministry or to the end of his life. *Telos* also means "fulfillment," "completion," or even "that which surpasses." Jesus loved them unto complete fulfillment. Jesus's *hour* is his death on the cross, the very thing that shows his ultimate love, the face of the Father as pure self-giving, and the paradoxical glory of God. Jesus loved them (us!) unto glory. "And during supper Jesus, knowing that the Father had given all things into his hands, and that he had come from God and was going to God, got up from the table. . . . Then he poured water into a basin and began to wash the disciples' feet" (13:2-5). Peter objects, "You will never wash my feet," to which Jesus answers, "Unless I wash you, you have no share in me" (13:6-8). "Do you know what I have done to you? You call me Teacher and Lord—and you are right, for that is what I am. So if I, your Lord and Teacher, have washed your feet, you also ought to wash one another's feet. For I have set you an example, that you also should do as I have done to you. Very truly, I tell you, servants are not greater than their master, nor are messengers greater than the one who sent them. If you know these things, you are blessed if you do them" (13:12-17).

There is much to unpack here. *Upodeigma*, which is translated as "an example," means more like "bring to light." Jesus, who *is* the light, is not simply attempting to pass on an ethical or moral example to follow. Rather, the nature of servanthood lies at the very heart of the Gospel. This foot washing expresses self-gift and intimate love. Jesus will later tell them that he no longer calls them servants but friends, "because a servant does not know what the master is doing; but I have called you friends, because I have made known to you everything that I have heard from my Father" (15:15). Buckley considers, "What gives such a mysterious influence of God its intelligibility, its urgency, its shape? It is the prior experience and awareness of having been touched—called, directed, loved, and cared for—by the Spirit of God. . . . This experience of prior care of Christ for us is the fundamental experience that makes any life of Christian ministry possible."[37] Acts of service can demonically morph into a kind of superiority or at least a debt that is owed. But acts of real love by someone who prefers another to oneself produces none of that. It only deepens the intimacy true friends have.[38]

John tells us that "Satan entered into him [Judas]. Jesus said to him, 'Do quickly what you are going to do'" (13:27). The other disciples imagine he was sent on an errand. Now Jesus is left with only faithful disciples; he tells them that he is about to leave them to return to the Father. "Where I am going, you cannot come. I give you a new commandment, that you love one another. Just as

I have loved you, you also should love one another" (13:33-34). This is no small challenge. It is hard enough to "love your neighbor as yourself." Now we are to love one another *as Jesus loves us.* St. Cyril of Alexandria, reflecting on this "new commandment" writes:

> *I give you a new commandment,* said Jesus: *love one another.* But how, we might ask, could he call this commandment new? . . . He showed the novelty of his command and how far the love he enjoined surpassed the old conception of mutual love by going on immediately to add: *Love one another as I have loved you.* . . . The law commanded people to love their brothers and sisters as they love themselves, but our Lord Jesus Christ loved us more than himself. He who was one in nature with God the Father and his equal would not have descended to our lowly estate, nor endured in his flesh such a bitter death for us, nor submitted to the blows given him by his enemies . . . nor, being rich, would he have become poor, had he not loved us far more than himself. It was indeed something new for love to go as far as that! . . . The Savior urges us to practice this love that transcends the law as the foundation of true devotion to God. He knew that only in this way could we become pleasing in God's eyes, and that it was by seeking the beauty of the love implanted in us by himself that we should attain to the highest blessings.[39]

Peter wants to know where Jesus is going, and Thomas wants to know the way there. "In my Father's house there are many dwelling places. . . . And if I go and prepare a place for you, I will come again and will take you to myself, so that where I am, there you may be also" (14:2-3). And to Thomas, "I am the way, and the truth, and the life. No one comes to the Father except through me" (14:6). And now Philip asks, "Lord, show us the Father, and we will be satisfied" (14:8). "Whoever has seen me has seen the Father. How can you say, 'Show us the Father'? Do you not believe that I am in the Father and the Father is in me?" (14:9-10).

Jesus must leave them to return to where he originally came from (1:1-2). There will be an in-between time from his leaving to his return to take us with him. This is the time of the church. It is during this protracted time that we must live in and through Jesus in a different way than when he was with us in his earthly ministry. Intimacy with God is through Jesus because he is the way, truth, and life, and knowing him is knowing the Father. The words he speaks are words of the Father and the deeds of Jesus are the works of the Father (14:10). "Believe me that I am in the Father and the Father is in me" (14:11). Francis Moloney writes, "Jesus not only announces who he is but also what he does."[40] St. Ambrose prays, "Yes, Lord Jesus, we do follow you, but we can only come at your bidding. No one can make the ascent without you, for you are our way, our truth, our life, our strength, our confidence, our reward. Be the way that receives us, the truth that strengthens us, the life that invigorates us."[41]

If Jesus is "going away" during this in-between time, what of us? "If you love me, you will keep my commandments. And I will ask the Father, and he will send you another Advocate, to be with you forever. This is the Spirit of truth. . . . The Advocate, the Holy Spirit, whom the Father will send in my name, will teach you everything, and remind you of all I have said to you" (14:15-17, 26). The term *paraklētos*, which is translated as "Advocate," can also be translated "Counselor" or "Guide." Thus, Jesus promises not to leave us orphaned or abandoned in this in-between time, but we will be led by the Holy Spirit. In this sense, the Holy Spirit will take over the role Jesus had. He is "another *paraklētos*" (14:16). The gift of the Holy Spirit, however, does not mean we lose Jesus. "Those who love me will keep my word, and my Father will love them, and we will come to them and make our home with them" (14:23). St. Bernard of Clairvaux: "It is necessary for a soul to grow and be enlarged until it is capable of containing God within itself. . . . It expands spiritually as it makes progress toward human perfection, which is measured by nothing less than the full stature of Christ, and so it grows into a temple sacred to the Lord."[42]

Thus, while being led by the Spirit, we can continue to have intimacy with both Father and Son. What we gain is the trinitarian *indwelling*. Jesus promises that we can be empowered to do even "greater works" than he (14:12). Such a claim seems impossible. And yet, as a church guided by the Holy Spirit and based on divine intimacy, we can heal, preach, and witness with our lives the kingdom of God and reveal the face of God as Jesus did, now throughout the world. We can be inspired and challenged by a famous poem attributed to St. Teresa of Avila:

Christ has no body but yours,
No hands, no feet on earth but yours,
Yours are the eyes with which he looks
Compassion on this world,
Yours are the feet with which he walks to do good,
Yours are the hands with which he blesses all the world.

The Final Discourse

Most biblical scholars see Jesus's last discourse and prayer to the Father as a series of teachings Jesus gave to his disciples during his last days among them. Throughout the Gospel of John there are "seams" that point to different sources John uses, including the chapters before us.[43] This makes for complicated reading with a good deal of redundancy, but it does not mean that these chapters are incoherent. Taken as a whole, they provide a lucid vision. What I intend here is a collection of Jesus's teachings in his final discourse and priestly prayer that I think will reveal this larger vision. Each passage is really its own meditation and ought to be treated as such.

1. I am the true vine, and my Father is the vinegrower. . . . Abide in me as I abide in you. Just as the branch cannot bear fruit by itself unless it abides in the vine, neither can you unless you abide in me. (15:1, 4)

2. As the Father has loved me, so I have loved you; abide in my love. If you keep my commandments, you will abide in my love, just as I have kept my Father's commandments and abide in his love. I have said these things to you so that my joy may be in you, and that your joy may be complete. (15:9-11)

3. If the world hates you, be aware that it hated me before it hated you. If you belonged to the world, the world would love you as its own. Because you do not belong to the world, but I have chosen you out of the world—therefore the world hates you. (15:18-19)

4. I have said these things to you to keep you from stumbling. They will put you out of the synagogues. Indeed, an hour is coming when those who kill you will think that by doing so they are offering worship to God. (16:1-2)

5. It is to your advantage that I go away, for if I do not go away, the Advocate will not come to you; but if I go, I will send him to you. . . . When the Spirit of truth comes, he will guide you into all the truth. (16:7, 13)

6. Very truly, I tell you, you will weep and mourn, but the world will rejoice; you will have pain, but your pain will turn into joy. . . . I will see you again, and your hearts will rejoice, and no one will take your joy from you. (16:20, 22)

7. I have said this to you, so that in me you may have peace. In the world you face persecution. But take courage; I have conquered the world! (16:33)

Jesus is talking directly to his disciples, but what he teaches is for the church at large as well. He will be with us, but in a different way than he was in his earthly ministry. The most important message is the imperative to always "abide" in him. Thus, he is available and present to us spiritually. With him, our lives are fruitful, and without him, there is nothing. But as important as this is, so is the peace he promises. Christ's peace is not a life without conflict. He regularly mentions in this discourse that standing up for his truth, the truth of the Father, is guaranteed to bring conflict (15:18-21; 16:1-2, 8-11, 20). The peace of Christ is that still, centered interior assurance of God's love and presence in our lives. This cannot be stolen, and it need not even be shaken. "Who will separate us from the love of Christ? . . . I am convinced that neither death, nor life, nor angels, nor rulers, nor things present, nor things to come, nor powers, nor height, nor depth, nor anything else in all creation, will be able to separate us from the love of God in Christ Jesus our Lord" (Rom 8:35, 38-39). "All that the Father has is mine" and "I have conquered the world" (John 16:15, 33). Jesus's final discourse is something like Matthew's Sermon on the Mount and Luke's Journey to Jerusalem; that is, it contains the heart of Jesus's spirituality and vision. In Jesus we encounter the fullness of divinity: we love because we are filled with divine love; we serve just as the Master serves. The indwelling of God not only constitutes our own glory but also creates unity and love within the church.[44]

Jesus's High Priestly Prayer

1. Father, the hour has come; glorify your Son so that the Son may glorify you, since you have given him authority over all people, to give eternal life to all whom you have given him. And this is eternal life, that they may know you, the only true God, and Jesus Christ whom you have sent. (17:1-3)

2. Holy Father, protect them in your name that you have given me, so that they may be one, as we are one. (17:11)

3. I ask not only on behalf of these, but also on behalf of those who will believe in me through their word, that they may all be one. As you, Father, are in me and I am in you, may they also be in us, so that the world may believe that you sent me. The glory that you have given me I have given them, so that they may be one, as we are one, I in them and you in me, that they may become completely one, so that the world may know that you have sent me and have loved them even as you have loved me. (17:20-23)

4. I made your name known to them, and I will make it known, so that the love with which you have loved me may be in them, and I in them. (17:26)

This is known as the *high priestly prayer* because Jesus acts as an intercessor for us. The Letter to the Hebrews frames Christ as holding the priesthood resembling that of Melchizedek from Genesis 14:18-20 and describes his eternal ministry: "But he holds his priesthood permanently, because he continues forever. Consequently he is able for all time to save those who approach God through him, since he always lives to make intercession for them" (Heb 7:24-25). This is indeed one long intercessory prayer. Jesus asks the Father to glorify him in his self-offering of love. This glory will be shared with those who love him. This love unites Jesus and the Father and Jesus and his disciples. We are ultimately called to union with God and even to live the divine life as God lives it, as a mutual indwelling. In describing the depth of intimacy possible, St. John of the Cross writes,

The movements of these divine flames [of love] . . . are not produced by the soul alone that is transformed in the flames of the

Holy Spirit, nor does the Holy Spirit produce them alone, but they are the work of both the soul and him. . . . Thus these movements of both God and the soul are not only splendors, but also glorifications of the soul. . . . A reciprocal love is thus actually formed between God and the soul, like a marriage union and surrender, in which the goods of both (the divine essence that each possesses freely by reason of the voluntary surrender between them) are possessed by both together.[45]

The Passion and the Glory (18:1–19:42)

The passion of Christ in the Synoptic Gospels highlights the horror of sin and the agony Jesus went through. This is Satan's imagined great feat: torturing and killing the Son of God. Jesus is willing to do whatever the Father desires but still asks that this *cup* be removed. Luke tells us that in the Garden his sweat became like great drops of blood. On the cross Matthew and Mark tell us that he cried out, "My God, my God, why have you forsaken me?" Jesus, taking on the sins of the world and the torturous ordeal of beatings, humiliations, scourging, and crucifixion, becomes an icon of what sin looks like and how it deforms the human condition. "Just as there were many who were astonished at him—so marred was his appearance, beyond human semblance, and his form beyond that of mortals. . . . He was despised and rejected by others; a man of suffering and acquainted with infirmity. . . . But he was wounded for our transgressions, crushed for our iniquities; upon him was the punishment that made us whole, and by his bruises we are healed" (Isa 52:14; 53:3, 5).

This is not how John takes us into the passion. Jesus has been preparing himself and his disciples for his *hour* where he will be "lifted up" and reveal the Father's glory as self-offering love.[46] Earlier, Jesus said, "And what should I say—'Father, save me from this hour'? No, it is for this reason that I have come to this hour. Father, glorify your name" (12:27-28). For John, Jesus is in total control of the situation. "For this reason the Father loves me, because I lay down my life in order to take it up again. No one takes it from me, but I lay it down of my own accord. I have power to lay it down, and I have power to take it up again" (10:17-18). Raymond Brown describes Jesus as "the sole master of his destiny."[47]

The Trials of the Face of God

Jesus takes his disciples to the Garden of Gethsemane, and Judas arrives with soldiers and temple police. " 'Whom are you looking for?' They answered, 'Jesus of Nazareth.' Jesus replied, 'I am he [*egō eimi*—I am]' " (18:4-5). John tells us that they stepped back and fell to the ground! Jesus is then led to Annas, the father-in-law of the high priest Caiaphas, while Peter waits in the courtyard. John takes us back and forth from Jesus to Peter. Contrary to Jesus's "I am" (*egō eimi*), we have Peter's denials of being a disciple of Jesus: "I am not" (*ouk eimi*). Jesus's interrogators get nothing out of him, who simply tells them that if they want to know his teachings they should ask everyone who heard them: "I have spoken openly to the world. . . . I have said nothing in secret" (18:20).

Then they take him to Pilate and the conversation is almost exclusively about being the "King of the Jews." His answer: "My kingdom is not from here [this world]" (18:36). Jesus is clearly the King, and he is clearly the Messiah, but he is not *their* kind of king or messiah. His kingdom is from above, not below. Just as there was a back and forth between Jesus and Peter at Annas's house, so too there is a back and forth in Jesus's trial with Pilate, this being *outside* and *inside* the Praetorium. It works as a *chiasm*, where a sequence is presented and then repeated in reverse order:

A: Outside—the charge: Jesus must die;

B: Inside—interrogation of kingship;

C: Outside—Pilate's declaration of Jesus's innocence;

D: Inside—Mocking the king;

C': Outside—Pilate's declaration of Jesus's innocence;

B': Inside—interrogation of power;

A': Outside—the verdict that Jesus must die.[48]

As we know from the Synoptic Gospels, Pilate has Jesus flogged and dressed in a purple—that is, royal—robe with a crown of thorns. Contra Matthew and Mark, these are not removed. He will go to Golgotha dressed as a king, even if the intention was pure mockery. In Jesus's dialogue with Pilate there are two poignant moments.

The first is when Jesus declares to him, " 'For this I was born, and for this I came into the world, to testify to the truth. Everyone who belongs to the truth listens to my voice.' Pilate asked him, 'What is truth?' " (18:37-38). Here is a governor who is charged by the Roman Empire to rule and adjudicate justice. And yet, he does not know what "truth" means. Later, after Pilate has had Jesus scourged and mockingly clothed in royalty, he announces to the crowd, "Here is the man!" (19:5). We typically know this as the Latin *Ecce homo*— Behold the man. If they had eyes to see, if they could recognize the icon of the Father; this would be to their salvation. But they do not recognize the Father in him. All they see is the threat to their own power and their perceptions of good and evil, of truth and falsehood. Francis Moloney sums the situation up elegantly:

> The account of Jesus before Pilate began with "the Jews" leading Jesus before the Roman authority. It concludes with the Roman authority handing Jesus over to them that they might lift up the Son of Man. The story has come full circle. Jesus has been proclaimed king both before and after his coronation, but the response of "the Jews" has been to choose false messianic hopes (Barabbas; Rome) and to seek the crucifixion of their king. The trial of Jesus before Pilate has really been a trial of Pilate and "the Jews." Both have been found wanting, and the irony of their failure is that Pilate hands Jesus over . . . to be crucified, to be lifted up.[49]

Jesus's response to Pilate that his kingdom does not belong to this world is an instance of the dualistic language of John's Gospel, where divisions are given sharp relief. Are you a child of God or of Satan? In the spirit or in the flesh? From above or from below? Of the light or of the darkness? Satan is depicted as the "ruler of this world" (12:31; 16:11). Such contrasts force us to make a decision on where we stand. The language is sharp, but it has to be understood rightly. This is not a decision between our bodies and souls or between the created world and heaven. "The earth is the LORD's and all that is in it, the world, and those who live in it" (Ps 24:1). Indeed, "God so loved the world that he gave his only Son" (John 3:16). The decision is about what rules our lives. To reject the *world* (worldliness) is to love creation; to renounce the *flesh* (disordered desires) is to honor the body; to reject the *ruler of this world* is to live here and now in the freedom of the children of God. The Catholic Church has a solemnity, Christ the King, instituted by Pope Pius XI. Pius wanted to address a world of suffering under the illusions of such false lords as consumerism, nationalism, exploitation, and secularism. In contrast to "strife and discord and hurrying along the road to ruin and death," Pius envisioned "a dominion by a King of Peace who came to reconcile all things, who came not to be ministered unto but to minister" with us "as instruments of justice unto God."[50]

To be a disciple of Jesus whose "kingdom does not belong to this world" is to embrace the world fully and lovingly. Vatican II's Pastoral Constitution on the Church in the Modern World asserts, "Far from diminishing our concern to develop this earth, the expectation of a new earth should spur us on, for it is here that the body of a new human family grows, foreshadowing in some way the age which is to come."[51] In Christ's kingdom we are called to consecrate and sanctify the world, offering it to God through the priesthood of Jesus Christ. The *world* is our altar, and our acts of love, compassion, and justice are the gifts we place on this altar, made sacred by God's presence within them and within us.[52]

The Lifting Up of the Son

John tells us that "Pilate also had an inscription written and put on the cross. It read, 'Jesus of Nazareth, the King of the Jews'" (19:19); this was written in Hebrew, Latin, and Greek, available to all in the Roman Empire. Thus, he unwittingly fulfills a prophecy of Jesus that when the Son is lifted up he would draw everyone to himself (11:49-52; 12:32). From the cross Jesus sees both his mother and the Beloved Disciple. In the narrative, we first meet the Beloved Disciple at the Last Supper. Many, including Raymond Brown, believe that this was a historical person, though not a formal member of the Twelve. But he also takes on a symbolic role as representing authentic discipleship and is even a symbol of the church itself.[53] "When Jesus saw his mother and the disciple whom he loved standing beside her, he said to his mother, 'Woman, here is your son.' Then he said to the disciple, 'Here is your mother.' And from that hour the disciple took her into his own home" (19:26-27). Following the symbolism here, Jesus gives Mary as mother to the church. Repetition is key to John's Gospel, and Jesus's "mother" is mentioned here in the space of three short verses five times. This is important. What we have is not only the foundation of the church as a new family under the cross of Christ; we also find the first of two gifts from Jesus on the cross. The second gift comes as Jesus dies: "When Jesus had received the wine, he said, 'It is finished.' Then he bowed his head and gave up his spirit" (19:30). On one level, we could say that John is simply telling us that Jesus died. We have a similar phrase: "gave up the ghost." But this cannot be John's primary intent here. The text literally reads, "gave over the spirit."[54] Jesus entrusts his Spirit to this newly formed family under the cross, a family of ideal discipleship and faithfulness.

John tells us that, because Friday night begins both sabbath and the Passover, they wanted to remove the bodies of the three men: Jesus and the thieves crucified with him. The thieves apparently were still alive, so the soldiers broke their legs, thus no longer allowing them an opportunity to breathe. "But when they came to Jesus and saw that he was already dead, they did not break his legs. Instead, one of the soldiers pierced his side with a spear, and at once blood and water came out" (19:33-34). So important is this event that the narrator breaks in to speak directly to the reader: "He who saw this has testified so that you also may believe. His testimony is true, and he knows that he tells the truth" (19:35). Certainly, blood and water could have come out of a corpse, so why the insistence? John continues, "These things occurred so that the scripture might be fulfilled, 'None of his bones shall be broken.' And again another passage of scripture says, 'They will look on the one whom they have pierced'" (19:36-37). The first reference comes directly from Psalm 34:20 and draws us to the insistence that the Passover lamb have none of its bones broken (Exod 12:46; Num 9:12). The second comes from Zechariah 12:10 describing the mourning of a defeated Israel.

Still, none of this actually addresses the blood and the water from Jesus's side. This is almost certainly a reference to the church's practice of the Eucharist and baptism. We must go back to Jesus during the Feast of Tabernacles when he proclaimed, "Let anyone who is thirsty come to me, and let the one who believes in me drink. As the scripture has said, 'Out of the believer's heart shall flow rivers of living water.' Now he said this about the Spirit, which believers in him were to receive; for as yet there was no Spirit, because Jesus was not yet glorified" (7:37-39). All this Jesus said before his *hour*. But now this is exactly his *hour*, and the Spirit (19:30) and the water (19:34) are poured out on the community. "God has been revealed in the pierced one, and this revelation of God continues in the flowing water and the spilled blood of Baptism and Eucharist as the worshiping community experiences the presence of the absent one."[55]

The Burial of Jesus of Nazareth, King of the Jews

Jesus had many disciples of various levels of understanding and commitment. One of them was "Joseph of Arimathea, who was a disciple of Jesus, though a secret one because of his fear of the Jews" (19:38); he got permission to take away Jesus's body. He is joined by Nicodemus, the Pharisee whose faith had been gradually increasing. He had come to Jesus at night and professed his belief that Jesus came from God (3:2) though he could not understand what the Lord was teaching. He was yet to be "born from above" (3:3). Later, we find him defending Jesus from being prejudged by other Pharisees, only to be ridiculed by them (7:50-52). Now he publicly joins Joseph of Arimathea in preparing Jesus's body for burial. He came, "bringing a mixture of myrrh and aloes, weighing about a hundred pounds. They took the body of Jesus and wrapped it with the spices in linen cloths" (19:39-40). This is an extraordinary amount of ointment, fit for a king. So, the paradoxes continue here. Jesus is proclaimed king by the people; Pilate mockingly clothes him in a royal robe and a crown of thorns; on the cross he founds his new community, blessing it with the Holy Spirit; and he is anointed with an extraordinary amount of oils and spices and then placed in a "new tomb." Jesus is buried as a king would be.

Jesus's whole ministry seems to have come to full completion: he showed the deepest of loves by offering his life; he has embraced his *hour* and been *lifted up*; he has revealed God as radical self-offering; he has given the gift of the Spirit to his newly forming church; he has been, ironically, proclaimed king. One might ask, if all this represents his glory and the glory of the Father, what is left regarding the resurrection? No, there is one thing more. "If Christ has not been raised, then our proclamation has been in vain and your faith has been in vain" (1 Cor 15:14).

The Resurrection: I Have Seen the Lord (20:1-29)

Throughout the Gospel of John we have seen various expressions of faith as well as degrees of faith. Perhaps only the faiths of the Beloved Disciple and Jesus's mother seem the purest. Mary's witness comes up in Jesus's first sign at Cana. Here hers is not an overwhelming realization or illumination. She simply had absolute confidence in her Son. The Beloved Disciple shows up late, but his presence is a constant. He is intimately at Jesus's side during the Last Supper and is the only male disciple mentioned at the foot of the cross. Every reference to him points to a constancy of trust. We see other representatives of resurrected faith in chapters 20–21.

Mary Magdalene first arrives at the tomb on Sunday at dawn, only to find the stone covering the tomb had been removed. But she does not know what this means. "They have taken the Lord out of the tomb, and we do not know where they have laid him" (20:2). Peter and the Beloved Disciple race to the tomb. Both look inside the tomb, but it is only the Beloved Disciple who sees what it means. "Then the other disciple, who reached the tomb first, also went in, and he saw and believed" (20:8). Mary apparently returned, for she was weeping in the garden. The risen Lord appeared to her, but she imagined he was the gardener. "Jesus said to her, 'Mary!' She turned and said to him in Hebrew, 'Rabbouni!' (which means Teacher). Jesus said to her, 'Do not hold on to me, because I have not yet ascended to the Father. But go to my brothers and say to them, 'I am ascending to my Father and your Father, to my God and your God.' Mary Magdalene went and announced to the disciples, 'I have seen the Lord'" (20:16-18).

Mary's path to full faith has seemingly been completed. She starts with wonderment. Then, with the call of her name, she knows Jesus is resurrected. Still, it is not complete. She wants to cling to him, but he has not yet ascended. Thus, his *hour* is still at hand, since his *hour* involves returning to the Father whence he originated. Further, Jesus, as he was known, can no longer be experienced in this way. In the resurrection accounts in all four Gospels, Jesus is certainly not a ghost or simply a resuscitated human being, as was Lazarus. He is both the same and not the same. This is why Mary did not at first recognize him, or in Luke why the disciples on the road to Emmaus did not realize it was he, or in Matthew why "some doubted." But with Mary's witness, she becomes the *apostola apostolorum*, the apostle to the apostles. Her faith is now complete. That very evening, John tells us, Jesus appeared to the disciples.

> "Peace be with you." After he said this, he showed them his hands and his side. Then the disciples rejoiced when they saw the Lord. Jesus said to them again, "Peace be with you. As the Father has sent me, so I send you." When he said this, he breathed on them and said to them, "Receive the Holy Spirit. If you forgive the sins of any, they are forgiven them; if you retain the sins of any, they are retained." (20:19-23)

The peace that constitutes intimacy with God, that peace so central to Jesus's final discourse, is the risen Lord's first word to them. In the context of this very intimacy of love, Jesus extends the gift of the Holy Spirit. Of course, we saw that Jesus "gave over the spirit" on the cross, this to Mary and the Beloved Disciple. But the gift of the Spirit is for the whole community, and Jesus's *hour* is still being extended until he ascends to the Father. The creation of humanity came about when "the LORD God formed man from the dust of the ground, and breathed into his nostrils the breath of life; and the man became a living being" (Gen 2:7). What we have now is a new creation. "So if anyone is in Christ, there is a new creation; everything old has passed away; see, everything has become new!" (2 Cor 5:17). Now, they are fully "born from above."

Thomas is not with them and refuses to believe that they have encountered the risen Lord. Thus, a week later (the eighth day) Jesus again appears and blesses them with peace. He then challenges Thomas, " 'Put your finger here and see my hands. Reach out your hand and put it in my side. Do not doubt but believe.' Thomas answered, 'My Lord and my God!' Jesus said to him, 'Have you believed because you have seen me? Blessed are those who have not seen and yet have come to believe' " (20:27-29). Now Thomas has come to the fullness of faith. He not only realizes that Jesus has risen but acknowledges him as one with the Father: My Lord and my God. Obviously, the underlying message is for Christians after the ascension who "have not seen and yet have come to believe."

The Beloved Disciple modeled this kind of faith. He believed when seeing the empty tomb but not yet having seen the risen Lord.

Now that the disciples are "born from above" they are empowered by Jesus and receive the authority to mediate divine forgiveness. This is not a biblical reference to the sacrament of penance, though that will be an expression of this empowerment. Rather, envision the disciples (all disciples of Jesus) manifesting his new, resurrected life and ministry in their own person. Jesus was breathing the spirit of his own mission and authority. Thomas should have been chastised, not because he was skeptical about accepting an outrageous claim with no evidence; rather, he *had* evidence but was blind to it. He should have seen that his companions were transformed from a group of people who were afraid, hopeless, guilty, and powerless into believers who were clear sighted, courageous, and hope filled; people who were forgiven and empowered to extend that forgiveness to others. Above all, their fear was replaced by the risen Lord's gift of peace. The evidence was overwhelmingly present to Thomas. He could have seen it in all that constitutes being a new creation in Christ.

Addendum: Jesus at the Sea of Tiberius (21:1-24)

The original Gospel of John seems to most scholars as having ended at 20:31. John tells us that Jesus did many other things, but these were written that you (the reader) "may come to believe that Jesus is the Messiah, the Son of God, and that through believing you may have life in his name" (20:31). Now we have yet another story as though there were not a conclusion: Jesus appears to seven disciples by the Sea of Tiberius (Sea of Galilee). They had gone fishing and caught nothing. Jesus calls out to them to cast again, and the haul is overwhelming. It is here that the Beloved Disciple says to Peter, "It is the Lord" (21:7). Jesus had prepared a breakfast of bread and fish over a charcoal fire. The last time Peter sat by a charcoal fire was at Annas's residence while denying Christ three times. Now three times Jesus asks him, "Simon son of John, do you love me more than these?" All three times Simon Peter assures Jesus that he does, even to his consternation that Jesus had to ask three times. At each assurance Jesus commands, "Feed my lambs," "Tend my sheep," "Feed my sheep." I assume that Peter was humiliated by the threefold question, particularly as he had failed Jesus on the night of his trial, and there is no reason to assume that he did not flee and thus was absent during Jesus's crucifixion.

Like many people, I am very conscious of my many failures over the years with the "shame of memories." I also go to Mass almost every day, and taking communion for me is both a humbling experience and also somewhat of a humiliation. I am not worthy, I know I am not worthy, and my history is littered with evidence that I am not worthy. It is an act of faith in a merciful God that I do so, hoping I do not "eat and drink judgment against" myself (1 Cor 11:29). I also see a value in this self-knowledge. It frees me somewhat from any delusions about myself, and it undermines my temptations to pride. More important, God's forgiveness of my sins helps me redefine myself as one living on God's mercy and love.

Jesus is charging Peter with a great deal. He is the first of the apostles and, as Jesus is the good shepherd, so Peter's role is to be so also. What Jesus wants from Peter is not a confession of sins, though that would be appropriate. Jesus wants Peter's love: Simon son of John, do you love me? "To accept the forgiveness of sins is to live habitually in the knowledge that even if there is or has been a vicious excision of goodness from our lives, God has continued faithfully to want us and to love us."[56] In Pope Benedict's encyclical *Deus Caritas Est* (God Is Love), he writes, "No longer is it a question, then, of a 'commandment' imposed from without and calling for the impossible, but rather of a freely-bestowed experience of love from within, a love which by its very nature must then be shared with others. Love grows through love. Love is 'divine' because it comes from God and unites us to God; through this unifying process it makes us a 'we' which transcends divisions and makes us one, until in the end God is 'all in all' (1 Cor 15:28)."[57]

Notes

Introduction

1. See Jerome's Commentary on Isaiah, cited in the Roman Office of Readings on his feast day, September 30.

2. *Dei Verbum*, nos. 2 and 4, in *Vatican Council II: Constitutions, Decrees, Declarations; The Basic Sixteen Documents*, ed. Austin Flannery (Collegeville, MN: Liturgical Press, 2014).

3. Peter Feldmeier, *The Christian Tradition: A Historical and Theological Introduction* (New York: Oxford University Press, 2017), 13.

4. I am broadly relying on Paul Ricoeur, *Interpretation Theory: Discourse and the Surplus of Meaning* (Fort Worth: Texas Christian University Press, 1976), and Paul Ricoeur, *Hermeneutics and the Human Sciences: Essays on Language, Action and Interpretation*, ed. and trans. John B. Thompson (Cambridge: Cambridge University Press, 1981).

5. Peter Feldmeier, *Christian Spirituality: Lived Expressions in the Life of the Church* (Winona, MN: Anselm Academic, 2015), 7.

6. Ewert Cousins, "Preface," in *Christian Spirituality*, ed. Bernard McGinn, John Meyendorff, and Jean Leclercq (New York: Continuum, 1988), 1:xiii.

7. Feldmeier, *Christian Spirituality*, 14–19.

8. Feldmeier, *Christian Spirituality*, 45–46.

9. Feldmeier, *Christian Spirituality*, 48–53, and *Christian Tradition*, 42–47.

10. Feldmeier, *Christian Spirituality*, 51.

11. Francis Moloney, *The Gospel of John* (Collegeville, MN: Liturgical Press, 1998), 5.

The Gospel of Matthew

1. See Matthew 2:5-6, 15, 17-18, 23; 4:14-16; 8:17; 12:17-21; 13:35; 21:4-5; 26:56; 27:9.

2. "A star shall come forth out of Jacob, and a scepter shall rise out of Israel" (Num 24:17).

3. This quip actually has several layers. That Herod had a stall of pigs while claiming to be Jewish shows his actual lack of Jewish observance. The obvious reference

is that he slaughtered more of his children than his swine, thus the pigs were safer. And then there is the pun: Better to be Herod's pig (*hus*) than his son (*huios*).

4. Pope Francis, Angelus, Feast of the Baptism of the Lord, January 12, 2014, in *The Gospel of Matthew: A Spiritual and Pastoral Reading* (Maryknoll, NY: Orbis Books, 2020), 36. Herein, this collection will only be cited by the occasion of Pope Francis's addresses.

5. Israel as God's son or children is a regular Old Testament theme. See Exodus 4:22-23; Deuteronomy 14:1; 32:6; 32:18-20; and Hosea 11:1.

6. The five are the *Sermon on the Mount* (5:3–7:27); the *Mission Sermon* (10:5-42); the *Sermon in Parables* (13:3-52); the *Sermon on the Church* (18:1-35); and the *Eschatological Sermon* (24:3–25:46).

7. John of the Cross, *The Dark Night* 12.4, in *The Collected Works of Saint John of the Cross*, trans. Kieran Kavanaugh and Otilio Rodriguez, rev. ed. (Washington, DC: ICS Publications, 1991).

8. John of the Cross, *Dark Night* 13.3.

9. Pope Francis, Homily, Solemnity of All Saints, November 1, 2015.

10. *Lumen Gentium*, no. 31, in *Vatican Council II: Constitutions, Decrees, Declarations; The Basic Sixteen Documents*, ed. Austin Flannery (Collegeville, MN: Liturgical Press, 2014).

11. Gerhard Lohfink, *The Our Father: A New Reading*, trans. Linda Maloney (Collegeville, MN: Liturgical Press, 2019), 6–7.

12. This is no isolated theme: "Therefore I tell you, the kingdom of God will be taken away from you and given to a people that produces the fruits of the kingdom" (21:43).

13. Pope Francis, Morning Meditation, Chapel of Domus Sanctae Marthae, "Founded on Rock," December 4, 2014.

14. See also Psalm 107:23-29, where God stills the waters, and Psalm 74:23-29, where God crushes the heads of Leviathan.

15. Francis continues, "Mercy first means treating the wounds. When someone is wounded, he needs immediate treatment, not tests for such things as cholesterol level and glucose tolerance. . . . There is a wound." Address to the Parish Priests of the Diocese of Rome, March 6, 2014.

16. Pope Francis, "*Introduzione*," in *Cambiamento (Le parole di Papa Francesco, 19)* (Milan: Corriere della Sera, 2014), 5–13.

17. Gerhard Lohfink, *The Forty Parables of Jesus*, trans. Linda Maloney (Collegeville, MN: Liturgical Press Academic, 2021), 53.

18. We see this in 1 Enoch 56:8, an influential intertestamental text, as well as Revelation 11:7; 17:8.

19. John Paul II, Homily at Belo Horizonte, July 1, 1980, cited by Francis Fernandez, *In Conversation with God*, 7 vols. (London: Scepter, 2000), 4:443.

20. Deut. Rab. 3.17. See *Jewish Annotated New Testament*, ed. Amy-Jill Levine and Marc Zvi Brettler, 2nd ed. (Oxford: Oxford University Press, 2017), 42.

21. Raymond Brown, *An Introduction to the New Testament* (New York: Doubleday, 1997), 194.

22. *Lumen Gentium*, nos. 39–40.

23. Amy-Jill Levine, *Short Stories by Jesus* (New York: HarperOne, 2014), 216.

24. Lohfink, *Forty Parables*, 92–93.

25. See Jeremiah 25:15; Lamentations 4:21; Isaiah 51:17; Habakkuk 2:15-16; and Psalm 75:8.

26. Daniel Harrington, *The Gospel of Matthew* (Collegeville, MN: Liturgical Press, 2007), 295.

27. St. Bonaventure, *The Tree of Life*, cited in Father Gabriel of St. Mary Magdalen, *Divine Intimacy*, 4 vols. (San Francisco: Ignatius Press, 1987), 2:106.

28. See Isaiah 62:4-5; Ezekiel 16:8-14; and Hosea 2:16-20.

29. See also Revelation 3:4–4:4; 6:11; 19:8; 22:14.

30. Here Jesus cites first Deuteronomy 6:5 and then Leviticus 19:18.

31. *Talmud Shabbat* 31a, cited in *The Talmud: Selected Writings*, trans. Ben Zion Bokser (New York: Paulist Press, 1989), 87.

32. Daniel Harrington and James Keenan, *Jesus and Virtue Ethics: Building Bridges between New Testament Studies and Moral Theology* (Lanham, MD: Sheed and Ward, 2002), 84–85.

33. Pope Francis, Angelus, October 26, 2014.

34. See, for example, Isaiah chapters 5, 10, 28, 30, 31; Amos 2:4-8; 4:6–5:6; 6:1-8; and Micah 2:1-2.

35. *Talmud Yoma* 72b in Levine and Brettler, *Jewish Annotated New Testament*, 23–24.

36. Thomas Merton, *New Seeds of Contemplation* (New York: New Directions, 1961), 21.

37. We see apocalyptic texts in the book of Daniel, the Dead Sea Scrolls, the Sibylline Oracles, 1 and 2 Baruch, 2 Enoch, the Assumption of Moses, the Book of Jubilees, the Testament of Benjamin, and the Psalms of Solomon. In the Christian tradition, there is the book of Revelation, which obviously made it into the New Testament. But there is also the Apocryphon of James, the Apocryphon of John, the Apocalypse of Paul, the First Apocalypse of James, the Second Apocalypse of James, the Apocalypse of Adam, and the Apocalypse of Peter.

38. See 1 Enoch 99:4-7; Jubilees 23; Sibylline Oracles 3:796–808; 4 Esdras 4:51; 8:63–9:6; and 2 Baruch 25-27. In 2 Ezra 9:3-4 we read, "There shall appear in the world earthquakes, tumult of peoples, intrigues of nations, wavering of leaders, confusion of princes." See Harrington, *Matthew*, 334.

39. See Isaiah 62:4-5; Jeremiah 2:2; Ezekiel 16:6-8; and Hosea 2:19-20.

40. See John 3:29; 2 Corinthians 11:2; Ephesians 5:21-33; and Revelation 21:2, 9; 22:17.

41. T. S. Eliot, *Four Quartets* (New York: Harcourt Brace Jovanovich, 1971), 59.

42. Think of this as both real and symbolic. By anointing his body, this really does seem to anticipate a preburial practice. Initially, though, Matthew says that she anointed his head, which is how kings were anointed when they took office. Here the kingship of Jesus, his being the Messiah, i.e., *anointed*, is united to his sacrificial death.

43. This may be a symbolic number. Zechariah acted as a shepherd to a doomed flock in imitation of God's dooming his people for faithlessness. Zechariah's pay was thirty shekels of silver, which he put into the treasury of the temple (Zech 11:12). Thirty pieces of silver is also the amount paid to a slave owner if his slave is gored by another's ox (Exod 21:32).

44. Raymond Brown, Joseph Fitzmyer, and Roland Murphy, eds., *New Jerome Biblical Commentary* (Englewood Cliffs, NJ: Prentice-Hall, 1990), 670.

45. See Genesis 9:4; Leviticus 17:10-14; and Deuteronomy 12:23-24.

46. Recall his rebukes: "Then he began to reproach the cities in which most of this deeds of power had been done, because they did not repent. 'Woe to you, Chorazin! Woe to you, Bethsaida!'" (11:20-21).

47. Week Three, Second Contemplation: *From the Last Supper to the Agony in the Garden*. See *The Spiritual Exercises of St. Ignatius*, trans. and ed. Louis J. Puhl (Chicago: Loyola Press, 1951), 83–84.

48. Two witnesses were necessary for a conclusive judgment of guilt. See Deuteronomy 19:55.

49. The great Jewish theologian and philosopher Philo describes Pilate's personality as "naturally inflexible, a blend of self-will and restlessness." Philo also charged him with briberies, insults, theft, cruelty, and executions without trial. See Harrington, *Matthew*, 391–92.

50. There is no extrabiblical text that references this practice, but amnesties on special occasions did sometimes happen in the ancient Roman world. See *New Jerome Biblical Commentary*, 671.

51. Pope Francis, "*Croce e senso bellico della vita*," in *Pace (Le parole di Papa Francesco, 5)* (Milan: Corriere della Sera, 2014), 31–46.

52. See Daniel 12:2 as well as John 11:23-26.

53. *Prayer of St. Bonaventure*, cited in Fernandez, *Conversation with God*, 2:289.

54. Dietrich Bonhoeffer, *The Cost of Discipleship* (London: SCM Press, 2015), 4.

55. Peter Feldmeier, *Christian Spirituality: Lived Expressions in the Life of the Church* (Winona, MN: Anselm Academic, 2015), 179.

The Gospel of Mark

1. John Donahue and Daniel Harrington, *The Gospel of Mark* (Collegeville, MN: Liturgical Press, 2002), 65.

2. Francis Watson, *The Fourfold Gospel: A Theological Reading of the New Testament Portraits of Jesus* (Grand Rapids, MI: Baker Academic, 2016), 54.

3. We see this in 1 Enoch 93:1-10; 91:12-17; and the Assumption of Moses 10. See Raymond Brown, Joseph Fitzmyer, and Roland Murphy, eds., *New Jerome Biblical Commentary* (Englewood Cliffs, NJ: Prentice-Hall, 1990), 599–600.

4. See Robert Putnam and David Campbell, *American Grace: How Religion Divides and Unites Us* (New York: Simon & Schuster, 2010).

5. Gerhard Lohfink, *Jesus of Nazareth: What He Wanted, Who He Was*, trans. Linda Maloney (Collegeville, MN: Liturgical Press, 2012), 30–31.

6. Jesus heals the Gerasene demoniac in 5:1-20, the Syrophoenician's daughter in 7:24-30, and the boy with an unclean spirit in 9:14-29.

7. Paul Achtemeier, "Invitation to Mark," in *Invitation to the Gospels* (New York: Paulist Press, 2002), 126–27. Interestingly, in the noncanonical Testament of Moses (10.1) the messianic age is one where Satan will be finally conquered and diseases cured. See Donahue and Harrington, *Mark*, 84.

8. See Exodus 34:6-7; Isaiah 43:25; 44:22.

9. See Isaiah 35:6; Jeremiah 31:8; Micah 4:6; and Zephaniah 3:19.

10. Donahue and Harrington, *Mark*, 104.

11. See also Jeremiah 2:2; 3:1, 14; Ezekiel 16:8-21; and Hosea 2:2-7.

12. This will be their charge against him when he is condemned to death (14:64).

13. This is an unusual name for the equivalent of Satan and probably goes back to the idolatry in ancient Canaanite worship.

14. John of the Cross, *The Dark Night* 1.3.1, in *The Collected Works of St. John of the Cross*, trans. Kieran Kavanaugh and Otilio Rodriguez, rev. ed. (Washington, DC: ICS Publications, 1991).

15. Teresa of Avila, *The Way of Perfection* 19.2, in *The Collected Works of St. Teresa of Avila*, trans. and ed. Kieran Kavanaugh and Otilio Rodriguez, vol. 2 (Washington, DC: ICS Publications, 1980).

16. Gregory the Great, *Forty Gospel Homilies*, cited in *Journey with the Fathers: Commentaries on the Sunday Gospels, Year A*, ed. Edith Barnecut (Hyde Park, NY: New City Press, 1994), 106–7.

17. Chrysostom was commenting on this same parable in Matthew's Gospel. See Chrysostom, *Commentary on Gospel of Matthew*, cited in Father Gabriel of St. Mary Magdalen, *Divine Intimacy*, 4 vols. (San Francisco: Ignatius Press, 1987), 3:116.

18. Pope Francis, Apostolic Exhortation, *Evangelii Gaudium*, nos. 278–79, https://www.vatican.va/content/francesco/en/apost_exhortations/documents/papa-francesco_esortazione-ap_20131124_evangelii-gaudium.html.

19. See Psalms 18:16; 69:2, 14-15.

20. *New Jerome Biblical Commentary*, 607.

21. Francis Fernandez, *In Conversation with God*, 7 vols. (London: Scepter, 2000), 3:638–39.

22. Donahue and Harrington, *Mark*, 178.

23. Peter Feldmeier, "Strength in Weakness," *America Magazine*, July 2, 2012, 30.

24. *Erāmos*, literally "desert," helps us to connect this feeding to God's feeding of Israel with manna in the desert.

25. *Dote* (give) *autois* (to them) *umeis* (yourselves) *phagein* (to eat).

26. See Josephus, *Antiquities* 13.297, cited in *The Pharisees*, ed. Joseph Sievers and Amy-Jill Levine (Grand Rapids, MI: Eerdmans, 2021), 56.

27. This comes from two of Pope Francis's reflections: "Two Identity Cards," Morning Meditation, February 10, 2015, and Angelus, September 2, 2018.

28. Peter Feldmeier, "It's About Holiness," *America Magazine*, August 27, 2012, 29.

29. See 1 Samuel 17:43; Isaiah 56:10-11; Matthew 7:6; 2 Peter 2:22; Philippians 3:2; and Revelation 22:15.

30. See Deuteronomy 18:20-22; 2 Kings 20:8-9; Isaiah 7:11-14; 55:13; and Ezekiel 12:11; 24:27.

31. Exodus 10:1, 20, 27; 11:10; 14:8; Ezekiel 3:7; 11:19. See Donahue and Harrington, *Mark*, 252.

32. Vincent Pizzuto, *Contemplating Christ: The Gospels and the Interior Life* (Collegeville, MN: Liturgical Press, 2018), 38.

33. Matthew has John *as* Elijah in 11:14; and Luke has John "with the spirit and power of Elijah" (1:17).

34. Donahue and Harrington, *Mark*, 273.

35. Pope Francis, Angelus, Second Sunday of Lent, March 16, 2014.

36. Matt Baglio, *The Rite: The Making of a Modern Exorcist* (London: Pocket Books, 2010), 175–92.

37. William Barry, *God and You: Prayer as a Personal Relationship* (New York: Paulist Press, 1987), 72–73.

38. Peter Feldmeier, "Standard Thinking," *America Magazine*, September 10, 2012, 38.

39. Deuteronomy 24:1-14; Joshua 22:8; Isaiah 61:6; and Wisdom 8:18.

40. Pope Francis, Angelus, October 11, 2015.

41. John of the Cross, *Collected Works*, 111.

42. John of the Cross, *Living Flame of Love* 3.10, in *The Collected Works of St. John of the Cross*, trans. Kieran Kavanaugh and Otilio Rodriguez, rev. ed. (Washington, DC: ICS Publications, 1991).

43. *New Jerome Biblical Commentary*, 619.

44. John Barton and John Muddiman, eds., *Oxford Bible Commentary* (Oxford: Oxford University Press, 2001), 909.

45. Josephus, *Josephus: The Essential Works*, trans. and ed. Paul Maier (Grand Rapids, MI: Kregel Publications, 1988), 265–66.

46. See Daniel 12:2; 2 Maccabees 7:9, 14, 29; and Wisdom 3:1-7.

47. Peter Feldmeier, "Love Grounds All," *America Magazine*, October 29, 2012, 31.

48. G. E. H. Palmer, Philip Sherrard, and Kallistos Ware, trans. and eds., *The Philokalia*, vol. 1 (London: Faber & Faber, 1979), 92.

49. See Isaiah 1:17, 23; Jeremiah 7:6; Ezekiel 22:7; and Zechariah 7:10.

50. See, for example, Jubilees, 1 Enoch, 4 Ezra, and 2 Baruch.

51. NRSV reads "like a human being," but most translations have it "like a Son of Man."

52. Peter Feldmeier, "Apocalyptic Vision," *America Magazine*, November 12, 2012, 31.

53. Cited in Donahue and Harrington, *Mark*, 400.

54. See also Isaiah 51:17 and Ezekiel 23:32-34.

55. Gerhard Lohfink, *No Irrelevant Jesus: On Jesus and the Church Today*, trans. Linda Maloney (Collegeville, MN: Liturgical Press, 2014), 101–2.

56. Lohfink, *No Irrelevant Jesus*, 99.

57. Lohfink, *Jesus of Nazareth*, 265.

58. Patrick Hartin, *Exploring the Spirituality of the Gospels* (Collegeville, MN: Liturgical Press, 2011), 37.

59. Donahue and Harrington, *Mark*, 414.

60. Jesus is identifying himself according to Daniel's vision in 7:13-14.

61. Donahue and Harrington, *Mark*, 445–46.

62. Donahue and Harrington, *Mark*, 446.

63. Cited in Donahue and Harrington, *Mark*, 428.

64. Donahue and Harrington, *Mark*, 429.

65. Venantius Fortunatus, "Sing, My Tongue, the Glorious Battle," trans. John Mason Neal (1818–1866), https://hymnary.org/hymn/GG2013/225.

The Gospel of Luke

1. Luke Timothy Johnson, *Living Jesus: Learning the Heart of the Gospel* (New York: HarperSanFrancisco, 1999), 161–63.

2. Luke Timothy Johnson, *The Gospel of Luke* (Collegeville, MN: Liturgical Press, 1991), 39.

3. The presence or work of the Holy Spirit is mentioned in Acts almost fifty times.

4. Raymond Brown, Joseph Fitzmyer, and Roland Murphy, eds., *New Jerome Biblical Commentary* (Englewood Cliffs, NJ: Prentice-Hall, 1990), 685.

5. Pope Francis, Angelus, December 13, 2015, in *The Gospel of Luke: A Spiritual and Pastoral Reading* (Maryknoll, NY: Orbis Books, 2021), 36. Herein, references from this collection will only be cited by the occasion of Pope Francis's addresses.

6. John Barton and John Muddiman, eds., *Oxford Bible Commentary* (Oxford: Oxford University Press, 2001), 932.

7. See also Exodus 9:29; Deuteronomy 10:14; Psalm 50:12; and 1 Corinthians 10:26.

8. See Gregory of Nazianzen, Homily 40, cited in *Journey with the Fathers, Year A*, ed. Edith Barnecut (Hyde Park, NY: New City Press, 1992), 37.

9. Johnson, *Luke*, 75.

10. See Luke 1:77; 3:3; 5:20; 24:47.

11. Brendan Byrne, *The Hospitality of God: A Reading of Luke's Gospel*, rev. ed. (Collegeville, MN: Liturgical Press, 2015), 60.

12. John Paul II, February 6, 1983, cited in Francis Fernandez, *In Conversation with God*, 7 vols. (London: Scepter, 2000), 3:236. I have adjusted the text for inclusivity.

13. John Henry Newman, *Meditations on Christian Doctrine* 1:2, cited in Father Gabriel of St. Mary Magdalen, *Divine Intimacy*, 4 vols. (San Francisco: Ignatius Press, 1987), 1:236.

14. Byrne, *Hospitality of God*, 70.

15. *New Jerome Biblical Commentary*, 695.

16. See Luke 4:18; 7:22; 14:13, 21; 16:20-22.

17. Gustavo Gutierrez, *We Drink from Our Own Wells: The Spiritual Journey of a People* (Maryknoll, NY: Orbis Books, 1983), 125.

18. John's ministry far outlasted John himself. In Acts, Paul discovers John's disciples as far away as Ephesus (see Acts 19:1).

19. See Isaiah 26:19; 25:5; 61:1.

20. Byrne, *Hospitality of God*, 85.

21. Pope Francis, General Audience, August 9, 2017.

22. Gerhard Lohfink, *The Forty Parables of Jesus*, trans. Linda Maloney (Collegeville, MN: Liturgical Press, 2021), 188.

23. Lohfink, *Forty Parables of Jesus*, 188.

24. Johnson, *Luke*, 113.

25. Johnson, *Luke*, 155.

26. John of the Cross, *Living Flame of Love* 1.19, in *The Collected Works of St. John of the Cross*, trans. Kieran Kavanaugh and Otilio Rodriguez, rev. ed. (Washington, DC: ICS Publications, 1991).

27. Luke reminds the reader a dozen times that he is on the way to Jerusalem.

28. Johnson, *Luke*, 164–65.

29. Byrne, *Hospitality of God*, 109.

30. Lohfink, *Forty Parables of Jesus*, 119.

31. Amy-Jill Levine, *Short Stories by Jesus* (New York: HarperOne, 2014), 81.

32. Origen, *On Luke's Gospel*, cited in *Journey with the Fathers: Commentaries on the Sunday Gospels, Year C*, ed. Edith Barnecut (Hyde Park, NY: New City Press, 1994), 99.

33. Emerson Powery, *The Good Samaritan: Luke 10 for the Life of the Church* (Grand Rapids, MI: Baker Academic, 2022), 155.

34. Elizabeth of the Trinity, *Letter* 133, February 24, 1903, cited in Father Gabriel, *Divine Intimacy*, 3:138.

35. Pope John Paul II, Homily, July 27, 1980, cited in Fernandez, *Conversation with God*, 4:239.

36. *New Jerome Biblical Commentary*, 703.

37. Pope Francis, Angelus, July 24, 2016.

38. Pope John Paul II, cited in Fernandez, *Conversation with God*, 4:241.

39. Byrne, *Hospitality of God*, 126–27.

40. Johnson, *Luke*, 201.

41. Pope Francis, *Laudato Si'*, no. 223, https://www.vatican.va/content/francesco /en/encyclicals/documents/papa-francesco_20150524_enciclica-laudato-si.html.

42. Johnson, *Luke*, 209.

43. Pope Francis, Angelus, August 18, 2013.

44. Consider other claims of Paul: Christ's cross leads to "justification and life for all" (Rom 5:18); God plans to "be merciful to all" (Rom 11:32); God will "unite all things in him" (Eph 1:10); God reconciles all things to himself (Col 1:19-20); and all will be made subject to God so that "God may be all in all" (1 Cor 15:20-29).

45. See Matthew 7:13-14; 10:28; 13:36-43. The ancient mind understood destruction not as eternal torment but *actual* destruction.

46. Byrne, *Hospitality of God*, 138–39.

47. Francis de Sales, *Introduction to the Devout Life*, trans. and ed. John Ryan (New York: Image Books, 1989), 135.
48. G. E. H. Palmer, Philip Sherrard, and Kallistos Ware, trans. and eds., *The Philokalia*, vol. 3 (London: Faber & Faber, 1984), 239.
49. Fernandez, *Conversation with God*, 4:514.
50. *Oxford Bible Commentary*, 947.
51. Robert Karris, "Invitation to Luke," in *Invitation to the Gospels* (New York: Paulist Press, 2002), 276.
52. Lohfink, *Forty Parables of Jesus*, 82.
53. Gerald O'Collins, *Jesus: A Portrait* (Maryknoll, NY: Orbis Books, 2008), 115–19.
54. O'Collins, *Jesus*, 95–97.
55. Lohfink, *Forty Parables of Jesus*, 177.
56. Pope John Paul II, General Audience, July 28, 1999.
57. Some ancient manuscripts read, "I saw one like a human being," but the Septuagint, which the evangelists relied on, has it literally as "Son of Man."
58. Cited in Father Gabriel, *Divine Intimacy*, 4:160.
59. Johnson, *Luke*, 312.
60. Johnson, *Luke*, 318.
61. Pope Francis, Homily for the Solemnity of Our Lord Jesus Christ, King of the Universe, November 20, 2016.
62. This was just as Jesus did in feeding the five thousand (9:16) and in the Last Supper (22:19).
63. See Acts 2:42, 46; 20:7.

The Gospel of John

1. The specified *signs* are: (1) turning water into wine (2:1-11); (2) healing a royal official's son (4:46-54); (3) healing the paralyzed man at the pool (5:1-15); (4) feeding the five thousand (6:1-15); (5) walking on the water (6:16-21); (6) healing the blind man (9:1-41); and (7) raising Lazarus from the dead (11:1-44).
2. Augustine, *Harmony of the Evangelists*, cited in Francis Watson, *The Fourfold Gospel: A Theological Reading of the New Testament Portraits of Jesus* (Grand Rapids, MI: Eerdmans, 2016), 94.
3. Stephen J. Binz, *Panorama of the Bible* (Collegeville, MN: Liturgical Press, 2016), 47.
4. Luke Timothy Johnson, *Living Jesus: Learning the Heart of the Gospel* (New York: HarperSanFrancisco, 1999), 182.
5. Francis J. Moloney, *The Gospel of John*, ed. Daniel J. Harrington (Collegeville, MN: Liturgical Press, 1998), 40.
6. Moloney, *John*, 41.
7. Around the time of Jesus there were Jewish miracle workers, such as Hone the "circle-drawer" and Hanina ben Dosa, both referred to as "Son of God."

8. In Revelation 19:7 we find: "Let us rejoice and exalt and give him the glory, for the marriage of the Lamb has come, and his bride has made herself ready."

9. Demetrius R. Dumm, *A Mystical Portrait of Jesus: New Perspectives on John's Gospel* (Collegeville, MN: Liturgical Press, 2001), 110.

10. Abraham Joshua Heschel, *The Sabbath: Its Meaning for Modern Man* (New York: Farrar, Straus and Giroux, 1951), 87–88.

11. Moloney, *John*, 170.

12. Consider Isaiah's denunciation of such presumption: "I will ascend to the tops of the clouds, I will make myself like the Most High" (Isa 14:14). Or Ezekiel's denunciation: "You have said, 'I am a god; I sit in the seat of the gods' . . . yet you are but a mortal, and no god" (Ezek 28:2).

13. Moloney, *John*, 171.

14. See Exodus 12:15-20; 23:14-15; and Leviticus 23:6-8.

15. Moloney, *John*, 212.

16. Moloney, *John*, 222.

17. Raymond Brown, *The Gospel According to John*, 2 vols. (Garden City, NY: Doubleday, 1966, 1970), 1:292–93, cited in Dumm, *A Mystical Portrait*, 122.

18. Moloney, *John*, 224.

19. This section is adapted from Peter Feldmeier, *The Christian Tradition: A Historical and Theological Introduction* (New York: Oxford University Press, 2017), 84–85.

20. Irenaeus of Lyons, *Against Heresies* 4.17.5–18.5, in *The Ante-Nicene Fathers*, ed. Alexander Roberts and James Donaldson, rev. ed. (Edinburgh: T & T Clark, 1996).

21. See Philadelphians, no. 4; Smyrnaeans, no. 6; and Ephesians, no. 20, in *The Apostolic Fathers*, trans. and ed. Michael Holmes, 3rd ed. (Grand Rapids, MI: Baker Academic, 2006).

22. Justin Martyr, First Apology, chap. 67, in *The Ante-Nicene Fathers*.

23. Augustine, *Confessions* 6.10, trans. Henry Chadwick (Oxford: Oxford University Press, 1991), 123–24.

24. See Deuteronomy 16:13; Leviticus 23:34; and Nehemiah 8:13-19.

25. Michael Buckley, *What Do You Seek?: The Questions of Jesus as Challenge and Promise* (Grand Rapids, MI: Eerdmans, 2016), 41–42.

26. Buckley, *What Do You Seek*, 49–50.

27. C. S. Lewis, *Mere Christianity* (New York: Macmillan, 1952; San Francisco: HarperSanFrancisco, 2001), 223–25.

28. Johnson, *Living Jesus*, 54.

29. Psalm 23:1; Isaiah 40:11; Jeremiah 31:10; and Sirach 18:13.

30. Jeremiah 3:15; 23:5; Ezekiel 34:23-24; and Micah 5:2-3.

31. Moloney, *John*, 314.

32. Moloney, *John*, 318.

33. Sandra Schneiders, *Written That You May Believe: Encountering Jesus in the Fourth Gospel*, rev. ed. (New York: Herder & Herder, 2003), 179–80.

34. Schneiders, *Written That You May Believe*, 183.

35. Buckley, *What Do You Seek*, 108.

36. Buckley, *What Do You Seek*, 110.

37. Buckley, *What Do You Seek*, 28–29.

38. Schneiders, *Written That You May Believe*, 194.

39. Cyril of Alexandria, *On John's Gospel*, cited in *Journey with the Fathers: Commentaries on the Sunday Gospels, Year C*, ed. Edith Barnecut (Hyde Park, NY: New City Press, 1994), 56–57.

40. Moloney, *John*, 395.

41. Ambrose, *Death as a Blessing*, cited in *Journey with the Fathers: Commentaries on the Sunday Gospels, Year A*, ed. Edith Barnecut (Hyde Park, NY: New City Press, 1994), 64–65.

42. Bernard of Clairvaux, *On the Song of Songs*, cited in Barnecut, *Journey with the Fathers, Year C*, 59.

43. Here are some examples: In chapter 2 we have the first sign, and chapter 4 we have the second sign, but in between people believed in Jesus because they saw the signs he was doing (2:23). In 2:23 Jesus is in Jerusalem until 3:21. But in 3:22 we read that Jesus then went into the land of Judea (where he already was). In 5:1 Jesus is in Jerusalem, but "after this, Jesus went to the other side of the Sea of Galilee." In the last discourse, Thomas asks Jesus where he is going (14:5), but in 16:5 Jesus states that "none of you asks me, 'Where are you going?'" In 14:31 Jesus tells them to "Rise, let us be on our way." Then he immediately launches into another long discourse and lengthy prayer only to repeat himself in 18:1: "Rise, let us go."

44. Patrick Hartin, *Exploring the Spirituality of the Gospels* (Collegeville, MN: Liturgical Press, 2011), 66–67.

45. John of the Cross, *Living Flame of Love* 3.10, 79, in *The Collected Works of St. John of the Cross*, trans. Kieran Kavanaugh and Otilio Rodriguez, rev. ed. (Washington, DC: ICS Publications, 1991).

46. See John 3:14; 8:28; 12:32-33 and 2:4; 7:6, 30; 8:20 and 17:1.

47. Brown, *Gospel According to John*, 2:917, cited in Moloney, *John*, 502.

48. George MacRae, "Invitation to John," in *Invitation to the Gospels* (New York: Paulist Press, 2002), 395.

49. Moloney, *John*, 497.

50. Pius XI, *Quas Primas* (1925), nos. 4, 20, 33; https://www.vatican.va/content/pius-xi/en/encyclicals/documents/hf_p-xi_enc_11121925_quas-primas.html.

51. *Gaudium et Spes*, no. 39, in *Vatican Council II: Constitutions, Decrees, Declarations; The Basic Sixteen Documents*, ed. Austin Flannery (Collegeville, MN: Liturgical Press, 2014).

52. Peter Feldmeier, "Living the Kingdom," *America Magazine*, November 19, 2012, 38.

53. Brown writes, "Other scholars (with whom I agree) theorize that the Beloved Disciple was a minor figure during the ministry of Jesus, too unimportant to be remembered in the more official tradition of the Synoptics. But since this figure became important in Johannine community history (perhaps the founder of the community), he became the ideal in its Gospel picture, capable of being contrasted

with Peter as closer to Jesus in love" (Raymond Brown, *Introduction to the New Testament* [New York: Doubleday, 1997], 369).

54. *Parédōken* (gave over) *to* (the) *pneuma* (spirit): notice the definite article "the."

55. Moloney, *John*, 506.

56. Buckley, *What Do You Seek*, 57.

57. Pope Benedict XVI, *Deus Caritas Est*, no. 18, https://www.vatican.va/content/benedict-xvi/en/encyclicals/documents/hf_ben-xvi_enc_20051225_deus-caritas-est.html.